AFRICAN POLITICAL SYSTEMS

D1355587

AFRICAN POLITICAL SYSTEMS

Edited by
M. FORTES, M.A., Ph.D.
and
E. E. EVANS-PRITCHARD, M.A., Ph.D.

Published for the
INTERNATIONAL AFRICAN INSTITUTE
by the
OXFORD UNIVERSITY PRESS
LONDON   OXFORD   NEW YORK
1970

Oxford University Press

LONDON OXFORD NEW YORK
GLASGOW TORONTO MELBOURNE WELLINGTON
CAPE TOWN SALISBURY IBADAN NAIROBI LUSAKA DAR ES SALAAM ADDIS ABABA
BOMBAY CALCUTTA MADRAS KARACHI LAHORE DACCA
KUALA LUMPUR SINGAPORE HONG KONG TOKYO

First published by
Oxford University Press, London, 1940

First issued as an
Oxford University Press paperback 1970

Reprinted Lithographically in Great Britain by
Ebenezer Baylis & Son Ltd.,
The Trinity Press, Worcester, and London

EDITORS' NOTE

THIS book is both an experiment in collaborative research and an attempt to bring into focus one of the major problems of African sociology. Many dogmatic opinions are held on the subject of African political organization and are even made use of in administrative practice; but no one has yet examined this aspect of African society on a broad, comparative basis. This book will, we hope, prove the need for and indicate some of the possibilities of such an investigation. Many of the problems it brings into the foreground can only be solved by further research; but the opportunity for such research is rapidly passing and if it is not grasped now may be lost for ever.

We regard this book as the first stage of a wider inquiry into the nature and development of African political systems. In addition to further research into native political systems, such an inquiry would include the study of the development of these systems under the influence of European rule. This problem is not only sociologically important, it is of pressing importance to the peoples of Africa and to those who are responsible for governing them.

We hope this book will be of interest and of use to those who have the task of administering African peoples. The anthropologist's duty is to present the facts and theory of native social organization as he sees them. It is no light duty; for a thorough training and laborious field investigations are indispensable to its proper performance. Whether or not an anthropologist's findings can be utilized in the practical tasks of administration must be left to the decision of administrators themselves.

We are grateful to the International African Institute for sponsoring the publication of this book. Though several of the contributors carried out their field research as Fellows of the Institute, it is in no way responsible for any points of view or opinions expressed in the book. We have to thank Professor Radcliffe-Brown for much help and advice, as well as for the Preface which he has kindly contributed. Our greatest debt is to our fellow workers. Without their collaboration the book would have been impossible. They will agree, we are sure, that it is an apposite contribution to social science at the present time.

M. F.
E. E. E.-P.

OXFORD,
  March, 1940.

CONTENTS

LIST OF MAPS

PREFACE

By PROFESSOR A. R. RADCLIFFE-BROWN

Tunc et amicitiam coeperunt jungere habentes
Finitima inter se, nec laedere, nec violare.
Non tamen omnimodis poterat concordia gigni;
Sed bona, magnaque pars servabant foedera casti:
Aut genus humanum jam tum foret omne peremptum,
Nec potuisset adhuc perducere saecla propago.

LUCRETIUS.

THE comparative study of political institutions, with special reference to the simpler societies, is an important branch of social anthropology which has not yet received the attention it deserves. The publication of this volume affords an opportunity for a brief statement of the nature of that study as it is conceived by the Editors and myself.

The task of social anthropology, as a natural science of human society, is the systematic investigation of the nature of social institutions. The method of natural science rests always on the comparison of observed phenomena, and the aim of such comparison is by a careful examination of diversities to discover underlying uniformities. Applied to human societies the comparative method used as an instrument for inductive inference will enable us to discover the universal, essential, characters which belong to all human societies, past, present, and future. The progressive achievement of knowledge of this kind must be the aim of all who believe that a veritable science of human society is possible and desirable.

But we cannot hope to pass directly from empirical observations to a knowledge of general sociological laws or principles. The attempt to proceed by this apparently easy method was what Bacon so rightly denounced as leading only to a false appearance of knowledge.[1] The immense diversity of forms of human society must first be reduced to order by some sort of classification. By comparing societies one with another we have to discriminate and define different types. Thus the Australian aborigines were

[1] *Novum Organum*, I, civ.

divided into some hundreds of separate tribes, each with its own language, organization, customs, and beliefs; but an examination of a sufficient sample shows that beneath the specific diversities there are such general similarities that we can constitute and describe in general terms an Australian type.[1] The type is of course an abstraction just as 'carnivore' or 'ungulate' is an abstraction, but it is an abstraction only a little way removed from the concrete reality. When a number of such types have been adequately defined they in turn can be compared one with another and a further step in abstraction can be made. By such a process, obviously requiring the labour of many students over many years, we may reach classifications and abstract concepts more precisely defined and more exactly representing empirical reality than the concepts indicated by such phrases as 'primitive society', 'feudal society', 'capitalist society', that occur so abundantly in contemporary writing.

In attempting to classify human societies, difficulties are met with of a kind that do not exist in other sciences, such as zoology or chemistry. Two societies or two types may resemble each other in one aspect of the total social system and differ in another. It is therefore necessary to compare societies with reference to some particular aspect or part of the whole social system, with reference, for example, to the economic system or the political system or the kinship system. Thus the present volume presents materials for the comparison of certain African societies with reference to their political organization alone.

This, of course, involves making an abstraction of a different kind. For in any social system the political institutions, the economic institutions, the kinship organization, and the ritual life are intimately related and interdependent. In science there are right and wrong ways of making abstractions; the right ways are profitable in that they lead us to important additions to our knowledge; the wrong ways are not merely unprofitable, but are sometimes obstructive. If we are to study political institutions in abstraction from other features of social systems we need to make sure that our definition of 'political' is such as to mark off a class of phenomena which can profitably be made the subject of separate theoretical treatment

The successful use of the comparative method depends, not

[1] Radcliffe-Brown, *Social Organization of Australian Tribes.*

only upon the quantity and quality of the factual material at our disposal, but also upon the apparatus of concepts and hypotheses which guide our investigations. The difficulty in science is not in finding answers to questions once they have been propounded, but in finding out what questions to ask. In a natural science of society the comparative method takes the place of the experimental method in other sciences and what Claude-Bernard said of the latter is equally true of the former. 'The experimental method cannot give new and fruitful ideas to men who have none; it can serve only to guide the ideas of men who have them, to direct their ideas and to develop them so as to get the best possible results. As only what has been sown in the ground will ever grow in it, so nothing will be developed by the experimental method except the ideas submitted to it. The method itself gives birth to nothing. Certain philosophers have made the mistake of according too much power to method along these lines.'

The factual material available for a comparative study of the political institutions of the simpler societies is inadequate both in quantity and quality. It is to be hoped that the publication of the essays contained in this volume may stimulate other anthropologists to give us similar descriptive studies. The quality of descriptive data, their value for comparative study, depends to a considerable extent on how the observer understands the theoretical problems for the solution of which the data he collects are relevant. In science, observation and the selection of what to record need to be guided by theory. In the study of the simpler societies the anthropologist finds that the concepts and theories of political philosophers or economists are unserviceable or insufficient. They have been elaborated in reference to societies of a limited number of types. In their place, the social anthropologist has to make for himself theories and concepts which will be universally applicable to all human societies, and, guided by these, carry out his work of observation and comparison.

In some regions of Africa, it is easy to define what may be called the 'political society'. This is so for the Ngwato, the Bemba, and Ankole, where we find a tribe or kingdom ruled over by a chief or king. But the difficulty that is presented in other regions is well illustrated by the discussion in Dr. Wagner's essay on the Bantu Kavirondo tribes.[1] Something of the same

[1] P. 199 ff.

difficulty occurs also with the Tallensi and Nuer described in this volume and with many other societies in various parts of the world. It would doubtless be possible to find a definition of the word 'state' such that we could say that certain African societies, such as Ankole or the Bemba, are states, while others are stateless societies. This does not help us, however, to solve our problems.

Every human society has some sort of territorial structure. We can find clearly-defined local communities the smallest of which are linked together in a larger society, of which they are segments. This territorial structure provides the framework, not only for the political organization, whatever it may be, but for other forms of social organization also, such as the economic, for example. The system of local aggregation and segregation, as such, has nothing specifically political about it; it is the basis of all social life. To try to distinguish, as Maine and Morgan did, between societies based on kinship (or, more strictly, on lineage) and societies based on occupation of a common territory or locality, and to regard the former as more 'primitive' than the latter, leads only to confusion.

In studying political organization, we have to deal with the maintenance or establishment of social order, within a territorial framework, by the organized exercise of coercive authority through the use, or the possibility of use, of physical force. In well-organized states, the police and the army are the instruments by which coercion is exercised. Within the state, the social order, whatever it may be, is maintained by the punishment of those who offend against the laws and by the armed suppression of revolt. Externally the state stands ready to use armed force against other states, either to maintain the existing order or to create a new one.

In dealing with political systems, therefore, we are dealing with law, on the one hand, and with war, on the other. But there are certain institutions, such as regulated vengeance, which come between the two. Let us first consider law, and within the field of law the machinery of repressive justice. Within a locally-defined community, an individual may commit some act or adopt some mode of behaviour which constitutes some sort of attack upon or offence against the community itself as a whole, and thereupon the offending person may be put to death or excluded from the community or in some way made to suffer. In simple societies the actions which are thus repressed, and which are therefore, in those societies, crimes or public delicts, are most commonly various forms of sacrilege, incest—which is itself generally conceived as a kind of sacrilege—witchcraft, in the sense of the exercise of evil magic against members of the same community, and sometimes the crime of being a bad lot, i.e. habitually failing to observe the customs of the community.

Dr. Wagner, in his essay on the Bantu Kavirondo, describes how offenders could be expelled from their group or could be put to death by what he speaks of as lynching, and writes[1]: 'Such group action in the face of threatened danger, taken spontaneously, i.e. without a hearing of the case and often on the spur of the moment, is clearly not the same as institutionalized jurisdiction of the tribal society through recognized judicial authorities.' But it seems highly likely that if such actions could have been carefully observed it would have been found that they were directed by leaders who had some measure of recognized authority. In the *kingole* of the Kamba and Kikuyu and in the *injoget* of the Kipsigis and Nandi, where individuals who had offended against the community were put to death or otherwise punished, this was done by an orderly procedure directed by men in authority.[2]

My own view is that in collective actions of this kind, in which it may be said that the community judges and the community inflicts punishment, we may see the embryonic form of criminal law. That there is often no trial results from the fact that the offence is often patent, well known to all the community. Otherwise the relatives and friends of the accused would come to his defence and the procedure would be checked. If there is doubt, then, in Africa, recourse may be had to some form of ordeal or oath. It would be a serious mistake, I believe, to accept Dr. Wagner's view and regard actions of this kind as fundamentally the same sort of thing as actions of retaliation by a person who has suffered injury in his rights against the person responsible for the injury. The punitive action is to be regarded as the direct expression of public sentiment.

Within small communities there may be little or no need for penal sanctions. Good behaviour may be to a great extent the

---

[1] *Infra*, p. 219.
[2] Lindblom, *The Akamba*, pp. 176–180; Dundas, 'History of Kitui', *Journal of the Royal Anthropological Institute*, vol. xliii, 1913, p. 514; Peristiany, *Social Institutions of the Kipsigis*, pp. 5, 192; Hollis, *Nandi*, pp. 75–6.

result of habit, of the conditioning of the individual by his early upbringing. In addition, there are two other kinds of sanctions. There is first the sanction of moral coercion as distinguished from physical coercion; the individual who does wrong is subjected to open expressions of reprobation or ridicule by his fellows and thus is shamed. What is effective here is the direct expression of public sentiment. When a person whose behaviour is unsatisfactory is subjected to some sort of boycott we have a condition intermediate between the moral and satirical sanctions and the penal sanctions proper.

Secondly, there are the various kinds of ritual or supernatural sanction. The most direct of these is constituted by the unquestioned belief that certain actions bring misfortune upon the person who is guilty of them. For us as Christians the expected misfortune is eternal torment in the fires of Hell; for an African it is most commonly sickness or death. In any particular instance, the mode of behaviour which is a failure to observe ritual obligations may or may not be also subject to a moral sanction; it may be reprehensible or it may be merely foolish; in the former case it is a sin, in the latter an unlucky act or failure to act. In other words, in the case of sin there is a moral sanction of reprobation added to the belief that the sin will lead to misfortune for the sinner.

When a person has committeed a ritual offence, his own concern if it is a matter of luck, or both that and public sentiment if it is one of sin, will induce him to perform some ritual act of expiation or purification by which the effects of his misdeed are believed to be obviated. In some societies the sinner must perform a penance, which may be regarded as a self-inflicted punishment.

But in some instances it may be believed that the effects of the sin will fall not only upon the sinner, but upon the whole community, or that the whole community is polluted by the sin; and the offending person may be put to death or driven out of the community as a collective act of expiation. Here we come back again to the penal sanction. Thus in Ashanti crimes such as incest or murder or sacrilege are sins—are conceived as offences against the gods—which bring misfortune upon the whole country, so that the criminal must be put to death in order that the misfortune may be avoided.

The kinds of belief which underlie the ritual or supernatural sanctions may provide a basis for what may be called indirect penal sanctions. Thus in some African tribes we find a regular practice of imprecation against wrongdoers. A person who has committed an offence, whether it is or is not known who he is, may be officially cursed by the elders or by persons having authority and power to act in this way. The curse is normally accompanied by some ritual or magical act through which it is effective. It is believed that the guilty person will fall sick and die unless the curse is removed.[1] Again, in many African societies a person who is accused or suspected of witchcraft or some other offence may be compelled to take an oath or submit to an ordeal, the belief being that if he is guilty he will fall sick and die.

Thus the rudiments of what in the more complex societies is the organized institution of criminal justice are to be found in these recognized procedures by which action is taken by or on behalf of the body of members of the community, either directly or by appeal to ritual or supernatural means, to inflict punishment on an offender or to exclude him from the community. In African societies the decision to apply a penal sanction may rest with the people in general, with the elders, as in a gerontocracy, with a limited number of judges or leaders, or with a single chief or king.

There is another side of law, in which we are concerned with conflicts between persons or groups, or with injuries inflicted by one person or group upon another, and with action by or on behalf of the community to resolve the conflict or to secure that satisfaction is given for the injury. In this field of law also we find a minimum of organization in some of the simpler societies; the effective force which controls or limits conflict, or which compels the wrong doer to give satisfaction to the person he has injured, is simply public opinion or, as it may perhaps better be called, public sentiment. A person who has suffered wrong or injury at the hand of another and cannot in any other way obtain satisfaction may take forcible action. If public sentiment is on his side, the conflict may be resolved in a way that is regarded as just, and so satisfies the community. There is often some conventionally recognized form of procedure by which an injured person may seek to get public sentiment on his side. Knowledge that such action of self-redress is possible is itself often sufficient to restrain those who might otherwise commit injurious acts or to induce them to

[1] For an example, see Peristiany, *Social Institutions of the Kipsigis*, pp. 87–8 188, 192.

offer satisfaction when they have been at fault. Public sentiment may be strong enough to compel the parties to a conflict to settle the matter by negotiation either directly or by means of a go-between.

A step towards the establishment of a judicial system is taken in some societies by the recognition of certain persons as having authority to act as arbitrators, or to give judgement on the rights and wrongs of a dispute submitted to them, and suggest a settlement, though they have no power of physical coercion by which to enforce that judgement. The authority of the judge or judges may be conceived in different ways. He or they may be thought of as the representatives of the community, giving voice to the public sentiment; or as persons whose wisdom enables them to settle disputes; or as having special knowledge of right custom; or, again, as having qualities that may be called 'religious,' similar to those of the priest or the medicine-man; and they may even be thought to be divinely inspired. Thus the court, if we may call it so, even where it has no coercive power, always does have authority.

Recourse may sometimes be had to ritual or supernatural sanctions in cases of disputed rights. If evidence is so conflicting that the judge or judges find it impossible to come to a decision they may resort to the application of an ordeal or oath. If a person refuses to abide by a decision of the court they may, by imprecation or the threat thereof, compel him to do so.

In a fully developed court of civil justice, the judge has power to enforce his judgement by some form of penal sanction. The chief of the Ngwato tribe, for example, has that power.

In seeking to define the political structure in a simple society, we have to look for a territorial community which is united by the rule of law. By that is meant a community throughout which public sentiment is concerned either with the application of direct or indirect penal sanctions to any of its own members who offend in certain ways, or with the settlement of disputes and the provision of just satisfaction for injuries within the community itself. Thus, for the Nuer, Dr. Evans-Pritchard has indicated that one character by which the political unit—the tribe—is to be defined is that it is the largest community which considers that disputes between its members should be settled by arbitration

But we have to recognize that in some societies such a political community is indeterminate. Thus amongst the Australian aborigines the independent, autonomous, or, if you will, the sovereign, group is a local horde or clan which rarely includes more than 100 members and often as few as thirty. Within this group, order is maintained by the authority of the old men. But for the celebration of religious rites a number of such hordes come together in one camp. In the community so assembled there is some sort of recognized machinery for dealing with injuries inflicted by one person or group on another. To give an example: if a man has had his wife stolen from him and the thief, from another horde, is present in the assembled camp, the injured man will make known his wrong by raising a clamour in the recognized, appropriate way. The public sentiment of the whole assembly, being appealed to, may compel the offender to submit to having a spear thrust into his thigh by the injured husband.

The point to be noted is that such assemblies for religious or ceremonial purposes consist on different occasions of different collections of hordes. Each assembly constitutes for the time being a political society. If there is a feud between two of the constituent hordes, it must either be settled and peace made or it must be kept in abeyance during the meeting, to break out again later on. Thus on different occasions a horde belongs temporarily to different larger temporary political groups. But there is no definite permanent group of this kind of which a horde can be said to be a part. Conditions similar to this are found in some parts of Africa—for example, among the Tallensi.[1]

There are exceedingly few human societies known to us in which there is not some form of warfare, and at least a good half of the history of political development is in one way or another a history of wars. The comparative study of war as a social institution has not yet been undertaken. Amongst the various different kinds of warfare that can be distinguished, what we may call wars of conquest have been important in Africa, as they have been in Europe. When such a war is successful it establishes one people as conquerors over another who are thus incorporated into a larger political society, sometimes in an inferior position as a subject people.

But the institution of war may take a different form in which

[1] *Infra*, p. 239 ff. Where a political structure of this kind exists, it is generally either ignored or completely misunderstood by colonial administrators.

two communities stand in a permanent relation such that war
between them is always a possibility and does from time to time
occur, though neither seeks to conquer the other and absorb it as a
conquered people in a larger political unity. In a political system
of which this is true, the occurrence or the possibility of war
gives us the readiest means of defining the political structure.

But it is very difficult to draw an exact dividing line, valid for all
societies, between war and feud. In a single society, as in some
parts of Australia, different kinds of armed conflict are recognized,
from duels between two groups by appointment as to time and
place, in which each side avoids, if possible, killing any of the
enemy, but seek to inflict non-mortal wounds, to 'wars to end war'
which only occur at relatively infrequent intervals and result in
many deaths.

There is one kind of feud which needs to be recognized as being
of importance in any attempt to define political structure in some
simple societies, viz. the institution of regulated retaliation for
homicide. Where that exists, when a man is killed, his relatives,
or the members of his clan or group, are entitled, or in some
societies obliged, by custom to take the life either of his killer or
of a member of his clan or group. Public sentiment regards such
vengeance as just and proper so long as the law of talion is
observed—that is, that the injury inflicted is equivalent to the
injury suffered, but not greater.

Feuds, or collective actions using force or the threat of force,
of the kind to which this example belongs cannot be regarded as
the same thing as war. The action is limited to obtaining satisfaction for a particular injury and is controlled by the general public
sentiment of the community in which it takes place. But, on the
other hand, though the idea of justice is involved, such actions
cannot be properly regarded as falling within the sphere of law.

Thus in simple societies the political structure in one of its
aspects, viz. as grouping together individuals within a territorial
framework, which implies, of course, the separation of group
from group within the total system, has to be described in terms
of war, feud, and the exercise of recognized authority in settling
disputes, finding remedies for injuries, and repressing actions
regarded as injuring not certain individuals, but the community
as a whole.

Amongst some writers on comparative politics, there is a

tendency to concentrate attention too much on what is called the 'sovereign state'. But states are merely territorial groups within a larger political system in which their relations are defined by war or its possibility, treaties, and international law. A political system of this kind, such as now exists in Europe, of sovereign nations linked by international relations, is only one type of political system. Political theory and political practice (including colonial administration) have often suffered by reason of this type of system being set up, consciously or unconsciously, as a norm.

There is a second aspect of political structure. The social structure of any society includes some differentiation of social role between persons and between classes of persons. The role of an individual is the part he plays in the total social life—economic, political, religious, &c. In the simplest societies, there is little more than the very important differentiation on the basis of sex and age and the non-institutionalized recognition of leadership in ritual, in hunting or fishing, in warfare, and so on, to which we may add the specialization of the oldest profession in the world, that of the medicine man. As we pass from the simpler to the more complex societies we find increasing differentiation of individual from individual and usually some more or less definite division of the community into classes.

As political organization develops there is an increasing differentiation whereby certain persons—chiefs, kings, judges, military commanders, &c.—have special roles in the social life. Each such person may be said to hold or fill an office—administrative, judicial, legislative, military, or other. The holder of an office in this sense is endowed with authority, and to the office there attach certain duties and also certain rights and privileges.

In Africa it is often hardly possible to separate, even in thought, political office from ritual or religious office. Thus in some African societies it may be said that the king is the executive head, the legislator, the supreme judge, the commander-in-chief of the army, the chief priest or supreme ritual head, and even perhaps the principal capitalist of the whole community. But it is erroneous to think of him as combining in himself a number of separate and distinct offices. There is a single office, that of king, and its various duties and activities, and its rights, prerogatives, and privileges, make up a single unified whole.

Besides the development of political office, though not independent of it, we have to take account of the various forms of political inequality. The simplest example of this is afforded by differentiation on the basis of sex and age; men usually take far more part than women, not only in war, but also in maintaining internal order, and older men, as a rule, have more authority than younger ones. Gerontocracy—rule by elders—is a form of political organization that is found in some parts of Africa. In some tribes of East Africa it is systematized by means of a definite structure of age-sets and age-grades. Where a society is under a chief or king, we may find an element of gerontocracy combined with the monarchical principle.

The Banyankole described in this book are an example of a division into politically unequal classes. The political power rests with the pastoral Bahima, who thus constitute a ruling class, while the agricultural Bairu are in an inferior position. In this instance and in a number of others there is good reason to believe that this differentiation into politically superior and inferior classes is the result of conquest, but it is going far beyond the evidence to assume that political inequality has in all instances arisen in this way. In the Banyankole and similar tribes, the political inequality is associated with other differences and the class structure is maintained by the difference in the mode of life of overlords and subjects and by the absence of intermarriage.

Thus in the comparative study of political systems we are concerned with certain special aspects of a total social structure, meaning by that term both the grouping together of individuals into territorial or lineage groups and also the differentiation of individuals by their social role either as individuals or on the basis of sex and age or by distinctions of social classes.

Social structure is not to be thought of as static, but as a condition of equilibrium that only persists by being continually renewed, like the chemical-physiological homostasis of a living organism. Events occur which disturb the equilibrium in some way, and a social reaction follows which tends to restore it. Sometimes a system may persist relatively unchanged for some length of time; after each disturbance the reaction restores it to very much what it was before. But at other times a disturbance of equilibrium may be such that it and the reaction which follows result in a modification of the system; a new equilibrium is reached which differs from the one previously existing. With a serious disturbance the process of readjustment may take a long time.

A political system, as we have seen, involves a set of relations between territorial groups. How the study of this as an equilibrium system may be approached in African societies is illustrated in the last two essays of this book, on the Nuer and the Tallensi. Within the community, the political constitution must also be studied as an equilibrium system. Dr. Gluckman's essay on the Zulu shows how the former system of a balance between the power of the chief, on the one side, and public sentiment, on the other, has been replaced by one in which the chief has to maintain as best he can some sort of balance between the requirements of the European rulers and the wishes of his people.

No attempt can be made to indicate the great variety of equilibrium situations that can be studied in the political systems of African peoples. It must suffice to draw attention to the need of studying political organizations from this point of view.

In writings on political institutions there is a good deal of discussion about the nature and the origin of the State, which is usually represented as being an entity over and above the human individuals who make up a society, having as one of its attributes something called 'sovereignty', and sometimes spoken of as having a will (law being often defined as the will of the State) or as issuing commands. The State, in this sense, does not exist in the phenomenal world; it is a fiction of the philosophers. What does exist is an organization, i.e. a collection of individual human beings connected by a complex system of relations. Within that organization different individuals have different roles, and some are in possession of special power or authority, as chiefs or elders capable of giving commands which will be obeyed, as legislators or judges, and so on. There is no such thing as the power of the State; there are only, in reality, powers of individuals—kings, prime ministers, magistrates, policemen, party bosses, and voters. The political organization of a society is that aspect of the total organization which is concerned with the control and regulation of the use of physical force. This, it is suggested, provides, for an objective study of human societies by the methods of natural science, the most satisfactory definition of the special class of social phenomena to the investigation of which this book is a contribution.

INTRODUCTION

By M. Fortes and E. E. Evans-Pritchard

I. Aims of this Book

ONE object we had in initiating this study was to provide a convenient reference book for anthropologists. We also hope that it will be a contribution to the discipline of comparative politics. We feel sure that the first object has been attained, for the societies described are representative of common types of African political systems and, taken together, they enable a student to appreciate the great variety of such types. As the sketch-map on p. 2 shows, the eight systems described are widely distributed in the continent. Most of the forms described are variants of a pattern of political organization found among contiguous or neighbouring societies, so that this book covers, by implication, a very large part of Africa. We are aware that not every type of political system found in Africa is represented, but we believe that all the major principles of African political organization are brought out in these essays.

Several contributors have described the changes in the political systems they investigated which have taken place as a result of European conquest and rule. If we do not emphasize this side of the subject it is because all contributors are more interested in anthropological than in administrative problems. We do not wish to imply, however, that anthropology is indifferent to practical affairs. The policy of Indirect Rule is now generally accepted in British Africa. We would suggest that it can only prove advantageous in the long run if the principles of African political systems, such as this book deals with, are understood.

II. A Representative Sample of African Societies

Each essay is a condensation of a detailed study of the political system of a single people undertaken in recent years by the most advanced methods of field-work by students trained in anthropological theory. A degree of brevity that hardly does justice to some important topics has been necessary for reasons of space.

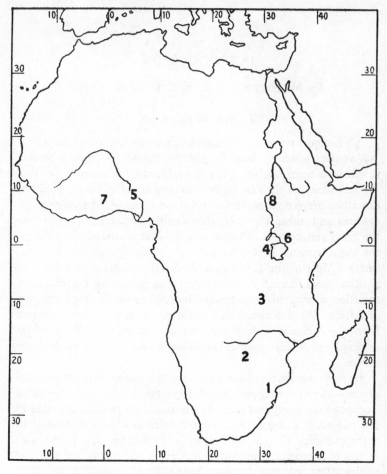

THE DISTRIBUTION OF THE PEOPLES DEALT WITH IN THIS BOOK

1. Zulu   4. Banyankole   7. Tallensi
2. Ngwato   5. Kede   8. Nuer
3. Bemba   6. Bantu Kavirondo

Each essay furnishes, nevertheless, a useful standard by which the political systems of other peoples in the same area may be classified. No such classification is attempted in this book, but we recognize that a satisfactory comparative study of African political institutions can only be undertaken after a classification of the kind has been made. It would then be possible to study a whole range of adjacent societies in the light of the Ngwato system, the Tale system, the Ankole system, the Bemba system, and so on, and, by analysis, to state the chief characters of series of political systems found in large areas. An analysis of the results obtained by these comparative studies in fields where a whole range of societies display many similar characteristics in their political systems would be more likely to lead to valid scientific generalizations than comparison between particular societies belonging to different areas and political types.

We do not mean to suggest that the political systems of societies which have a high degree of general cultural resemblance are necessarily of the same type, though on the whole they tend to be. However, it is well to bear in mind that within a single linguistic or cultural area we often find political systems which are very unlike one another in many important features. Conversely, the same kind of political structures are found in societies of totally different culture. This can be seen even in the eight societies in this book. Also, there may be a totally different cultural content in social processes with identical functions. The function of ritual ideology in political organization in Africa clearly illustrates this. Mystical values are attached to political office among the Bemba, the Banyankole, the Kede, and the Tallensi, but the symbols and institutions in which these values are expressed are very different in all four societies. A comparative study of political systems has to be on an abstract plane where social processes are stripped of their cultural idiom and are reduced to functional terms. The structural similarities which disparity of culture conceals are then laid bare and structural dissimilarities are revealed behind a screen of cultural uniformity. There is evidently an intrinsic connexion between a people's culture and their social organization, but the nature of this connexion is a major problem in sociology and we cannot emphasize too much that these two components of social life must not be confused.

We believe that the eight societies described will not only give the student a bird's-eye view of the basic principles of African political organization, but will also enable him to draw a few, perhaps elementary, conclusions of a general and theoretical kind. It must be emphasized, however, that all the contributors have aimed primarily at giving a concise descriptive account and have subordinated theoretical speculations to this end. In so far as they have allowed themselves to draw theoretical conclusions, these have been largely determined by the view they have taken of what constitutes political structure. They do not all take the same view on this matter. In stating our own views we have found it best to avoid reference to the writings of political philosophers, and in doing so we feel sure that we have the support of our contributors.

III. Political Philosophy and Comparative Politics

We have not found that the theories of political philosophers have helped us to understand the societies we have studied and we consider them of little scientific value; for their conclusions are seldom formulated in terms of observed behaviour or capable of being tested by this criterion. Political philosophy has chiefly concerned itself with how men *ought* to live and what form of government they *ought* to have, rather than with what *are* their political habits and institutions.

In so far as political philosophers have attempted to understand existing institutions instead of trying to justify or undermine them, they have done so in terms of popular psychology or of history. They have generally had recourse to hypotheses about earlier stages of human society presumed to be devoid of political institutions or to display them in a very rudimentary form and have attempted to reconstruct the process by which the political institutions with which they were familiar in their own societies might have arisen out of these elementary forms of organization. Political philosophers in modern times have often sought to substantiate their theories by appeal to the facts of primitive societies. They cannot be blamed if, in doing so, they have been led astray, for little anthropological research has been conducted into primitive political systems compared with research into other primitive institutions, customs, and beliefs, and still less have comparative studies of them been made.[1] We do not consider that the origins of primitive institutions can be discovered and, therefore, we do not think that it is worth while seeking for them. We speak for all social anthropologists when we say that a scientific study of political institutions must be inductive and comparative and aim solely at establishing and explaining the uniformities found among them and their interdependencies with other features of social organization.

IV. The Two Types of Political System Studied

It will be noted that the political systems described in this book fall into two main categories. One group, which we refer to as Group A, consists of those societies which have centralized authority, administrative machinery, and judicial institutions—in short, a government—and in which cleavages of wealth, privilege, and status correspond to the distribution of power and authority. This group comprises the Zulu, the Ngwato, the Bemba, the Banyankole, and the Kede. The other group, which we refer to as Group B, consists of those societies which lack centralized authority, administrative machinery, and constituted judicial institutions—in short which lack government—and in which there are no sharp divisions of rank, status, or wealth. This group comprises the Logoli, the Tallensi, and the Nuer. Those who consider that a state should be defined by the presence of governmental institutions will regard the first group as primitive states and the second group as stateless societies.

The kind of information related and the kind of problems discussed in a description of each society have largely depended on the category to which it belongs. Those who have studied societies of Group A are mainly concerned to describe governmental organization. They therefore give an account of the status of kings and classes, the roles of administrative officials of one kind or another, the privileges of rank, the differences in wealth and power, the regulation of tax and tribute, the territorial divisions of the state and their relation to its central authority, the

[1] We would except from this stricture Professor R. H. Lowie, though we do not altogether accept his methods and conclusions. See his works *Primitive Society* (1920) and *Origin of the State* (1927). We are referring only to anthropologists. The work of the great legal and constitutional historians like Maine, Vinogradoff, and Ed. Meyer falls into another category. All students of political institutions are indebted to their pioneer researches.

rights of subjects and the obligations of rulers, and the checks on authority. Those who studied societies of Group B had no such matters to discuss and were therefore forced to consider what, in the absence of explicit forms of government, could be held to constitute the political structure of a people. This problem was simplest among the Nuer, who have very distinct territorial divisions. The difficulty was greater for the Logoli and Tallensi, who have no clear spatially-defined political units.

V. Kinship in Political Organization

One of the outstanding differences between the two groups is the part played by the lineage system in political structure. We must here distinguish between the set of relationships linking the individual to other persons and to particular social units through the transient, bilateral family, which we shall call the kinship system, and the segmentary system of permanent, unilateral descent groups, which we call the lineage system. Only the latter establishes corporate units with political functions. In both groups of societies kinship and domestic ties have an important role in the lives of individuals, but their relation to the political system is of a secondary order. In the societies of Group A it is the administrative organization, in societies of Group B the segmentary lineage system, which primarily regulates political relations between territorial segments.

This is clearest among the Ngwato, whose political system resembles the pattern with which we are familiar in the modern nation-state. The political unit is essentially a territorial grouping wherein the plexus of kinship ties serves merely to cement those already established by membership of the ward, district, and nation. In societies of this type the state is never the kinship system writ large, but is organized on totally different principles. In societies of Group B kinship ties appear to play a more prominent role in political organization, owing to the close association of territorial grouping with lineage grouping, but it is still only a secondary role.

It seems probable to us that three types of political system can be distinguished. Firstly, there are those very small societies, none of which are described in this book, in which even the largest political unit embraces a group of people all of whom are united to one another by ties of kinship, so that political relations are coterminous with kinship relations and the political structure and kinship organization are completely fused. Secondly, there are societies in which a lineage structure is the framework of the political system, there being a precise co-ordination between the two, so that they are consistent with each other, though each remains distinct and autonomous in its own sphere. Thirdly, there are societies in which an administrative organization is the framework of the political structure.

The numerical and territorial range of a political system would vary according to the type to which it belongs. A kinship system would seem to be incapable of uniting such large numbers of persons into a single organization for defence and the settlement of disputes by arbitration as a lineage system and a lineage system incapable of uniting such numbers as an administrative system.

VI. *The Influence of Demography*

It is noteworthy that the political unit in the societies with a state organization is numerically larger than in those without a state organization. The largest political groups among the Tallensi, Logoli, and Nuer cannot compete in numbers with the quarter to half million of the Zulu state (in about 1870), the 101,000 of the Ngwato state, and the 140,000 of the Bemba state. It is true that the Kede and their subject population are not so populous, but it must be remembered that they form part of the vast Nupe state. It is not suggested that a stateless political unit need be very small —Nuer political units comprise as many as 45,000 souls—nor that a political unit with state organization need be very large, but it is probably true that there is a limit to the size of a population that can hold together without some kind of centralized government.

Size of population should not be confused with density of population. There may be some relation between the degree of political development and the size of population, but it would be incorrect to suppose that governmental institutions are found in those societies with greatest density. The opposite seems to be equally likely, judging by our material. The density of the Zulu is 3·5, of the Ngwato 2·5, of the Bemba 3·75 per square mile, while that of the Nuer is higher and of the Tallensi and Logoli very much higher. It might be supposed that the dense permanent settlements of the Tallensi would necessarily lead to the development of a centralized form of government, whereas the wide dispersion of shifting villages among the Bemba would be incompatible with centralized rule. The reverse is actually the case. In addition to the material collected in this book, evidence from other African societies could be cited to prove that a large population in a political unit and a high degree of political centralization do not necessarily go together with great density.

VII. The Influence of Mode of Livelihood

The density and distribution of population in an African society are clearly related to ecological conditions which also affect the whole mode of livelihood. It is obvious, however, that mere differences in modes of livelihood do not determine differences in political structure. The Tallensi and the Bemba are both agriculturalists, the Tallensi having fixed and the Bemba shifting cultivation, but they have very different political systems. The Nuer and Logoli of Group B and the Zulu and Ngwato of Group A alike practise mixed agriculture and cattle husbandry. In a general sense, modes of livelihood, together with environmental conditions, which always impose effective limits on modes of livelihood, determine the dominant values of the peoples and strongly influence their social organizations, including their political systems. This is evident in the political divisions of the Nuer, in the distribution of Kede settlements and the administrative organization embracing them, and in the class system of the Banyankole.

Most African societies belong to an economic order very different from ours. Theirs is mainly a subsistence economy with a rudimentary differentiation of productive labour and with no machinery for the accumulation of wealth in the form of commercial or industrial capital. If wealth is accumulated it takes the form of consumption goods and amenities or is used for the support of additional dependants. Hence it tends to be rapidly dissipated again and does not give rise to permanent class divisions. Distinctions of rank, status, or occupation operate independently of differences of wealth.

Economic privileges, such as rights to tax, tribute, and labour, are both the main reward of political power and an essential means of maintaining it in the political systems of Group A. But there are counterbalancing economic obligations no less strongly backed by institutionalized sanctions. It must not be forgotten, also, that those who derive maximum economic benefit from political office also have the maximum administrative, judicial, and religious responsibilities.

Compared with the societies of Group A, distinctions of rank and status are of minor significance in societies of Group B. Political office carries no economic privileges, though the possession of greater than average wealth may be a criterion of the qualities or status required for political leadership; for in these economically homogeneous, equalitarian, and segmentary societies the attainment of wealth depends either on exceptional personal qualities or accomplishments, or on superior status in the lineage system.

VIII. Composite Political Systems and the Conquest Theory

It might be held that societies like the Logoli, Tallensi, and Nuer, without central government or administrative machinery, develop into states like the Ngwato, Zulu, and Banyankole as a result of conquest. Such a development is suggested for the Zulu and Banyankole. But the history of all the peoples treated in this book is not well enough known to enable us to declare with any degree of certainty what course their political development has taken. The problem must therefore be stated in a different way. All the societies of Group A appear to be an amalgam of different peoples, each aware of its unique origin and history, and all except the Zulu and Bemba are still to-day culturally heterogeneous. Cultural diversity is most marked among the Banyankole and Kede, but it is also clear among the Ngwato. We may, therefore, ask to what extent cultural heterogeneity in a society is correlated with an administrative system and central authority. The evidence at our disposal in this book suggests that cultural and economic heterogeneity is associated with a state-like political structure. Centralized authority and an administrative organization seem to be necessary to accommodate culturally diverse groups within a single political system, especially if they have different modes of livelihood. A class or caste system may result if there are great cultural and, especially, great economic divergencies. But centralized forms of government are found also with peoples of homogeneous culture and little economic differentiation like the Zulu. It is possible that groups of diverse culture are the more easily welded into a unitary political system without the emergence of classes the closer they are to one another in culture. A centralized form of government is not necessary to enable different groups of closely related culture and pursuing the same mode of livelihood to amalgamate, nor does it necessarily arise out of the amalgamation. The Nuer have absorbed large numbers of conquered Dinka, who are a pastoral people like themselves with a very similar culture. They have incorporated them by adoption and other ways into their lineage system; but this has not resulted in a class or caste structure or in a centralized form of government. Marked divergencies in culture and economic pursuits are probably incompatible with a segmentary political system such as that of the Nuer or the Tallensi. We have not the data to check this. It is clear, however, that a conquest theory of the primitive state—assuming that the necessary historical evidence is available—must take into account not only the mode of conquest and the conditions of contact, but also the similarities or divergencies in culture and mode of livelihood of conquerors and conquered and the political institutions they bring with them into the new combination.

IX. *The Territorial Aspect*

The territorial aspect of early forms of political organization was justly emphasized by Maine in *Ancient Law* and other scholars have given much attention to it. In all the societies described in this book the political system has a territorial framework, but it has a different function in the two types of political organization. The difference is due to the dominance of an administrative and judicial apparatus in one type of system and its absence in the other. In the societies of Group A the administrative unit is a territorial unit; political rights and obligations are territorially delimited. A chief is the administrative and judicial head of a given territorial division, vested often with final economic and legal control over all the land within his boundaries. Everybody living within these boundaries is his subject, and the right to live in this area can be acquired only by accepting the obligations of a subject. The head of the state is a territorial ruler.

In the other group of societies there are no territorial units defined by an administrative system, but the territorial units are local communities the extent of which corresponds to the range of a particular set of lineage ties and the bonds of direct co-operation.

Political office does not carry with it juridical rights over a particular, defined stretch of territory and its inhabitants. Membership of the local community, and the rights and duties that go with it, are acquired as a rule through genealogical ties, real or fictional. The lineage principle takes the place of political allegiance, and the interrelations of territorial segments are directly co-ordinated with the interrelations of lineage segments.

Political relations are not simply a reflexion of territorial relations. The political system, in its own right, incorporates territorial relations and invests them with the particular kind of political significance they have.

X. *The Balance of Forces in the Political System*

A relatively stable political system in Africa presents a balance between conflicting tendencies and between divergent interests. In Group A it is a balance between different parts of the administrative organization. The forces that maintain the supremacy of the paramount ruler are opposed by the forces that act as a check on his powers. Institutions such as the regimental organization of the Zulu, the genealogical restriction of succession to kingship or chiefship, the appointment by the king of his kinsmen to regional chiefships, and the mystical sanctions of his office all reinforce the power of the central authority. But they are counterbalanced by other institutions, like the king's council, sacerdotal officials who have a decisive voice in the king's investiture, queen mothers' courts, and so forth, which work for the protection of law and custom and the control of centralized power. The regional devolution of powers and privileges, necessary on account of difficulties of communication and transport and of other cultural deficiencies, imposes severe restrictions on a king's authority. The balance between central authority and regional autonomy is a very important element in the political structure. If a king abuses his power, subordinate chiefs are liable to secede or to lead a revolt against him. If a subordinate chief seems to be getting too powerful and independent, the central authority will be supported by other subordinate chiefs in suppressing him. A king may try to buttress his authority by playing off rival subordinate chiefs against one another.

It would be a mistake to regard the scheme of constitutional checks and balances and the delegation of power and authority to regional chiefs as nothing more than an administrative device. A general principle of great importance is contained in these arrangements, which has the effect of giving every section and every major interest of the society direct or indirect representation in the conduct of government. Local chiefs represent the central authority in relation to their districts, but they also represent the people under them in relation to the central authority. Councillors and ritual functionaries represent the community's interest in the preservation of law and custom and in the observance of the ritual measures deemed necessary for its well-being. The voice of such functionaries and delegates is effective in the conduct of government on account of the general principle that power and authority are distributed. The king's power and authority are composite. Their various components are lodged in different offices. Without the co-operation of those who hold these offices it is extremely difficult, if not impossible, for the king to obtain his revenue, assert his judicial and legislative supremacy, or retain his secular and ritual prestige. Functionaries vested with essential subsidiary powers and privileges can often sabotage a ruler's acts if they disapprove them.

Looked at from another angle, the government of an African state consists in a balance between power and authority on the one side and obligation and responsibility on the other. Every one who holds political office has responsibilities for the public weal corresponding to his rights and privileges. The distribution of political authority provides a machinery by which the various agents of government can be held to their responsibilities. A chief or a king has the right to exact tax, tribute, and labour service from his subjects; he has the corresponding obligation to dispense justice to them, to ensure their protection from enemies and to safeguard their general welfare by ritual acts and observances. The structure of an African state implies that kings and chiefs rule by consent. A ruler's subjects are as fully aware of the duties he owes to them as they are of the duties they owe to him, and are able to exert pressure to make him discharge these duties.

We should emphasize here, that we are talking of constitutional arrangements, not of how they work in practice. Africans recognize as clearly as we do that power corrupts and that men are liable to abuse it. In many ways the kind of constitution we find in societies of Group A is cumbrous and too loosely jointed to prevent abuse entirely. The native theory of government is often contradicted by their practice. Both rulers and subjects, actuated by their private interests, infringe the rules of the constitution. Though it usually has a form calculated to hold in check any tendency towards absolute despotism, no African constitution can prevent a ruler from sometimes becoming a tyrant. The history of Shaka is an extreme case, but in this and other instances where the contradiction between theory and practice is too glaring and the infringement of constitutional rules becomes too grave, popular disapproval is sure to follow and may even result in a movement of secession or revolt led by members of the royal family or subordinate chiefs. This is what happened to Shaka.

It should be remembered that in these states there is only one theory of government. In the event of rebellion, the aim, and result, is only to change the personnel of office and never to abolish it or to substitute for it some new form of government. When subordinate chiefs, who are often kinsmen of the king, rebel against him they do so in defence of the values violated by his malpractices. They have an interest greater than any other section of the people in maintaining the kingship. The ideal constitutional pattern remains the valid norm, in spite of breaches of its rules.

A different kind of balance is found in societies of Group B. It is an equilibrium between a number of segments, spatially juxtaposed and structurally equivalent, which are defined in local and lineage, and not in administrative terms. Every segment has the same interests as other segments of a like order. The set of intersegmentary relations that constitutes the political structure is a balance of opposed local loyalties and of divergent lineage and ritual ties. Conflict between the interests of administrative divisions is common in societies like those of Group A. Subordinate chiefs and other political functionaries, whose rivalries are often personal, or due to their relationship to the king or the ruling aristocracy, often exploit these divergent local loyalties for their own ends. But the administrative organization canalizes and provides checks on such inter-regional dissensions. In the societies without an administrative organization, divergence of interests between the component segments is intrinsic to the political structure. Conflicts between local segments necessarily mean conflicts between lineage segments, since the two are closely interlocked; and the stabilizing factor is not a superordinate juridical or military organization, but is simply the sum total of inter-segment relations.

XI. The Incidence and Function of Organized Force

In our judgement, the most significant characteristic distinguishing the centralized, pyramidal, state-like forms of government of the Ngwato, Bemba, &c., from the segmentary political systems of the Logoli, the Tallensi, and the Nuer is the incidence and function of organized force in the system. In the former group of societies, the principal sanction of a ruler's rights and prerogatives, and of the authority exercised by his subordinate chiefs, is the command of organized force. This may enable an African king to rule oppressively for a time, if he is inclined to do so, but a good ruler uses the armed forces under his control in the public interest, as an accepted instrument of government—that is, for the defence of the society as a whole or of any section of it, for offence against a common enemy, and as a coercive sanction to enforce the law or respect for the constitution. The king and his delegates and advisers use organized force with the consent of their subjects to keep going a political system which the latter take for granted as the foundation of their social order.

In societies of Group B there is no association, class, or segment which has a dominant place in the political structure through the command of greater organized force than is at the disposal of any of its congeners. If force is resorted to in a dispute between segments it will be met with equal force. If one segment defeats another it does not attempt to establish political dominance over it; in the absence of an administrative machinery there is, in fact, no means by which it could do so. In the language of political philosophy, there is no individual or group in which sovereignty can be said to rest. In such a system, stability is maintained by an equilibrium at every line of cleavage and every point of divergent interests in the social structure. This balance is sustained by a distribution of the command of force corresponding to the distribution of like, but competitive, interests amongst the homologous segments of the society. Whereas a constituted judicial machinery is possible and is always found in societies of Group A, since it has the backing of organized force, the jural institutions of the Logoli, the Tallensi and the Nuer rest on the right of self-help.

XII. *Differences in Response to European Rule*

The distinctions we have noted between the two categories into which these eight societies fall, especially in the kind of balance characteristic of each, are very marked in their adjustment to the rule of colonial governments. Most of these societies have been conquered or have submitted to European rule from fear of invasion. They would not acquiesce in it if the threat of force were withdrawn; and this fact determines the part now played in their political life by European administrations.

In the societies of Group A, the paramount ruler is prohibited, by the constraint of the colonial government, from using the organized force at his command on his own responsibility. This has everywhere resulted in diminishing his authority and generally in increasing the power and independence of his subordinates. He no longer rules in his own right, but as the agent of the colonial government. The pyramidal structure of the state is now maintained by the latter's taking his place as paramount. If he capitulates entirely, he may become a mere puppet of the colonial government. He loses the support of his people because the pattern of reciprocal rights and duties which bound him to them is destroyed. Alternatively, he may be able to safeguard his former status, to some extent, by openly or covertly leading the opposition which his people inevitably feel towards alien rule. Very often he is in the equivocal position of having to reconcile his contradictory roles as representative of his people against the colonial government and of the latter against his people. He becomes the pivot on which the new system swings precariously. Indirect Rule may be regarded as a policy designed to stabilize the new political order, with the native paramount ruler in this dual role, but eliminating the friction it is liable to give rise to.

In the societies of Group B, European rule has had the opposite effect. The colonial government cannot administer through aggregates of individuals composing political segments, but has to employ administrative agents. For this purpose it makes use of any persons who can be assimilated to the stereotyped notion of an African chief. These agents for the first time have the backing of force behind their authority, now, moreover, extending into spheres for which there is no precedent. Direct resort to force in the form of self-help in defence of the rights of individuals or of groups is no longer permitted; for there is now, for the first time, a paramount authority exacting obedience in virtue of superior force which enables it to establish courts of justice to replace self-help. This tends to lead to the whole system of mutually balancing segments collapsing and a bureaucratic European system taking its place. An organization more like that of a centralized state comes into being.

XIII. The Mystical Values Associated with Political Office

The sanction of force is not an innovation in African forms of government. We have stressed the fact that it is one of the main pillars of the indigenous type of state. But the sanction of force on which a European administration depends lies outside the native political system. It is not used to maintain the values inherent in that system. In both societies of Group A and those of Group B European governments can impose their authority; in neither are they able to establish moral ties with the subject people. For, as we have seen, in the original native system force is used by a ruler with the consent of his subjects in the interest of the social order.

An African ruler is not to his people merely a person who can enforce his will on them. He is the axis of their political relations, the symbol of their unity and exclusiveness, and the embodiment of their essential values. He is more than a secular ruler; in *that* capacity the European government can to a great extent replace him. His credentials are mystical and are derived from antiquity. Where there are no chiefs, the balanced segments which compose the political structure are vouched for by tradition and myth and their interrelations are guided by values expressed in mystical symbols. Into these sacred precincts the European rulers can never enter. They have no mythical or ritual warranty for their authority.

What is the meaning of this aspect of African political organization? African societies are not models of continuous internal harmony. Acts of violence, oppression, revolt, civil war, and so forth, chequer the history of every African state. In societies like the Logoli, Tallensi, and Nuer the segmentary nature of the social structure is often most strikingly brought to light by armed conflict between the segments. But if the social system has reached a sufficient degree of stability, these internal convulsions do not necessarily wreck it. In fact, they may be the means of reinforcing it, as we have seen, against the abuses and infringements of rulers actuated by their private interests. In the segmentary societies, war is not a matter of one segment enforcing its will on another, but is the way in which segments protect their particular interests within a field of common interests and values.

There are, in every African society, innumerable ties which counteract the tendencies towards political fission arising out of the tensions and cleavages in the social structure. An administrative organization backed by coercive sanctions, clanship, lineage and age-set ties, the fine-spun web of kinship—all these unite people who have different or even opposed sectional and private interests. Often also there are common material interests such, as the need to share pastures or to trade in a common market-place, or complementary economic pursuits binding different sections to one another. Always there are common ritual values, the ideological superstructure of political organization.

Members of an African society feel their unity and perceive their common interests in symbols, and it is their attachment to these symbols which more than anything else gives their society cohesion and persistence. In the form of myths, fictions, dogmas, ritual, sacred places and persons, these symbols represent the unity and exclusiveness of the groups which respect them. They are regarded, however, not as mere symbols, but as final values in themselves.

To explain these symbols sociologically, they have to be translated into terms of social function and of the social structure which they serve to maintain. Africans have no objective knowledge of the forces determining their social organization and actuating their social behaviour. Yet they would be unable to carry on their collective life if they could not think and feel about the interests which actuate them, the institutions by means of which they organize collective action, and the structure of the groups into which they are organized. Myths, dogmas, ritual beliefs and activities make his social system intellectually tangible and coherent to an African and enable him to think and feel about it. Furthermore, these sacred symbols, which reflect the social system, endow it with mystical values which evoke acceptance of the social order that goes far beyond the obedience exacted by the secular sanction of force. The social system is, as it were, removed to a mystical plane, where it figures as a system of sacred values beyond criticism or revision. Hence people will overthrow a bad king, but the kingship is never questioned; hence the wars or feuds between segments of a society like the Nuer or the Tallensi are kept within bounds by mystical sanctions. These values are common to the whole society, to rulers and ruled alike and to all the segments and sections of a society.

The African does not see beyond the symbols; it might well be held that if he understood their objective meaning, they would lose the power they have over him. This power lies in their symbolic content, and in their association with the nodal institutions of the social structure, such as the kingship. Not every kind of ritual or any sort of mystical ideas can express the values that hold a society together and focus the loyalty and devotion of its members on their rulers. If we study the mystical values bound up with the kingship in any of the societies of Group A, we find that they refer to fertility, health, prosperity, peace, justice—to everything, in short, which gives life and happiness to a people. The African sees these ritual observances as the supreme safeguard of the basic needs of his existence and of the basic relations that make up his social order—land, cattle, rain, bodily health, the family, the clan, the state. The mystical values reflect the general import of the basic elements of existence: the land as the source of the whole people's livelihood, physical health as something universally desired, the family as the fundamental procreative unit, and so forth. These are the common interests of the whole society, as the native sees them. These are the themes of taboos, observances and ceremonies in which, in societies of Group A, the whole people has a share through its representatives, and in societies of Group B all the segments participate, since they are matters of equal moment to all.

We have stressed the fact that the universal aspect of things like land or fertility are the subjects of common interest in an African society; for these matters also have another side to them, as the private interests of individuals and segments of a society. The productivity of his own land, the welfare and security of his own family or his own clan, such matters are of daily, practical concern to every member of an African society; and over such matters arise the conflicts between sections and factions of the society. Thus the basic needs of existence and the basic social relations are, in their pragmatic and utilitarian aspects, as sources of immediate satisfactions and strivings, the subjects of private interests; as common interests, they are non-utilitarian and non-pragmatic, matters of moral value and ideological significance. The common interests spring from those very private interests to which they stand in opposition.

To explain the ritual aspect of African political organization in terms of magical mentality is not enough; and it does not take us far to say that land, rain, fertility, &c., are 'sacralized' because they are the most vital needs of the community. Such arguments do not explain why the great ceremonies in which ritual for the common good is performed are usually on a public scale. They do not explain why the ritual functions we have been describing should be bound up, always, with pivotal political offices and should be part of the political theory of an organized society.

Again, it is not enough to dismiss these ritual functions of chief-ship, kingship, &c., by calling them sanctions of political authority. Why, then, are they regarded as among the most stringent respon-sibilities of office? Why are they so often distributed amongst a number of independent functionaries who are thus enabled to exercise a balancing constraint on one another? It is clear that they serve, also, as a sanction against the abuse of political power and as a means of constraining political functionaries to perform their administrative obligations as well as their religious duties, lest the common good suffer injury.

When, finally, it is stated as an observable descriptive fact that we are dealing here with institutions that serve to affirm and pro-mote political solidarity we must ask why they do so. Why is an all-embracing administrative machinery or a wide-flung lineage system insufficient by itself to achieve this?

We cannot attempt to deal at length with all these questions. We have already given overmuch space to them because we consider them to be of the utmost importance, both from the theoretical and the practical point of view. The 'supernatural' aspects of African government are always puzzling and often exasperating to the European administrator. But a great deal more of research is needed before we shall be able to understand them fully. The hypothesis we are making use of is, we feel, a stimulating starting-point for further research into these matters.

That part of it which has already been stated is, perhaps, least controversial. But it is incomplete.

Any item of social behaviour, and therefore any political relation, has a utilitarian or pragmatic content. It means that material goods change hands, are disbursed or acquired, and that the direct purposes of individuals are achieved. Items of social behaviour and therefore political relations have also a moral aspect; that is, they express rights and duties, privileges and obligations, political sentiments, social ties and cleavages. We see these two aspects clearly in such acts as paying tribute to a ruler or handing over blood-cattle in compensation for murder. In political relations, consequently, we find two types of interests working conjointly, material interests and moral interests, though they are not separated in this abstract way in native thought. Natives stress the material components of a political relation and generally state it in terms of its utilitarian and pragmatic functions.

A particular right or duty or political sentiment occurs as an item of behaviour of an individual or a small section of an African society and is enforceable by secular sanctions brought to bear on these individuals or small sections. But in a politically organized community a particular right, duty, or sentiment exists only as an element in a whole body of common, reciprocal, and mutually balancing rights, duties, and sentiments, the body of moral and legal norms. Upon the regularity and order with which this whole body of interwoven norms is maintained depends the stability and continuity of the structure of an African society. On the average, rights must be respected, duties performed, the sentiments binding the members together upheld or else the social order would be so insecure that the material needs of existence could no longer be satisfied. Productive labour would come to a standstill and the society disintegrate. This is the greatest common interest in any African society, and it is this interest which the political system, viewed in its entirety, subserves. This, too, is the ultimate and, we might say, axiomatic set of premisses of the social order. If they were continually and arbitrarily violated, the social system would cease to work.

We can sum up this analysis by saying that the material interests that actuate individuals or groups in an African society operate in the frame of a body of interconnected moral and legal norms the order and stability of which is maintained by the political organization. Africans, as we have pointed out, do not analyse their social system; they live it. They think and feel about it in terms of values which reflect, in doctrine and symbol, but do not explain, the forces that really control their social behaviour. Outstanding among these values are the mystical values dramatized in the great public ceremonies and bound up with their key political institutions. These, we believe, stand for the greatest common interest of the widest political community to which a member of a particular African society belongs—that is, for the whole body of interconnected rights, duties, and sentiments; for this is what makes the society a single political community. That is why these mystical values are always associated with pivotal political offices and are expressed in both the privileges and the obligations of political office.

Their mystical form is due to the ultimate and axiomatic character of the body of moral and legal norms which could not be kept in being, as a body, by secular sanctions. Periodical ceremonies are necessary to affirm and consolidate these values because, in the ordinary course of events, people are preoccupied with sectional and private interests and are apt to lose sight of the common interest and of their political interdependence. Lastly, their symbolic content reflects the basic needs of existence and the basic social relations because these are the most concrete and tangible elements of all social and political relations. The visible test of how well a given body of rights, duties, and sentiments is being maintained and is working is to be found in the level of security and success with which the basic needs of existence are satisfied and the basic social relations sustained.

It is an interesting fact that under European rule African kings retain their 'ritual functions' long after most of the secular authority which these are said to sanction is lost. Nor are the mystical values of political office entirely obliterated by a change of religion to Christianity or Islam. As long as the kingship endures as the axis of a body of moral and legal norms holding a people together in a political community, it will, most probably, continue to be the focus of mystical values.

It is easy to see a connexion between kingship and the interests and solidarity of the whole community in a state with highly centralized authority. In societies lacking centralized government, social values cannot be symbolized by a single person, but are distributed at cardinal points of the social structure. Here we find myths, dogmas, ritual ceremonies, mystical powers, &c., associated with segments and defining and serving to maintain the relationship between them. Periodic ceremonies emphasizing the solidarity of segments, and between segments, as against sectional interests within these groups, are the rule among the Tallensi and Logoli no less than among the Bemba and Kede. Among the Nuer, the leopard-skin chief, a sacred personage associated with the fertility of the earth, is the medium through whom feuds are settled and, hence, inter-segment relations regulated. The difference between these societies of Group B and those of Group A lies in the fact that there is no person who represents the political unity of the people, such unity being lacking, and there may be no person who represents the unity of segments of the people. Ritual powers and responsibility are distributed in conformity with the highly segmentary structure of the society.

XIV. The Problem of the Limits of the Political Group

We conclude by emphasizing two points of very great importance which are often overlooked. However one may define political units or groups, they cannot be treated in isolation, for they always form part of a larger social system. Thus, to take an extreme example, the localized lineages of the Tallensi overlap one another like a series of intersecting circles, so that it is impossible to state clearly where the lines of political cleavage run. These overlapping fields of political relations stretch almost indefinitely, so that there is a kind of interlocking even of neighbouring peoples, and while we can see that this people is distinct from that, it is not easy to say at what point, culturally or politically, one is justified in regarding them as distinct units. Among the Nuer, political demarcation is simpler, but even here there is, between segments of a political unit, the same kind of structural relationship as there is between this unit and another unit of the same order. Hence the designation of autonomous political groups is always to some extent an arbitrary matter. This is more noticeable among the societies of Group B, but among those of Group A also there is an interdependence between the political group described and neighbouring political groups and a certain overlapping between them. The Ngwato have a segmentary relationship to other Tswana tribes which in many respects is of the same order as that between divisions of the Ngwato themselves. The same is true of the other societies with centralized governments.

This overlapping and interlocking of societies is largely due to the fact that the point at which political relations, narrowly defined in terms of military action and legal sanctions, end is not the point at which all social relations cease. The social structure of a people stretches beyond their political system, so defined, for there are always social relations of one kind or another between peoples of different autonomous political groups. Clans, age-sets, ritual associations, relations of affinity and of trade, and social relations of other kinds unite people of different political units. Common language or closely related languages, similar customs and beliefs, and so on, also unite them. Hence a strong feeling of community may exist between groups which do not acknowledge a single ruler or unite for specific political purposes. Community of language and culture, as we have indicated, does not necessarily give rise to political unity, any more than linguistic and cultural dissimilarity prevents political unity.

Herein lies a problem of world importance: what is the relation of political structure to the whole social structure? Everywhere in Africa social ties of one kind or another tend to draw together peoples who are politically separated and political ties appear to be dominant whenever there is conflict between them and other social ties. The solution of this problem would seem to lie in a more detailed investigation of the nature of political values and of the symbols in which they are expressed. Bonds of utilitarian interest between individuals and between groups are not as strong as the bonds implied in common attachment to mystical symbols. It is precisely the greater solidarity, based on these bonds, which generally gives political groups their dominance over social groups of other kinds.

THE KINGDOM OF THE ZULU OF SOUTH AFRICA[1]

By MAX GLUCKMAN

I. Historical Introduction

I DESCRIBE Zulu political organization at two periods of Zulu history—under King Mpande and to-day under European rule. Zulu history has been well described by Bryant and Gibson, and I here give only a bare outline which can be filled in by referring to their books.[2] I have used historical records partly to illustrate the functioning of the organization in each period and partly to discuss changes in the nature of the organization.

The Nguni family of Bantu-speaking people who later formed the Zulu nation migrated into south-eastern Africa about the middle of the fifteenth century. They were pastoralists practising a shifting cultivation. They lived in scattered homesteads occupied by male agnates and their families; a number of these homesteads were united under a chief, the heir of their senior line, into a tribe. Exogamous patrilineal clans (men and women of common descent bearing a common name) tended to be local units and the cores of tribes. A tribe was divided into sections under brothers of the chief and as a result of a quarrel a section might migrate and establish itself as an independent clan and tribe. There was also absorption of strangers into a tribe. Cattle raids were frequent, but there were no wars of conquest. By 1775 the motives for war changed, possibly owing to pressure of population. Certain tribes conquered their neighbours and small kingdoms emerged which

[1] The information contained in this article was largely collected during fourteen months' work in Zululand (1936–8), financed by the National Bureau of Educational and Social Research of the Union of South Africa (Carnegie Fund). I wish to thank the Bureau for its grant. I have also used many books, dispatches, and reports about Zululand in the last 100 years. For a bibliography of these, and an account of Zulu society, see E. J. Krige's *Social Systems of the Zulu* (Longmans, 1936).

[2] A. T. Bryant, *Olden Times in Zululand and Natal* (Longmans, 1938); J. Y. Gibson, *The Story of the Zulus* (Longmans, 1911). The account of the Zulu nation in this article is reconstructed from histories, contemporaneous records, and my questionings of old men.

came into conflict. In this struggle Shaka, head of the Zulu tribe, was victorious; by his personal character and military strategy, he made himself, in ten years, master of what is now Zululand and Natal,[1] and his troops were campaigning far beyond his boundaries. He organized a nation out of all the tribes he had subjected. His chief interest was in the army and he made whole-time warriors of his men; he developed the idea of regiments formed of men of the same age, and quartered them, for most of the year, in large barracks built in different parts of his country. They trained there for war, herded the king's cattle and worked his fields. The men were forbidden to marry till the king gave them permission, as a regiment, to marry into a certain age-regiment of girls. Shaka's rule was tyrannous and he fought a war every year; therefore, when in 1828 he was assassinated by his brother, Dingane, the people gladly accepted Dingane as king.

During Shaka's life English traders settled at Port Natal on friendly terms with the Zulu. Later the Boers entered Natal, defeated the Zulu in 1838, and confined them north of the Tugela River. Dingane's rule was also tyrannous and his people began to turn from him to his brother, Mpande. Dingane plotted to kill Mpande, who fled with his followers to the Boers in Natal; from there he attacked and routed Dingane and became king. The Zulu now entered on a period of comparative peace, for Mpande only occasionally raided the Swazi and Tembe (Thonga); to south and west were European states and the strongly entrenched Basuto. However, during his reign two of his sons fought for his heirship; Cetshwayo was victorious and he became king when Mpande died in 1872.

In 1880 the British defeated the Zulu, deposed Cetshwayo and divided the nation into thirteen kingdoms. Three years later they tried to reinstate Cetshwayo; for various reasons civil war broke out between the Usuthu (the Royal) section of the nation and tribes ruled, under the King, by the Mandlakazi Zulu house, which was united to the royal house in Mpande's grandfather. The king died but his son, Dinuzulu, with Boer help defeated the rebels who fled to the British. In 1887 the British established a magistracy in

---

[1] An area of some 80,000 square miles, occupied, according to Bryant's estimate, by about 100,000 people. I think this figure is too low. It may be noted that tribes fleeing from Shaka established the Matabele, Shangana, and Nguni nations.

Zululand and restored the Mandlakazi to their homes. Dinuzulu resisted, was defeated and exiled. The Zulu were divided into many tribes and white rule was firmly established. Dinuzulu was later appointed chief over a small tribe (the Usuthu), but was again exiled after the Bambada Rebellion in 1906. He died in exile and his heir was appointed Usuthu chief; on his death he was succeeded by his full-brother as regent. The government has

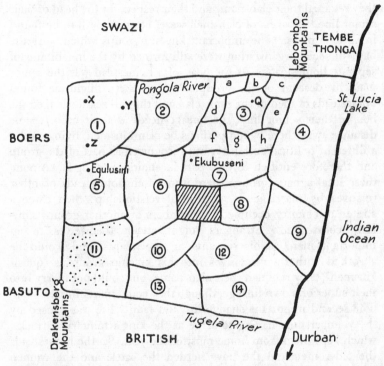

This is a sketch of the territorial organization of the Zulu nation under King Mpande. It is presented only as a plan, and not as a map.

The shaded area is the King's, containing his capital, other royal homesteads, and military barracks (which are also royal homesteads). Numerals show tribal areas: there were many more than fourteen.

In tribe 3, of which Q is the capital, small letters show wards under indunas.

In tribe 1, X, Y, and Z are the homesteads of the chief and two of his important brothers: the men of the tribe are attached to these homesteads to constitute the military divisions of the tribe.

In tribe 11, the dots represent homesteads spread over the country. Equlusini and Ekubuseni are royal homesteads which were heads of national army divisions, though they lay outside the King's area.

passed from Britain to Natal and in 1910 to the Union of South Africa.

II. The Zulu King and the State

Certain kinship groupings persisted through the devastating wars and the great change in political organization of Shaka's and Dingane's reigns. The clans had disappeared as units, and members of a single clan might be widely dispersed over Zululand: they retained their clan-name and their respect for the head of their senior line.[1] Pockets of clansmen were, however, still to be found in various parts. The important kinship groups which were the basis of social organization were still formed by the inhabitants of separate homesteads. At the head of a homestead was the senior male by descent of the group. Nearby there might be found homesteads of men of the same clan and they all acknowledged the heir of their senior line (the lineage-head) as their head. Some distance away there would perhaps be clan-kinsmen, living under a different political authority, but recognized as part of the group and therefore entitled to take part in affairs affecting it. Among these local agnatic groups there were often homesteads of other relatives by marriage or matrilineal relationship: then came a stretch of country occupied by members of another group, similarly constituted. Strangers might attach themselves to an important man, as his servants or dependants, and would be absorbed with their relatives into his kinship group as 'quasi-kinsmen'; they retained their clan-name, but could not marry into their superior's own lineage, though they could marry into his clan. The second important change in Zulu family life was caused by the younger men having to serve at the king's military barracks, which kept them from home most of the year. In the homesteads the older men and the boys herded the cattle and the women worked the fields. Each homestead had its own fields and cattle-fold. A demographic survey would show the homesteads scattered at some distance apart (a few hundred yards to a mile or two) along the hills which, intersected by deep bush-filled valleys, characterized the interior of Zululand. The fields were mostly

[1] Men and women with the same clan-name could not marry one another. No new clans have been formed in the period since the clans ceased to be local, political units, as in the past a chief desiring to marry a woman of his clan would split off her lineage and make of it a separate clan. Dinuzulu attempted unsuccessfully to form a new clan of a Mandlakazi lineage into which he married.

along the ridges and the banks of streams; the low valleys, uninhabited because of fever, were winter-grazing and hunting grounds.
The coastal tribes lived, similarly distributed, on the malarial
sandy plain between the hills and the sea. Communication between different parts of Zululand was fairly easy; men went from
all parts to the King's barracks and marriage between members of
widely separated homesteads was common.

The Zulu nation thus consisted of members of some hundreds of
clans, united by their allegiance to the king. The people belonged
to the king and he therefore took the fine in cases of assault or
murder. In the earlier period of Nguni history, political allegiance tended to coincide with kinship affiliation. Thus the Zulu
tribe (*abakwazulu*) consisted originally largely of descendants of
Zulu, a junior son of Malandela, as distinguished from the Qwabe
tribe, the descendants of Qwabe, the senior son of Malandela.
To-day the term *abakwazulu* still means the members of the Zulu
clan, but it has also the wider meaning of all the people who pay
allegiance to the Zulu king. Collectively, whatever their clan
names, they are politely addressed as 'Zulu'. Political and kinship
affiliation came to be distinct also in the smaller political groups
into which the nation was divided. These were composed of
members of many clans, though they might have a core of kinsmen: members of a single clan might be found in many political
groups. While the kinship basis of political groups disappeared, the
new ones which emerged were described in kinship terms, for any
political officer was spoken of as the father of his people, and his
relationship to them was conceived to be similar to that of a father
and his children. The territory of king or chief may be referred to
as *umzi kaMpande* (the homestead of Mpande) or *umzi kaZibebu*
(the homestead of Zibebu), as *umzi kabani* is the family homestead
of So-and-So. The children of the king are not supposed to refer
to him as 'father', for, 'is not the king father of his people, not of
his family only'.

The king also owned the land. All who came to live in Zululand
had to acknowledge his sovereignty. *Abakwazulu* has too the
meaning of the people of Zululand (*Kwazulu*) and the Zulu word
izwe means nation, tribe, or country.[1] The same rule applied to

---

[1] It must be noted that the Zulu form of describing the clan is locative:
abakwàzulu, 'the people of the Zulu clan', literally, 'the people of the place
of Zulu', not genitive, *abakaZulu*, 'the descendants of Zulu'.

the smaller political groupings and to find out who a man's chief is, one asks either 'Who is your chief?' or 'Of whose district are you?' The relation of the political unit to land may be defined: any one coming on to land belonging to a political authority became subject to that authority, and all his subjects were entitled to land in his area.

The Zulu nation may therefore be defined as a group of people owing allegiance to a common head (the king) and occupying a defined territory. They combined under the king to attack or defend themselves against outside groups. In addition to controlling relations with other Bantu-speaking peoples and the Europeans, the king exercised judicial, administrative, and legislative authority over his people, with power to enforce his decisions. He performed religious ceremonies and magical acts on behalf of the nation. All the tribes which made up the nation spoke dialects of the same language and had a common culture.

The kings Mpande and Cetshwayo had no subjects directly under their control. They lived in a tract of land occupied only by royal homesteads and military barracks[1]: outside of this tract Zululand was divided into a large number of political groups. The inhabitants of the largest divisions of the nation I call 'tribes', and their heads I call 'chiefs'. The tribes were divided into smaller groups (wards) under relatives of the chief or men of other clans (indunas), responsible to the chiefs.

The king was approached with ceremonious salutations and titles of respect which, say the Zulu, increased his prestige. He was addressed as the nation. What tradition and history was common to all the Zulu had to be told in the names of the Zulu kings and it was largely their common sentiment about the king and his predecessors which united all Zulu as members of the nation. At the great first-fruits ceremonies and in war-rites, the king was strengthened and cleansed in the name of the nation. He possessed certain objects, inherited from his ancestors, and the welfare of the country was held to depend on them. This ceremonial position of the king was backed by his ancestral spirits. They were supposed to care for the whole of Zululand, and in the interests of the nation the king had to appeal to them in drought, war, and at the planting and first-fruits seasons. They were

---

[1] All military barracks were royal homesteads. They were built on the plan of ordinary homesteads but were very large, housing some thousands of men.

praised against the ancestors of other kings. The king was in charge of, and responsible for, all national magic. Shaka expelled all rainmakers from his kingdom, saying only he could control the heavens. The king possessed important therapeutic medicines with which he would treat all his ailing important people. All skilled leeches had to teach the king their cures. Finally, when people died and a person was accused of killing them by sorcery, no sentence was supposed to be executed unless the king's witch-doctors confirmed the verdict. These religious and magical duties of the king, in performing which he was assisted by special, hereditary magicians, were vested in the office of kingship; though a king might be killed, his successor took over these duties, and the spirits of tyrants were even supposed to become a source of good to the people who had slain them.

The ritual of these national ceremonies was similar to that of tribal ceremonies of pre-Shaka times, but Shaka militarized them and the men paraded for them in regiments. The ceremonies were chiefly designed to strengthen the Zulu at the expense of other people, who were symbolically attacked in them. It was this military orientation of Zulu culture under the king which largely unified his people. A man was called *isihlangu senkosi* (war-shield of the king). The dominant values of Zulu life were those of the warrior, and they were satisfied in service at the king's barracks and in his wars. To-day old men talking of the kings get excited and joyful, chanting the king's songs and dances, and all Zulu tend, in conversation, to slip into tales of the king's wars and affairs at his court.

The regiments belonged to the king alone. They lived in barracks concentrated about the capital; the chiefs had no control over the regiments and assembled their own people in territorial, not age, divisions. This organization probably persisted from the period before Shaka[1] began to form 'age regiments'. In those times the chief of a tribe seems to have assembled his army in divisions which he constituted by attaching the men of certain areas to certain of his important homesteads. The tribes within the Zulu nation were (and to-day still are) organized for fighting and hunting on this basis. The king alone could summon the age regiments. The nation also was divided for military purposes in the same way as a tribe was divided. For the king attached

[1] The idea of age regiments was originally developed on the basis of old age-grades by a chief, Dingiswayo, who was Shaka's patron.

certain groups of tribes to certain of his royal homesteads. I call each of these divisions and the royal homestead (*ikhanda*, head) to which it was attached a 'head'. Most of the homesteads which were 'heads' were in the king's area; one or two lay outside it. Some were also barracks in which were quartered particular regiments. The division into 'heads' was not purely territorial, for once a man was attached to a 'head' he could not change his attachment even if he moved into a tribal area attached to a different 'head'. His sons inherited his attachment; when they were ready to be enrolled as soldiers, they went to the 'head' to which their father belonged, and later from all the 'heads' the king assembled all the young men and formed them into a new regiment with its own barracks. Therefore each 'head' contained members of all regiments and each regiment contained members of all the 'heads'. In a barracks or on parade, the 'heads' within a regiment had set places according to the seniority of establishment of their respective royal homesteads. The members of a 'head' supported the prince of their royal homestead; King Cetshwayo, therefore, when he succeeded to the throne, strengthened his own head by attaching to it more tribes. Each regiment had commanders who were usually princes, chiefs, or the brothers of important chiefs, but were sometimes brave commoners.

This centralization of the regiments in the king's area gave him a position in Zulu life entirely different from that of any of his chiefs. It continually brought the men close to his capital, where they lived on the bounty of his cattle and grain, supplemented by food sent from their homes. But though it brought the regiments under the king's control, it robbed him of personal followers, since all the men were attached to some chief. It may be noted that this centralization seems to have been effected when the Zulu were fighting few wars but maintaining a large standing army; Zulu prestige was so great that there was little likelihood of other Bantu raiding them, even though the Zulu troops were stationed far from the borders.[1]

The king was also the supreme court of the nation and appeals from the chiefs' courts went to him. He was called on to decide

[1] This organization may be contrasted with a lack of similar organization among the Tswana and Sotho and is perhaps a reflection of the scattered establishment of the Zulu. In the large Tswana towns the men could easily be summoned to the chief's home. But chiefs of tribes such as the Swazi and Thonga seem to have kept only one or two regiments near them: the concentration of the whole Zulu army about the king is unique in southern Africa.

difficult cases. There were always in residence at his capital some *indunas* of cases (*izinduna zamacala*) who heard these cases and gave verdicts in the king's name. Most of these *indunas* were chiefs ruling areas of their own; others were sons, brothers, and uncles of the king, and there were commoners 'lifted up' by the king for their wisdom and knowledge of law. In all the councils of men throughout the land, the *indunas* were supposed to mark men skilful in debate and law and their ability might get them into the king's council. Two of his *indunas* were more important than the others : the one was more specifically commander of the army and was a chief or prince; the other was called the 'great *induna*' (prime minister) and had weightiest voice in discussing affairs of state. He was always an important chief, never a member of the royal family.

The king was supposed to maintain the customary law. Zulu have illustrated this to me by quoting a case in which Mpande had to decide against one of his favourites and then sent men to wipe out the successful litigant's family so as to make it impossible for the decision to be carried out. But he could not decide, against the law, for his favourite. Nevertheless, the king could in deciding a case create new law for what he and his council considered good reason.

The king was supposed to follow the advice of his council. If he did not, it is said that the council could take one of his cattle. The Zulu believed that the welfare of the country depended on the king's having wise and strong councillors ready to criticize the king. In council the king (or a chief) was supposed to put the matter under discussion before the council and himself speak last so that no one would be afraid to express his own opinion. The king might inform his close councillors of his views and they could put these to the council; he should not put himself in a position where he would be contradicted. But no councillor should express a strong opinion; he should introduce his points with some oblique phrase deferring to the king. The king ended the discussion and, if he were wise, adopted the views of the majority. The council could also initiate discussions on matters of tribal or national interest. It seems that in fact the king did consider his councillors' views and did not act autocratically. Sometimes he would excuse an action by saying that it had been done by his *indunas* without his authority, and this does seem to have happened; and in dealing with Europeans on occasion the kings said they were willing to do something, and then backed out on the plea that their *indunas* had decided against it. The king's power and the councillors' insistence on their rights and jealousy of one another might all affect the course of discussion and the decision on any matter or case.

From his subjects' point of view, one may say that the main duty they owed the king was military service, including labour service. The king was also entitled to certain royal game, though he had to reward the hunters. In addition, it was customary to give him gifts of grain, beer, cattle and, some say, girls. As he also received most of the cattle and women captured in war and fines for certain offences, he was easily the richest man in the nation.[1] In return for this, he was expected to feed and help his people generously. He had to care for his regiments and give them their shields; in famine he was expected to help all his people and also at all times those in difficulties. Thus if the king ruled according to tradition, he was generous to his subjects, using his wealth for them; he gave them justice; he protected their interests; and through him they hoped to satisfy their ambitions on battlefield and in forum.

III. Status and Political Power

All the members of Shaka's family enjoyed a higher status as a result of his victories. Neither he nor Dingane had any children and it was the descendants of Mpande who came to form the royal family, though certain important collateral lines were regarded as princes. Any child of these lines, and the children of their daughters and adopted women, were referred to as *abant-wana* (=children, but is equivalent to princes and princesses). They formed the superior rank in Zulu society, in status above even the chiefs; some of them also ruled as chiefs of tribes. Princes of the Zulu lines, and chiefs of other clan lines who were princes by royal women, were among the most powerful chiefs in the land. But the closer a royal prince was (and is) by birth to the reigning king the higher his social status, though he might exert less influence in the nation than other princes or even commoners. To a lesser extent the same rules applied to the reigning families within the tribes; the close relatives of a chief were the aristocracy in his tribe.

---

[1] Shaka made all trade with Europeans pass through his hands; and later only important people were allowed to buy certain goods from traders.

Any member of the Zulu royal family had to be greeted ceremonially by commoners, including chiefs. Any royal prince
might also be greeted by some of the praise names of the king,
such as 'source of the country', if the king were not there, though
the royal salute, *Bayede*, and the names *inkosi* (king), *ingonyama*
(lion), should be strictly reserved for the king himself. This
status of the princes brought some of them political power. Shaka's
brothers became chiefs in the areas in which they settled. Mpande
followed the practice of big, polygynous chiefs and settled his sons
in various areas as chiefs there. The king was therefore head by
descent of the powerful aristocratic Zulu lineage which was looked
up to by all Zulu, and his position in the national organization was
strengthened, since tribes scattered through Zululand were ruled
by his close relatives, who were bound to him by strong kinship
ties of mutual assistance and by their common membership of the
royal lineage. Marriage between the royal family and families of
chiefs established similar ties. The king would marry off a sister,
a daughter, or even some girl belonging to him, to a chief, and her
son (who ranked as a prince in the nation) should be heir. However, the princes might draw to themselves followers beyond those
given them by the king, and as in the past brothers of tribal chiefs
had broken away to establish independent tribes, so the princes
within the nation were a potential threat to the king, especially if he
misruled. They were ready to intrigue against him and take advantage of the people's dislike of him. Zulu custom says the king
should not eat with his brothers, lest they poison him. His relatives on his mother's side and by marriage were said to be his
strongest supporters, for their importance in national life came
from their relationship to him, rather than their relationship to the
royal lineage.

Zulu therefore state, on the one hand, that the king rules with
the support of his brothers and uncles, and, on the other hand,
that the king hates his brothers and uncles, who may aspire to the
throne. In practice, it appears that more often the princes and
chiefs competed for importance at court, i.e. they intrigued against
one another, rather than against the king. While Mpande lived his
sons also struggled for power. The most important of these
struggles was for Mpande's heirship. The rule of succession is that
the heir is born of the woman whom the king makes his chief wife.
Mpande first appointed Cetshwayo heir, for Cetshwayo was born

of a wife given him by Dingane. Then he began to favour Mbuyazi, son of his most beloved wife. Each son had his own following. Cetshwayo was supported by his most important brothers and the big chiefs, and he routed Mbuyazi: from that time he began to rule. Zulu succession has been very chequered: the first two kings were ousted by a brother, and Cetshwayo fought for the kingdom. When the British deposed him, his chief wife had had no children, so he appointed Dinuzulu, then about seventeen, heir. A son was born to the chief wife after Cetshwayo's death and was made a chief by the British; Dinuzulu objected, as he feared his brother would come to be a rival.

Royal rank therefore tended to carry political power either in the form of a personal following or else of great weight in tribal and national councils. Otherwise high rank in the nation, with respect, was accorded to all political officers, whether they were chiefs or councillors of the king, and to his important servants and brave warriors.

One other principle also gave high rank—namely, kinship seniority within any kinship group. As stated above, Zulu, the founder of the Zulu clan, was the junior brother of Qwabe, the founder of the Qwabe clan. To-day the Qwabe chief is one of the few chiefs who will not recognize the superiority of the Zulu king: he claims that he himself is superior by birth. People to whom I have put his claim consider that it is invalid: Shaka founded the Zulu nation and therefore his heirs are entitled to rule it. Nevertheless, they say, the king should 'respect' the kinship seniority of the Qwabe chief. This principle worked through all the clans. Independently of political power or boundaries, the people continued to pay respect to the lineal head of their clan. They might take inheritance cases to him and assist him with the bride-wealth for his chief wife, even if they lived under a chief of another clan line.

IV. The Tribes within the Nation

Zululand was divided into a large number of tribes of varying sizes.[1] In Zulu theory the chiefs (or their ancestors) of all these tribes were 'raised up' by one or other of the kings. By this the

[1] Estimate of population: The nation about 1870 probably numbered a quarter to half a million; tribes varied from a few hundreds to several thousands. The later regiments consisted of nearly 8,000 men.

Zulu mean that they held power subject to the king and that ultimately, at the time when the Zulu nation was being created and consolidated, Shaka or his succeeding brothers made their ancestors into chiefs, or allowed them to continue their rule in a particular area. The kings either recognized existing chiefs or sent some man with a following to colonize an uninhabited area. One of the important ways in which a man obtained political status was by royal birth, as described in the preceding section. Other men were the heads of the remnants of tribes which had been independent before Shaka's conquest and there were clan-heads to whom, in the years after the initial wars had scattered their people, their followers returned. The kings on occasion also rewarded personal body-servants, brave warriors, and learned councillors by putting them in charge of districts. But usually the chiefs were princes or the heads of clans. The lineal heads of certain clans had no political power; other clans were represented by chiefs in various parts of Zululand. It was even expedient for the kings to recognize clan-heads as chiefs since kinship affiliation was still a principle uniting people and cognizance had to be taken of the groups thus formed.

From the earliest times political officers had been succeeded by their sons and under the kings this rule continued to be recognized. Zulu still say that an *induna* or chief had his position because he was given it by the king; but if he died his heir, unless hopelessly incompetent, should succeed him. And, failing the heir, the king (or chief) should appoint a close relative to act as regent and the position return to the main line if possible. Zulu say the heir has a right to be appointed, but it depends on the king's will; yet it is recognized that if the heir is passed over he and his followers may cause trouble. For example, I heard an important chief discussing with two of his brothers the appointment of a successor to a recently deceased *induna* of the X—— clan. The brothers were against a descendant being appointed, as they held that the dead man had intrigued with the local magistrate to be recognized as independent. The chief replied that there was no proof that his sons would act in that way because he had; in any case, the area was thickly populated by the X—— people and he asked his brother how they would like it if a stranger were put in control of their own area? He concluded: 'If we do that, we shall have trouble with the X—— people.' (I need scarcely note that the magistrate was not party to this intrigue.) Nevertheless, in a small *induna*'s area the king (or chief) had power to appoint a parvenu: the king would hesitate to interfere directly in the succession to a large tribal chieftainship, or a chief with a powerful *induna*, for a number of the people might remain loyal to the man whom they considered the rightful heir. There were occasions, however, on which the king favoured one or other claimant to a chieftainship to suit his own ends. If the homestead of an important son of the king or a chief (especially a Zulu clan chief) was built in a commoner *induna*'s area the prince became political head there and the *induna* became his *induna*. However when Mpande wanted to settle one of his sons as a chief, he asked a chief for land for him.

The chiefs had certain powers delegated to them by the king. Their most important duties were judicial and administrative. They tried cases coming to them on appeal from their *indunas*' courts and investigated breaches of the law. Though in theory all fines for bodily hurts went to the king, in fact the chiefs seem to have kept these; however, they periodically sent large herds of cattle as gifts to the king. They were supposed to forward difficult cases and cases involving important estates to the king. In their decisions they were bound to follow laws issued by the king and from them appeal lay to his court. They had power to execute judgement, but no power of life and death. In practice, some powerful chiefs were fairly independent and are said to have executed sorcerers and adulterers. As judicial heads in their districts, they had to report to the king all grave misdemeanours and they had to watch over the public weal. An example of how the king delegated administrative duties to his chiefs is Cetshwayo's appointing a coastal chief to facilitate the passage of labourers from Thongaland to Natal through Zululand, which he had agreed to do for the Natal Government. As the chiefs were often in attendance on the king, they could not perform these duties themselves, but delegated them to trusted relatives and *indunas*.

The king communicated with his chiefs by runners. To impersonate a king's messenger was punishable by death. Thus orders to mobilize at the capital, projected laws and matters of national import were announced to the people by the king through his chiefs, though many announcements were made at the first-fruits ceremony. When necessary, the chiefs passed on these orders to their *indunas* in charge of wards and these reported to the heads of lineage groups and homesteads. All the people were entitled to express their opinion on affairs and they did this through the heads of their kinship groups and then their immediate political officers. In addition, the chiefs and *indunas* had administrative duties within their own districts, including the allocation of land, the maintenance of order, trying of cases, watching over their districts' welfare, taking ritual steps to protect the crops, looking for sorcerers. Chiefs, like the king, received gifts of corn and cattle, but they levied no regular tribute. They could call out their subjects to work their fields, build their homesteads, arrest malefactors, or hunt. In turn, they were expected to reward these workers with food and to help their people who were in trouble. Like the king, too, they were bound to consult and listen to a council composed of their important men.

Thus authority from the king was exercised through the chiefs, his representatives in various districts. They ruled through their brothers and *indunas* of smaller districts, under whom were the lineage- and homestead-heads. Zulu political organization may therefore be seen as delegated authority over smaller and smaller groups with lessening executive power. From inferior officers there was an appeal to higher ones; in theory the king's will was almost absolute. At the bottom were the heads of kinship groups who could issue orders and arbitrate in disputes within their groups, but who could not enforce their decisions, except over women and minors. On the other hand, as the groups became smaller the ties of community and kinship grew stronger, and as force lessened as a sanction other social sanctions increased in importance. The dependence of men on their senior relatives in religious and economic matters, as well as in trouble, was strong; even at the barracks they shared huts with their kinsmen and relied on them for food and support in quarrels. In kinship groupings the main integrating activities and social sanctions were based on reciprocity and communal living. Some kinship rules were backed by judicial sanctions, but when these obligations were enforced at law, force was used on the chief's judgement. not on the obligation itself.

I have described the tribes and smaller groups as part of a pyramidal organization with the king at the top in order to bring out the administrative framework which ran through the social groupings, but the position of the head of each group in the series

was different, for he was related to the members of his group by
different ties from those linking them to the head of the larger
group of which it was part. Besides the ties of sentiment, homestead and lineage, heads exercised authority because of their
kinship status and their importance in their inferiors' social and
economic life; *indunas* and their followers shared in common
social, and often economic, activities, as well as political affairs;
tribesmen were attached to their chiefs mainly by political bonds;
and all Zulu to the king by their military duties. The average
Zulu's importance decreased the bigger the group of which he was
a member. The king's position in the state was essentially his
establishment in the 'barrack area'. He symbolized for the Zulu
their identity as a nation as against the Swazi and other Bantu, and
European, Powers. The nation was a federation of tribes whose
separate identities were symbolized by their chiefs. The tribes
were even autonomous within the national organization for on
occasion many tribesmen supported their chiefs in quarrels with
the king, though some were swayed by national loyalties.[1] However, it was in the relations between tribes that tribal identities
mainly appeared. There existed between the tribes a strong
hostility which radically affected the course of Zulu history after
the Zulu War of 1880; it was mirrored at court in the competition
of the chiefs for power. For the people of any tribe of some
strength were proud of their traditions and their chiefly line, were
loyal to their chief and quick to resent any attempt by other chiefs
to interfere in their tribal affairs. Occasionally, especially on the
borders of tribes, this hostility broke out in affrays. It appeared
most clearly in the people's attachment to their own chief as against
other chiefs. Therefore, as will be seen in the next section, the
chiefs tried by ruling well to win adherents from other chiefs.
Nevertheless, the chiefs were often related to one another and on
friendly terms. As part of the administrative machinery they
served together on the king's council and they might even combine
to constrain the king.

Within a tribe, there was a similar opposition between sections.
The tribes were divided, as described in the paragraphs on the
Army, into sections attached to homesteads of the chief, his

---

[1] This is how Zulu describe it; in fact, they may have been moved by self-
interest or other motives, but their actions are described in terms of tribal and
national values.

brothers, and his uncles; the adherents of each of these homesteads were very jealous of their 'prince's' prestige and felt a local
loyalty to him as against the adherents of other 'princes'. Before
and after the death of a chief, these groups vied with one another
to have their 'prince' nominated as heir, and were even ready on
occasion, despite their tribal loyalties, to support him against the
heir when he assumed power. Faction fights between these sections continue to-day, often flaring up over trivial matters; and
when Government assumed rule in Zululand it inherited a rich
legacy of their feuds and of inter-tribal feuds. Even the members
of wards under commoner *indunas* often came to blows, for at
weddings and hunts they assembled as members of military sections or wards, and if a fight started between two men their fellow
members would support them. Thus in every Zulu political group
there was opposition between its component sections, often mani-
fested through their leaders, though they co-operated in matters
affecting the welfare of the whole group.

The opposed groups within the nation were united by the
common service of their leaders in the council of the larger group
of which they were part. The administration ran in separate
threads from king to a particular chief, to a particular *induna*, to a
particular lineage-head; all these threads were woven together in
the council system. Though the group-heads were the main part
of what bureaucracy there was in the simple Zulu social organization, their functions as bureaucrats and as group-heads were not
entirely identical. In previous paragraphs some of their functions
as group-heads have been reviewed. As administrators, they
watched their people's interests and ruled them according to the
orders of their superiors, and they also used their people's backing
in their struggles for administrative power, perhaps against the
people's interests. They and the officers about a court were the
link between a ruler and his subjects, but frequently tended to
become a barrier between them, for they were jealous of their
rights, resented any encroachment on their privileges and sometimes acted independently of the ruler. The people had to consider
these officials in approaching their rulers, the rulers were largely
compelled to conduct their relations with the people through them.
There was therefore an unstable balance of duties and interests
between the group-heads acting as courtiers and other courtiers,
and the rulers and the people.

V. Sanctions on Authority and the Stability of the State

The king was bound to consider custom and his council. The Zulu king rarely called full meetings of the nation for discussion; he consulted their wishes through the chiefs. The people could not themselves criticize the king, but he might suffer if he disregarded their feelings entirely. The king was supposed to be just and generous and princes and chiefs were educated in, and conscious of, the tradition of good rule. The Zulu point to their history and show its lessons. Was not Shaka killed because he oppressed the people, so that Dingane did not fear to kill him? In turn, many people supported Mpande against Dingane. Mpande, the just and generous king, ruled long I have been told that if a chief troubled his people, his family and *indunas* would poison him, but my informants could not give me a case in which this was done.

It required a long period of suffering before the people would turn against their rulers. Kings and chiefs were said to have many spies, and it was difficult to organize armed resistance to the king, though Zulu point out that all Shaka's spies did not save him from assassination. The king was backed with great force and a rebellion required that jealous chiefs and princes should unite. An early European visitor to Shaka records that his policy was to keep his chiefs at loggerheads with one another, and the Zulu admit this as a method of rule, pointing out that Government uses it to-day in dividing up Natal and Zululand into 300 chieftainships. Outside of the royal family there was no one who could hold together the nation and this was recognized by the chiefs.

The people depended for leadership against an oppressive ruler on their nearer political officers. The Zulu had no idea of any political organization other than hereditary chieftainship and their stage of social development did not conduce to the establishment of new types of régime. Their only reaction to bad rule was to depose the tyrant and put some one else in his place with similar powers, though individuals could escape from Zululand to other nations' protection; that is, the people could take advantage of the princes' and chiefs' intrigues for power and the latter in intriguing sought to win the backing of the people. The king's policy was therefore to prosecute any one who threatened to be able to take his place: he had to meet rivals, not revolutionaries.

The kings killed all brothers whose rivalry they feared. Uncles (fathers in the kinship system) were less likely to oust the king, and while the people should not complain against the king to his brothers they could appeal to one of his uncles. The kings, and all officers, were always on the watch for these threats to them. As the medicines of a ruler were believed to make him immune to the influence of his inferiors, if he felt ill in the presence of some person he could accuse the latter of sorcery.

The king had to treat all his brothers (and chiefs) carefully, lest they became centres of disaffection against him. The tension between the king and his brothers was a check on the king's rule because his subjects could shift their allegiance to his brothers. In addition, because the Zulu were strongly attached to their immediate political heads, the chiefs, and would even support them against the king, the chiefs had power to control the actions of the king. On the other hand, the chiefs remained dependent on the king. He could enlarge the powers of his favourites or assist the rivals of a recalcitrant chief.

Within tribes the chiefs held power under similar conditions. They could use armed force against disobedient or rebellious subjects though they had to inform the king that they were doing this. There were stronger checks on their rule. Their subjects could complain to the king if they were misruled. Though a man could in theory sue the king, he was not likely to do so; a chief could be brought before the king's court. Misrule by a chief would strengthen the hands of his brothers within the tribe and these brothers, unless the king intervened, might seize power. A quarrel with an important brother or subject might induce him to live elsewhere with his personal adherents. While misrule drove subjects to other chiefs a good and generous rule would attract followers. The Zulu have it that a chief should be free and generous with his people and listen to their troubles, then they will support him in war and 'not stab him in his hut'. The forces of fission and integration which marked the early political organization were still at work in the Zulu nation and to benefit by them it behoved a chief to rule wisely and justly in accordance with the wishes of his people.

The Zulu had loyalties to their various political heads. While these loyalties did not generally conflict, if king, chief, or *induna* abused his power the people would support one of their other

political heads against him, and in their intrigues for power the
political heads were ready to take advantage of this. Thus the
potential conflict of these loyalties was a strong check on misrule
and gave the people some control over their rulers.

VI. The People and Their Leaders

The working of these forces depended on the fact that political
leadership was personal. In theory, any one could approach his
superiors through their courtiers, though it might take some days.
A chief (and even the king) was supposed to deal with his people
himself and should not altogether delegate this duty. Chiefs and
indunas knew most of their subjects, with their relationships and
ancestry; if a stranger arrived at a capital all details about him
were asked. To a lesser extent this applied to the king. The chief
attended his people's weddings and sent his condolences, or
visited them, if a relative died. The Zulu sum this up by saying
'the people respect their chief, but the chief ought to respect his
people'.

This intimacy between the chief and his people, despite the
ceremonial which surrounded him, was largely possible because
there was no class snobbery among the Zulu. The chief was still
regarded and treated as the 'father of his people'; 'they are your
father's people', he was told; 'care for them well'. And did not the
chief belong to the tribe, especially if it had subscribed the bride-
wealth for his mother? There was no insurmountable barrier to
marriage between his and any of his subjects' families. Though
the courtiers had greater knowledge of affairs than the provincials
had, the Zulu all had the same education and lived in the same
way; and any one could take his part in the chief's council or
assist in judging a case. Birth, age, courage, and wisdom all
affected the attention a man would get; but every one could speak.
Wealth brought a chief closer to, did not remove him from, his
people. For under the conditions of Zulu life wealth did not give
a chief opportunity to live at a higher level than his inferiors. He
had more wives and bigger homesteads, but he could not surround
himself with luxuries, for there were none. Wealth, in the form of
well-filled granaries and large herds of cattle, gave a man power
only to increase the number of his dependants and to dominate
many inferiors. From the point of view of the chief, it may be said
that he had to be rich in order to support his dependants; and

besides this there was no use for wealth.[1] On the other hand, the wealth of a commoner attracted dependants and gave the rich man political status. Moreover, the kinsman of a wealthy man would not quarrel readily with him, so that there was little likelihood of his kinship group breaking up. However, there were few ways in which a commoner could acquire wealth: he might by magical practice, or as a reward from king or chief for some deed, or as booty in war. I have been told that only important men owned cattle. The rich Zulu loaned out cattle to other people to herd for him; they could use the milk, and also the meat of animals which died, and this contract made them dependent on the cattle-owner because he could inflict great hardship on them by taking away his cattle. When the chief did this, it gave him a hold over his people and prevented them from easily changing their allegiance and going to some other chief.[2] Wealth therefore attracted followers, and as they increased and had children the wealthy man could collect about him a substantial group of dependants which was a political unit. Kinship alone, within a lineage, also created political units; even the head of a homestead had political duties. A notable feature of Zulu political organization throughout Zulu history is the creation of new groups as people moved about, settled and increased, and the heads of all these groups were minor political officers who might in time achieve prominence. Since leadership was personal, these groups were not merely absorbed into existing political groups; their leaders became officers within the organization.

There was thus a constant creation of new officials which, with the rise in rank of brave warriors and wise men, permitted of a high degree of social mobility. Any man, whatever his rank by birth, could become politically important if he had the ability, though those already established in high positions watched jealously over their rights and privileges. Thus it is said that sometimes if a chief became jealous of an inferior he would kill him on a trumped-up charge of sorcery, though it seems that more often these charges were brought by other men in the chief's court. They were (and are) frequent in court circles.

[1] To-day the position is different. Wealthy men can build European houses and buy motor-cars, clothes, ploughs, &c.

[2] A certain chief in Zululand to-day has a remarkable hold over his people: he has 16,000 cattle (out of a tribal total of 54,000) loaned out among them.

The Zulu say that to-day there is more security of life than in olden times, when a man might be killed for anything. Despite this, and despite accounts of lawlessness and favouritism, the old Zulu declare that they got justice from their chiefs and help in times of trouble. They deny that chiefs could be bribed. Mpande and Cetshwayo both gave decisions against important chiefs. The chiefs were undoubtedly cruel and capricious on occasion, but they were generous, though one old man who had been much at court said to me sadly: 'There is no chief who is kind.' The old Zulu generally shake their heads over the harsh rule of the past; and then speak of the glories under it. The life of the subjects seems to have varied with the character of their chief.

During the time of the kings, the State bulked large in the people's lives. In council and on the battle-field only could high ambitions be satisfied. In the smaller districts the men were always busy on administrative and judicial affairs when they were at home, especially after they retired from the active service, during which they had to spend a large part of their time at the military barracks. Here they starved for days, then feasted royally on meat. They lounged with their fellows, hunted, danced before the king, paraded for the national ceremonies. The king would sit and talk with his important men, discussing the law, mighty deeds, and history. Tribal and ward capitals were the centres of social life in their districts. The evolution of the barrack system affected Zulu social life considerably: it controlled marriages, and, though the old sexual labour division values remained, it was necessary for girls to assist in the work of herding and milking. The young men were not available for work at home and food had to be sent to them at the barracks. For the moment when they would be enrolled as warriors they waited eagerly, longing to join a regiment.

VII. The Period of European Rule[1]

Between 1887–8 the British Government finally took over the rule of Zululand, despite Dinuzulu's armed opposition. In

[1] My observations on modern Zulu politics have been made especially in the districts of Nongoma, Mhlabatini, and Hlabisa, and to a lesser extent in Ngotshe, Vryheid, Ingwavuma, and Ubombo. Certain observations have also been made in towns, on travels in more southerly districts, and at gatherings of chiefs and Zulu with Mshiyeni, the Regent of the Zulu royal house.

a short time Government rule was confirmed.[1] To-day it is a vital part of Zulu life: of ten matters I heard discussed one day in a chief's council seven were directly concerned with Government. Fifty years of close contact with Europeans have radically changed Zulu life along the lines known all over South Africa.[2] The military organization has been broken and peace established. The adoption of the plough has put agricultural labour on to the men, and they go out to work for Europeans in Durban, Johannesburg, and elsewhere. The development of new activities and needs, the work of various Government departments, missions, schools, stores, all daily affect the life of the modern Zulu. Communication has become easier, though pressure on the land is greater. Money is a common standard of value. The ancestral cult and much old ceremonial have fallen into disuse.

Zululand is divided into a number of magisterial districts, which are divided into tribes under chiefs,[3] who are granted a limited judicial authority and who are required to assist the Government in many administrative matters.[4] Within a district the magistrate is the superior political and judicial officer. He is the representative of Government. His court applies European law and is a court of first instance and of appeal from chiefs in cases between Natives decided according to Zulu law. He co-operates with other Government departments, and with the chiefs and their *indunas*. This, according to statute, is the political system: the chiefs are servants of Government under the magistrate, whom they are bound to obey. In Zulu life the magistrate and the chief occupy different, and in many ways opposed, positions.

The modern Zulu political system is ultimately dominated by the force of Government, represented in the district by the police. They are few in number, for the area and population they control,

---

[1] I lack space to discuss historically the way in which Government rule has been accepted, but have tried to make this implicit in my account of the system to-day.

[2] See I. Schapera (Editor), *Western Civilization and the Natives of South Africa* (Routledge, London, 1934).

[3] For population figures and maps see N. J. van Warmelo, *A Preliminary Survey of the Bantu Tribes of South Africa* (Union Government Printer, Pretoria, 1935). Magisterial districts comprise about 30,000 people; tribes vary from tens of to a few thousand taxpayers.

[4] These duties are defined by the Natal Code of Native Law, Proclamation No. 168/1932. See W. Stafford, *Native Law as Practised in Natal* (Witwatersrand University Press, Johannesburg, 1935).

but behind them lies the overwhelming military power of the Europeans. The magistrate is backed by this power and he is vested with all the authority of the white upper class in the South African community. In the development of new activities which has marked the change in Zulu life, Government has played a leading role. It has established peace, encouraged men to go to work for Europeans, supported schools, started health, veterinary, and agricultural services. The magistrate, therefore, not only applies Government regulations, but he is also the chief head of the organization which is bringing new enterprise and some adaptation to new conditions to the Zulu.[1] He has to do many things which the chief cannot do for lack of power, organization, and knowledge. People go to the magistracy with questions and troubles. Thus the magistracy has come to stand for many of the new values and beliefs which to-day affect Zulu behaviour.

However, while the Zulu acknowledge and use the magistracy, their attitude to Government is mainly hostile and suspicious. They blame it for the new conflicts in their community; they point to laws which they consider oppressive;[2] they regard measures which Government intends in their interests as being designed to take from them their land and cattle, and cite in argument the encroaching of whites on Zululand in the past and what they regard as a series of broken promises to them. Moreover, many of these measures conflict with their pleasures, beliefs, and mode of life, as, for example, the forbidding of hemp-smoking and of sorcery trials, and the dipping of cattle and control of cattle movements. Therefore while Government requires the chiefs to support its measures, the people expect their chiefs to oppose them. And, indeed, the chiefs are usually opposed to them. This position was clearly emphasized in 1938, when a chief who opposed the building of cattle paddocks to prevent soil-erosion was praised by his people, but condemned by officials; a chief who asked for a cattle paddock was praised by officials, but condemned by his people. They complained against him to the Zulu king. For

[1] I lack space to discuss the relations of different Government departments or the role of missionaries, and the reaction of the Zulu to changes, many of which have not been purposefully made.

[2] See D. D. T. Jabavu on 'Bantu Grievances' in *Western Civilization and the Natives of South Africa,* op. cit. These are outlined from the point of view of an educated Native.

the people look to their native leaders to examine Government projects and 'stand up for the people' against them.

The imposition of white rule and the development of new activities have radically curtailed and altered the chief's powers. He is subordinate to Government rule; he cannot compel, though he levies, labour service; he still owns the land, but it is less and subject to Government control; he has lost his relatively enormous wealth and often uses what he has in his own, and not his subjects' interests; he is surpassed in the new knowledge by many of his people. The men now have less time to devote to their chief's interests. A chief may try to enforce old forms of allegiance which some subjects will not render and this leads to conflict between them. If he tries to exploit or oppress a man, the latter can turn to the magistrate who will protect him. This last important point needs no elaboration, though it may be noted that as far back as the civil wars the different factions tried to persuade the British Government that they were in the right and should be helped. The chief can compel only that allegiance which Government, in its desire to rule through the chiefs, will make the people render, though his disapproval is a serious penalty in public life. Nevertheless, the chief still occupies a vital position in the people's life. Not only does he lead them in their opposition to Government, but he also has for them a value the magistrate cannot have. The magistrate cannot cross the barrier between white and black. He talks with his people and discusses their troubles, but his social life is with other Europeans in the district. The chief's social life is with his people. Though he is their superior, he is equal with them as against the whites and 'feels together' with them. 'He has the same skin as we have. When our hearts feel pain, his heart feels pain. What we find good, he finds good.' A white man cannot do this, cannot represent them. The Zulu are ignorant of European history and it can have no value for them: the chiefs, and especially the king, symbolize Zulu traditions and values. They appreciate with their people the value of cattle as ends in themselves and of customs like bride-wealth which are decried by Europeans. The chief is related to many of them by kinship ties and any man may become so related by marriage; the social and endogamous barrier between whites and blacks cannot be satisfactorily crossed. The Zulu acknowledge their chiefs' position largely through conservatism and partly because Government recognizes it. But a chief is usually chief by inheritance: 'he has the blood and the prestige of chieftainship and they extend to his relatives; the magistrate has only the prestige of his office.' By this contrast Zulu express the chief's position as it exists independently of Government's acknowledgement and rooted in the values and habits of the people. Chiefs and members of the royal family are greeted with traditional modes of respect. Their family history is retailed. Their capitals are centres of social life. They are given loyalty and tribute.

I have outlined the opposed positions of chief and magistrate: the balance between them is the dominant characteristic of the political system. However, it shifts from situation to situation in Zulu life. A certain minimum of allegiance to both magistrate and chief is legally enforced by Government; the influence of each may vary above that minimum with their characters and relations to each other, or according to the matter considered. A sympathetic magistrate who understands the Zulu will draw them to him, especially from a chief who is unsatisfactory; a harsh magistrate keeps people away from him and they go more to their chiefs. Even more the balance shifts for different individuals in different situations. A man who considers the chief to be biassed against him, favours the magistrate as impartial; but for him the chief is the source of justice when the magistrate enforces an unwelcome law. The people rally to the chief when they oppose measures such as the reduction of bride-wealth. If the chief tries to force labour from people, they compare him unfavourably with the magistrate who pays for the labour he employs. Though in many situations it cannot be done, the Zulu constantly compare Native and European officers and switch their allegiance according to what is to their own advantage or by what values they are being guided on different occasions.

It has been necessary for this analysis to emphasize the opposition between chief and magistrate. It is strong, and appears in the jealousy each often has of the other's power. But in routine administration the system functions fairly well. Chiefs and *indunas* actively assist in the administration of law and the carrying out of certain activities. The magistrates, keen on their work and anxious to see their districts progress, may as individuals win the trust of their people, though it is never complete and the fundamental attitude to Government remains unchanged. They represent their people to Government, and the administration, in developing the Native reserves, seems to be coming into conflict with Parliament in so far as Parliament represents white interests. But though in general the system works, the opposition between the two sets of authorities becomes patent over major issues. Then ultimately the superior power of Government can force a measure through unless it depends on the willing co-operation of people and chief. The Zulu now have little hope of resisting Government rule and sullenly accept Government decisions. In the chiefs' councils, they vent their opposition in talk.

In evaluating this reaction to modern political institutions it is necessary to distinguish between two groups of Zulu, the pagan and the Christian (or schooled). Any schooled Zulu is in general much readier to accept European innovations than are the pagans. However, the majority of Christians have the same attitudes as the pagans, though their complaints against Government and whites may be differently formulated. Some better educated Christians measure the chief's value by the materialistic standard of the practical work done by Government and hold that the chiefs are reactionaries opposing progress and they favour a system like the Transkeian Bunga. They are possibly moved by desire for power themselves. In general it may be said that most schooled Zulu regard the magistracy with more favour than do pagans, but among the best educated Zulu, who come most strongly against the colour bar, there is a tendency to a violent reaction to their own people and culture and values away from the Europeans. Nevertheless, it is through the Christians that the Europeans introduce most new ideas into Zulu life. This is causing hostility between pagans and Christians and creating, on the basis of differences in education, adaptability, enterprise, and values, a new opposition in the nation. Aside from these Christians, there are the pagans who attend on whites, seeking some advantage and trying to profit from the political situation: thus Zulu unity against the whites is weakened. The people tend not to see a conflict in their own actions, though they feel and suffer under it, but often they criticize other Zulu for their allegiance to the whites, saying that they are selling their people to the white man.

Though all Zulu tend to be united against the Europeans, old tribal loyalties and oppositions are still at work and faction fights frequently occur. Tribes are often hostile to one another, but they are again beginning to support the Zulu king. He is recognized legally only as the head of a small tribe in Nongoma district, though Government recognizes his superior status and through him speaks to, and hears from, the Zulu people. He has been used on several occasions to settle disputes in other tribes and always gets precedence over other chiefs. The present Regent is Government's nominee to the Union Native Representative Council. Government thus recognizes the continued existence of the Zulu nation. The strength of Zulu nationalism is growing after a period of weakness. The head of the royal house is again the king (*inkosi*); other chiefs are *abantwana* (princes) or *abanumzana* (big people). He exercises influence, aside from what Government allows him, in other tribes. Nearly all the tribes of Zululand and Natal and some in the Transvaal acknowledge him as their king, though many of them were never ruled by the kings and fought in various wars for the whites against them. The king's present power is partly due to the fact that he symbolizes the great tradition of the Zulu kings, which gives the Zulu their greatness as against other peoples, such as the Swazi. Bantu national loyalties, pride, and antagonisms are still strong despite a growing sense of black unity. The king's power is also part of the reaction against white domination, for the Zulu feel that he has the ear of Government and therefore power to help them in their present difficulties, and that he has the courage and strength to oppose Government. Nevertheless, under Government each chief is independent. Jealousy and desire for power still divide the chiefs, but only the Mandlakazi and Qwabe chiefs are jealous of the king, though he could not get all the tribes to adopt his nominee to represent the Natal Natives in the Union Senate; but other chiefs, find that, as representatives of the king, their position among their people is stronger than it is as independent Government chiefs. As such, their people suspect them of being afraid to criticize Government. The allegiance they give the king varies from constant consultation to recognition when he travels. All Zulu crowd to see him when they can and heap gifts on him.

Within a tribe there remains the divisions into sections under brothers of the chief or *indunas* which sometimes leads to fighting. The chief must rule according to tradition or the tribe will support his brothers and weaken his court, though the magistrate is, as pointed out, the strongest sanction on misrule. If a chief palters to Government, his subjects may turn from him to a more obdurate brother, or sometimes if the chiefs say they approve of a measure, the people may accept it. The chief has to pick his way between satisfying Government and his people and has to control political officers over whom he has only slight material sanction, though, since these officials and the councils of the people are not legally constituted by Government, he may disregard them.

I am unable, for lack of space, to examine the way in which the political system functions in modern Zulu social and economic life; or the effect on the political situation of the division of the white colour-group into Afrikaans-speakers and English-speakers, and other divisions within it. Briefly, it should be noted that the white group itself has contradictory values in approaching the Natives; though many Europeans are influenced by both sets of values, the missionaries, various other Europeans, and administrators, educationalists, and people in similar positions give more active expression to the Christian and liberal values. Many of these Europeans are on very friendly terms with Zulu. They fight for Zulu interests and the Zulu recognize this to some extent, though they still regard them as whites and therefore suspect. In economic life the ties between Europeans and Zulu are strong. This may be seen in the traders who have to compete for Zulu customers and in the various labour employers competing with each other for the limited supply of labour. They attempt to get the goodwill of chiefs in their enterprises and at the Rand mines members of the royal family are employed to control Zulu workers as well as to attract them there. Meanwhile, the recognition accorded by these labour employers and traders, and also by missionaries, to the chiefs adds to their powers in the present situation, even while the labour flow and Christianity are weakening in other ways the tribal organization.

VIII. Conclusion

Zulu political organization has been twice radically altered. On both occasions the people quickly acknowledged their new rulers' power and the new organization functioned fairly well; but the old organization, which retained its values and significance, affected the functioning of the new one of which it was made a part. Meantime, despite the changes brought about by the centralization of authority and the regimental system under the kings, and to-day by the labour flow and the development of new social groups and values and modes of behaviour, the smaller social groups have remained relatively constant.

The essence of both the systems described is the opposition of like groups and the potentially conflicting loyalties of the people to different authorities. The nation was a stable organization, for this opposition was principally between the tribes which were united in the king's position and his regiments. The circulation of the rulers' wealth was necessary to enable them to maintain their close relationship with their people. The conflict of loyalties to officials of different rank, often intriguing against one another, came into the open as a check on misrule. Therefore, despite the apparent autocracy of king and chiefs, ultimately sovereignty in the State resided in the people. However, though a ruler might be deposed, the office was not affected. In actual administration, the loyalties of the people and the competition of officers did not often conflict, since the administrative machinery worked through the heads of groups of different type: the main opposition was between similar groups, co-operating as parts of a larger group.

To-day the system is not stable, for not only is Zulu life being constantly affected and changed by many factors, but also the different authorities stand for entirely different, even contradictory, values. The Zulu, with their strong political organization, have reacted against white domination through their political authorities, who were incorporated in Government administration. The modern political organization of Zululand is the opposition between the two colour-groups represented by certain authorities. Each group makes use of the leaders of the other group if it can for its own purposes. The opposition between the two groups is not well-balanced, for ultimately it is dominated by the superior force of Government, against which the only reaction of the Zulu is acceptance or passive disobedience. The threat of this force is necessary to make the system work, because Zulu values and interests are so opposed to those of the Europeans that the Zulu do not recognize a strong moral relationship between themselves and Government, such as existed, and exists, between themselves and their king and chiefs. They usually regard Government as being out to exploit them, regardless of their interests. Government is now largely a sanction on oppressive chiefs, but the old checks on the chiefs act to prevent them becoming merely subordinate tools of Government. Government, too, does much work that the chiefs cannot do.

The opposition is synthesized by co-operation in everyday activities; by the position that an individual white official wins in the people's esteem so that he comes even to stand for them against Government, i.e. he enters the black, as opposed to the white, colour-group; and by the attempt of the people to exploit the opposed political authorities to their own advantage. In addition, divisions of each large group into political groups and opposed groups with conflicting ideals and interests act to weaken each group within itself and to lessen the main opposition. Members of dissident black groups, or individuals supporting Government in some matter, may be said to be supporters of the magistrate against the chief. In these ways social, economic, and other ties between Zulu and Europeans are bringing the Zulu more and more to accept white rule.

Within the one political organization there are officials, white and black, who have entirely different positions in the people's life and whose bases of power are different. These officials represent values which may be contradictory. By their allegiance in different situations to the officials representing each set of values, the people are prevented from being faced with a patent conflict of these values. Nevertheless, as the chief's material power is puny compared with Government's, the position he occupies is largely a centre for psychological satisfaction only and white domination is accepted by the Zulu, resignedly hostile.[1]

---

[1] Since this essay was written, Dr. Hilda Kuper's book *An African Aristocracy: Rank Among the Swazi*, has appeared (1947). Dr. Kuper's book gives important comparative material for an understanding of the political institutions of the Nguni-speaking Bantu.

THE POLITICAL ORGANIZATION OF THE NGWATO
OF BECHUANALAND PROTECTORATE[1]

By I. SCHAPERA

I. Ethnic Composition and Territorial Constitution

THE Native inhabitants of Bechuanaland Protectorate, most of whom belong to the Tswana (Western Sotho) cluster of Bantu-speaking peoples, are politically divided into eight separate tribes (*merafe*, sing. *morafe*). Each has its own name, occupies its own territorial reserve within which no European may own land, and, subject to the overriding authority of the British Administration, manages its own affairs under the direction of a chief (*kgosi, morêna*), who is independent of the rest. The Ngwato (commonly termed BaMangwato) are the largest and historically the best-known of these tribes. Their great chief, Kgama III (c. 1837–1923), attained world-wide prominence as a zealous convert to Christianity, a fanatical prohibitionist of alcoholic liquor, and a strong supporter of British imperialism in central South Africa. He promoted in various ways the economic progress of his people, and keenly encouraged the spread of education. The latest census, in May, 1936, showed that no less than 28 per cent. of the population was literate—a factor considerably affecting the modern relationship between the chief and his subjects.[2] Kgama's innovations were not confined to this partial acceptance of Western civilization, but included several changes in the legal and administrative system of the tribe. As a result of both this and the active intervention of the British Administration, the Ngwato have departed considerably from their traditional system of government, and so offer an interesting field for the study of African political development.

The tribe occupies a reserve 39,000 square miles in extent,

---

[1] This article is based upon field investigations made in 1935 for the Bechuanaland Protectorate Administration. For a more detailed account of Tswana social and political organization in general, the reader is referred to my *Handbook of Tswana Law and Custom* (Oxford, 1938), chaps. i–vi, xvi.

[2] The corresponding figures for other Tswana tribes are: Kgatla, 28 per cent.; Ngwaketse, 15 per cent.; Kwena, 9 per cent.; Tawana, 1·9 per cent.

much less than the territory it claimed when the Protectorate was established in 1885. Its population, returned in 1936 as 101,481, is by no means homogeneous. Only one-fifth belongs to the nuclear community, comprising the ruling dynasty and other descendants of the people who founded the tribe by separating early in the eighteenth century from the Kwena.[1] The remainder are *bafaladi* (foreigners, 'refugees'), who became subject to the Ngwato chiefs at various times through conquest in war, voluntary submission, flight from an invading enemy, or secession from some other tribe. Most of them retain sufficient corporate life to be regarded as separate communities or groups of communities within the tribe. Some, like the Kaa, Phaleng, Pedi, Tswapong, Kwena, Seleka, Khurutshe, Birwa, and Kgalagadi, are themselves of Tswana origin, or come from the closely allied Northern Sotho cluster. Others are linguistically and culturally distinct. The Kalaka (who actually outnumber the Ngwato proper), Talaote, and Nabya belong to the Shona group of Southern Rhodesia, and the Rotse, Kuba, and Subia to the peoples of north-western Rhodesia; the Herero are refugees from South-West Africa, and the Sarwa are Bushmen with a large admixture of Bantu blood and culture.

Practically all the Ngwato proper, members of the dominant community, are concentrated round the chief in the capital town of Serowe (pop., 25,000).[2] Serowe also contains many groups of foreigners. But the great majority of these are scattered over the rest of the reserve, people of the same stock tending to inhabit the same localities. They live in some 170 villages, ranging in size from small settlements, of less than 100 people each, to such relatively large centres as Shoshong, Mmadinare, Bobonong, and Tonôta, with populations of 2,000 or more. For administrative purposes, the villages some distance away from Serowe were gradually grouped by Kgama and his successors into districts, based partly upon geographical convenience and partly upon ethnic considerations.[3] The district of Shoshong is inhabited

[1] The Kwena (living in a reserve immediately south of the Ngwato) are generally regarded as the parent stock from which the Ngwaketse, Ngwato, and Tawana are derived.

[2] Built in 1902. Before that the tribal head-quarters was located at Palapye, built in 1889, and before that at Shoshong.

[3] The districts already existed, in the sense that people of the same stock inhabited the same part of the tribal territory; but Kgama gave them concrete form by appointing men specially to administer the outlying parts of the Reserve for him (see below, p. 61).

F

mainly by Kaa, Phaleng, and Kgalagadi; Matšhana and Maga-
lapye by Herero and Kgalagadi; Tswapong by Tswapong, with
smaller groups of Birwa, Rotse, and Seleka; Bobonong by Birwa;
Mmadinare by Talaote, Seleka, and Tswapong; Tonôta by
Khurutshe and Kalaka; BoKalaka by Kalaka; and BoTletle and
Matšha by many small groups of Kalaka, Khurutshe, Herero,
Kuba, Nabya, Subia, and Kgalagadi. The Sarwa are not confined
to any particular district, but are scattered widely over the whole
reserve.

The inhabitants of a small village generally belong to the same
tribal community. For administrative purposes they are held to
constitute a single 'ward' (motse, 'village'), under the leadership
and authority of an hereditary headman. The ward is a patrilineal
but non-exogamous body, most of whose members belong to the
family-group of the headman, but normally it also includes several
other families or family-groups[1] attached to him as dependants.
The bigger settlements all contain a number of wards, not necessarily of the same community. The village in such cases must be
regarded, not as a local unit divided for convenience into smaller
segments, but as a cluster of self-contained social groups inhabiting one centre. Within it each ward has its own hamlet, clearly
separated from the rest, and its own kgotla (council-place), where
lawsuits and other local business are dealt with. Altogether there
are some 300 wards in the tribe, of which no less than 113 are
located in Serowe. They vary considerably in size, but on the
average contain from 200 to 400 people each.

This grouping into wards, common to all the Tswana, explains
the facility with which immigrants or conquered peoples were
absorbed into the tribe. Single families or family-groups of
strangers were placed by the chief in some existing ward, i.e. under
the immediate control of a particular ward-head. A larger group
would be recognized as a separate ward in itself, with its leader as
headman, or divided into a number of wards, according to its size
and existing kinship or territorial organization. Every person in
the tribe must belong to a ward and, save in exceptional circumstances, he must always live in the same place as his fellow
members.

---

[1] A family-group (kgotlana) is a collection of households whose heads are all
descended in the male line from a common grandfather or great-grandfather.
The senior descendant in line of birth is the 'elder' (mogolwane) of the group.

Among the Ngwato proper, as contrasted with the foreigners, there are two main categories of wards, distinguished according to their mode of origin. In the days when polygamy was still practised, a chief would group his sons by one wife into a single body, under the authority of the eldest, and attach to them some people of common birth as servants. The present headmen of the wards thus created, all descendants of former chiefs, are accordingly known as *dikgosana*, 'royal headmen' (sing. *kgosana*, 'prince, chieftain').[1] Each chief would also allocate the supervision of his own cattle among several faithful commoners; each of whom, with his immediate relatives and the cattle herds placed under him, thus became the nucleus of a new ward. The headman of such a ward is termed a *motlhanka*, 'common headman' (lit., 'servant'). Many wards, both Ngwato and foreign, have since their foundation become subdivided, one or more family-groups seceding because of internal disputes or some similar factor. Such offshoots might then be recognized by the chief as new wards, and given land on which to erect their own village or hamlet.

Within a ward each family-group manages its own affairs, under the leadership of its elder, and settles by arbitration disputes involving any of its people. But all members of the ward fall under the general control of their headman. He allocates land to them for residence, cultivation, and grazing, can freely command their services for all public purposes, is their official representative and spokesman, and supports and protects them in their dealings with outsiders. He must see that they carry out the commands of his political superiors, and formerly also collected the tribute they paid to the chief. He judges cases which the other elders of his ward have not been able to settle, or which are beyond their competence to try; and, unlike them, can impose fines and thrashings as punishments. He also conducts various religious and magical ceremonies on behalf of the ward as a whole, although with the spread of Christianity his functions in this direction are disappearing. His close paternal relatives, the elders of the remaining family-groups, and any other men of repute and ability

[1] Thus, the headmen of the Tshosa, Kgope, and Mauba wards are descended from Chief Kesitilwe; the headmen of the Maeketso, Seetso, Mokomane, Sedihelo, Tshweu, and Seiswana wards from his son, Makgasana; the headmen of the Morwakwena and Rammala wards from the latter's son, Molete; and the headmen of the Ramere, Monageng, Mmualefe, Modimoeng, and Ramasuga wards from Molete's son, Mathiba.

in his ward assist and advise him; and during his absence, or after his death, the man next to him in line of succession, normally his eldest son by his first wife, automatically takes his place.[1] Matters of importance are discussed at a general meeting of the men in the ward, the opinions they express helping the headman to reach a decision.

Where a ward has become subdivided, the headman of the parent group is the first court of appeal from the verdicts of the others. In the bigger centres outside Serowe, the ward-head senior to the rest in birth is also the headman of the whole village. As such, he can hear appeals from the verdicts of his colleagues, and has an overriding authority in all other matters, e.g. the distribution of land and the organization of collective undertakings. He is also the medium through whom the chief communicates with the inhabitants of the village.

The hereditary chieftain of each foreign community continues to rule over his people according to their own laws and customs. He controls the activities of his dependent ward and village headmen, tries cases they are unable to settle or appealed from their verdicts, and deals with other matters pertaining to the community as a whole. But he is himself subject to the authority of the chief, to whom he is responsible for the general order, peace, and good government of his adherents, and to whom also there is an appeal from his decisions.

Each community living outside tribal head-quarters was formerly placed under the protection of some prominent Ngwato *motlhanka* (common headman) resident in the chief's town. This man, whose responsibilities were hereditary, was expected to keep in touch with the people and their affairs, visit them periodically to collect tribute for the chief, and while there try cases brought to him on appeal. He also informed them of developments at head-quarters, looked after them whenever they came there, and transmitted their grievances to the chief. In time it became evident, with the expansion of the tribe, that many subject communities lived too far away from head-quarters for this method

---

[1] This hereditary principle runs right through the Ngwato political system. It means in effect that the administration of any group is vested not so much in one particular person, as in the whole family of which he is the head; and that the leading member of this family present on any occasion when action must be taken is able, by virtue of his birthright, to exercise authority over the other people of the group.

of supervision to be sufficiently effective. Kgama therefore devised a more direct system of administration. He grouped the more remote communities into the districts to which reference has already been made, and in each placed a resident governor, usually a member of his own family, but sometimes a prominent and reliable common headman. His successors have continued and extended this policy.

The governor is accompanied to his district by his immediate relatives, who assist and advise him. His main duties are to communicate the chief's orders and messages to the people under his control, hear appeals from the verdicts of their chieftains, settle disputes between different communities, organize and direct local public undertakings, supervise the collection of hut-tax and tribal levies, and advise the chief on local political and economic conditions. All matters that he cannot himself settle he must refer to the chief, to whom there is also an appeal from his own decisions. Should he abuse his authority, or otherwise prove incompetent, he may be recalled by the chief, as has happened on several occasions within recent years. Some other man is then sent to take his place. Failing this, his appointment tends to be permanent, and may even become hereditary, unless the chief sees reason to intervene. The 'protector' of a foreign community continues to represent it at Serowe, and is still the medium through whom its people must approach the chief when they come there to appeal against their district governor or for some other official purpose. But he no longer visits them to claim tribute, the collection of which was abandoned by Kgama, nor does he try the cases in which they are involved. He is now little more than their 'consular agent', his administrative duties having been taken over by the district governor.

All the wards in the tribe, both Ngwato and foreign, are finally grouped into four parallel 'sections' (*dikgotla*, sing. *kgotla*), named respectively, after the leading ward in each, Ditimamodimo, Basimane, Maalosô, and Maalosâ-a-Ngwana. The origin of this grouping is not clearly known, but it seems to have arisen from the practice of giving the heir to the chieftainship a large cattle post and creating a new ward of commoners to look after it. The Ditimamodimo cattle post, and the ward created for and named after it, are said to have been established by Chief Molete for his son, Mathiba; the Basimane by Mathiba for his son, Kgama I;

the Maalosô by Kgama I for his son, Kgari; and the Maalosô-a-Ngwana for Kgari's son, Sekgoma I (father of Kgama III). The heir, on coming to the chieftainship, relied considerably upon the assistance and support of the retainers thus attached to him, and as a rule placed under their supervision all the wards originating in his reign. .The creation of new sections ceased in the reign of Sekgoma I, who consolidated the system into its present form. All wards since created were placed, at the discretion of the chief, within one or other of the existing sections.

In Serowe each section has its own quarter of the town, within which its component wards are located. The headman of the nuclear ward in each is also headman of the whole section. Associated with him in the administration of its affairs is the senior *kgosana* of the section, i.e. the royal headman most closely related to the chief.[1] These two men act together as the senior judges of the section. They hear all cases referred to them directly or on appeal from the other ward-heads of their section in Serowe, or from a district governor where members of their section are involved; and until they have done so the case cannot come before the chief. As heads of the section they also command much greater influence in the tribe than do the other ward-heads. The chief frequently consults them on questions of tribal policy, and may depute them to deal on his behalf with important administrative matters. They speak for their people at tribal meetings where the opinions of each section are separately canvassed, and can also summon meetings of their own to discuss matters of sectional or tribal interest. The section to which the chief himself belongs—and, as already indicated, different chiefs have belonged to different sections—is generally regarded during his reign as the ruling section of the tribe. He relies more upon its senior headmen for help in formulating tribal policy, and looks to them particularly for support in all his plans and undertakings.

[1] The descendants of Sekgoma I, who are all more closely related to the chiei than other royal headmen, are associated with him in the central government of the tribe, and do not take part in the sectional administration. The next senior royal headman in each section is regarded as its responsible royal headman. This position is held in Ditimamodimo by the headman of Ditlharapa ward, in Basimane by the headman of Tshisi ward, in Maalosô by the headman of Maboledi ward, and in Maalosô-a-Ngwana by the headman of Menyatso ward, all of whom are descendants of Kgama I.

II. The Administrative System

The administrative system just described, and the social organization upon which it is directly based, separate the members of the tribe into groups distinguished one from another by local powers and loyalties. In certain respects each section, district, community, village, ward, and family-group is independent of the rest, managing its own affairs under the direction of a recognized head whose authority extends over almost every sphere of public life. The many communities of which the tribe is composed frequently also differ from one another in language, custom, and tradition, and so have not even a common cultural background. We must now consider how all these groups are welded together and given a solidarity and cohesion enabling the tribe as a whole to present a united front to the outside world in defence or aggression, maintain law and order and adjust disputes between the members of one group and another, and carry on large collective undertakings.

One of the mechanisms through which this is achieved is the administrative hierarchy into which the various forms of local authority are graded. In Serowe, as we have indicated, the elder of a family-group is directly subordinate to his ward-head. The ward-head, in turn, is subordinate, either directly or through the headman of the ward from which his own is derived, to the headman of the nuclear ward in the same section.[1] The sectional headman, finally, is subordinate to the chief. In the outlying districts, the ward-head is, either directly or through his village headman, subordinate to the hereditary chieftain of his tribal community. The latter, again, is subordinate to the district governor, who is finally subordinate to the chief. In each case the superior authority has powers overriding those of the lesser authorities in his own group. The latter must obey his commands and carry out his instructions, must refer to him all cases which they are unable to settle or with which they are not competent to deal, and there is an appeal to him from all their judicial and executive decisions.

The judicial system is fundamentally the same for all courts. The victim of a civil wrong, such as breach of contract, seduction,

[1] In the foreign communities living in Serowe, the local chieftain of each is intermediate between the ward-head and the sectional headman.

adultery, trespass, damage to property, theft, or defamation, may either pass it over or, through the elder of his family-group, try to arrive at an agreed settlement with the offender. Failing this, he takes the matter to the court of defendant's ward-head. Crimes, such as offences against political authorities acting in their official capacity, breaches of the laws decreed by the chief, rape, assault, homicide, and sorcery, can never be compounded, but must always come to trial. All trials are heard in public, and any member of the tribe has the right to attend and take part in the proceedings, no matter in what court they are held. The parties concerned and their respective witnesses are heard in succession, listened to intently and uninterruptedly, and closely questioned by the people present. The judge then throws the matter open for general discussion, and the merits of the case are publicly argued by those wishing to do so. This is one of the principal functions of his personal advisers. Finally he sums up, in the light of the opinions thus expressed, and either pronounces his verdict or, if he feels that the case is too important or difficult, refers it to the court of his political superior. If either party is dissatisfied with the verdict, he can likewise appeal against it. The case is then heard again from the very beginning at the superior court, pending whose decision action is suspended. A case originating in a family-group may thus pass through three or four grades of intermediate court before ultimately reaching the chief.

In effect, therefore, the existing social and territorial organization is used to delegate matters of more purely local concern to the subordinate authorities, but the government of the tribe as a whole is concentrated in the hands of the chief and his personal advisers. The chief is the central figure round whom the tribal life revolves, and through whom the activities of the tribe are ordered and controlled. He is at once its ruler and judge, maker and guardian of its law, and director of its economic life, and in the olden days was also its leader in war and its principal priest and magician. It is primarily through allegiance to him that the members of the tribe express their unity. He calls and signs himself '*Kgosi ya baNgwato*', 'Chief of the Ngwato people'; he is ceremonially addressed, by the personification of the tribal name, as '*MoNgwato*'; the tribe itself is named after his ancestor, the legendary founder of the royal line; and he is its representative and spokesman in all its external relations. Like his subordinate authorities, he is assisted in his work by his close paternal relatives and other personal advisers. But on occasion he also invokes the aid of wider councils and other forms of assembly drawn from the tribe as a whole, and so binding its people together still further.[1] Sometimes he consults the headmen alone, but more frequently he summons all the men of Serowe, or even of the whole tribe, to a meeting where public business is discussed, while through the regimental organization he may bring them together for work or, in the olden days, for war. These forms of assembly cut across the parochial loyalties of ward, village, and community, and so are among the most conspicuous means of uniting the members of the tribe.

This system of central administration still prevai s, but since the establishment of the Protectorate it has been somewhat modified. The European Administration has not only limited the powers of the chief and other tribal authorities, and altered the structure of their courts; it has also introduced its own governmental institutions. The Ngwato are now ruled by both European and Native authorities, and the latter occupy the subordinate position. It will be as well, therefore, to review briefly the part played by the European Administration in the regulation of tribal affairs before we proceed to discuss in more detail the past and present powers and functions of the chief and his councils.

Bechuanaland Protectorate, together with Basutoland and Swaziland, is under the general legislative and administrative control of a High Commissioner responsible to the Secretary of State for Dominion Affairs in Great Britain. The Territory itself is directly governed by a Resident Commissioner, with headquarters at Mafeking.[2] The Ngwato Reserve, one of the twelve administrative districts into which it is divided, is under the immediate jurisdiction of a District Commissioner stationed at Serowe. He is assisted to maintain law and order, and carry out his other duties, by a small body of police and a few subordinate European and Native officials. Some technical officers representing the medical, agricultural, and veterinary branches of the

[1] For a more detailed sketch of these advisers and councils, see below, pp. 71-2.
[2] Mafeking, oddly enough, is located in the Union of South Africa, and not in Bechuanaland Protectorate itself, whose southern border is twelve miles north of the town. This anomalous position is a survival of the days (1885-95) when what is now British Bechuanaland, in the northern Cape Colony, was included in the Protectorate.

Administration also live and work in the Reserve. Its total European population, comprising not only Government officials, but the London Missionary Society staff, traders, railway employees, and others, was 376 in 1936, men, women, and children included.

The general policy of the Administration, in dealing with the Natives, has been 'to preserve the tribal authority of the chiefs and the laws and customs of the people, subject to the due exercise of the power and jurisdiction of the Crown, and subject to the requirements of peace, order, and good government'. It early took away from the chiefs the right to make war or enter into independent political agreements, removed cases of murder and culpable homicide, as well as all cases involving Europeans, to the jurisdiction of the European courts, allowed appeals from the verdicts of the chiefs in very serious cases, defined the boundaries of the tribal territories, and imposed a regular annual tax upon all adult male Natives. But for many years thereafter the manner in which the chief administered the tribe was not a matter of Government concern, except when it led to open trouble, and in most cases the tendency was to support him as far as possible in his dealings with his people. More recently, however, the chief's judicial powers were further curtailed. In 1919 provision was made for hearing appeals from his verdicts in any type of case, civil or criminal, by the establishment of a combined court presided over jointly by him and by the local District Commissioner. In 1926 divorce proceedings between Natives married according to European civil law were also brought under the jurisdiction of the District Commissioner's Court, and in 1927 the trial of alleged sorcerers was removed from the tribal courts when the imputation or practice of 'witchcraft' was made a statutory offence. These encroachments did not pass unchallenged. Tshekedi, who became Regent in 1926 for his fraternal nephew Serêtsê (son of Kgama's son, Sekgoma II), joined the chiefs of several other tribes in protesting against them, but they were nevertheless made law.

Finally, in 1934, the powers of the chief were for the first time clearly defined, and the status and powers of the tribal courts regularized. The Native Administration Proclamation (No. 74 of 1934) specifies the rights, powers, and duties of the chief and other tribal authorities, makes succession to and tenure of the chieftainship subject to the approval of the Administration, which has the power to pass over an unsuitable heir or suspend an incompetent or otherwise unsatisfactory chief, provides machinery whereby the tribe can depose a chief, makes conspiracy against the chief a statutory offence, and establishes a formal Tribal Council to assist him in the execution of his duties. The Native Tribunals Proclamation (No. 75 of 1934) removes from the jurisdiction of the tribal courts all cases in which the accused is charged with treason, sedition, murder or attempted murder, culpable homicide, rape or attempted rape, assault or intent to do grievous bodily harm, conspiracy against the chief, and a variety of statutory offences. All other cases, both civil and criminal, in which Natives only are concerned, can still be tried by the tribal courts according to Tswana law and custom. But, in place of the many grades of court in the tribal system, the Proclamation recognizes only three whose decisions are legally binding. These are styled Junior and Senior Native Tribunals and the Chief's Tribunal respectively. From the last there is an appeal to the District Commissioner's Court and thence, under certain conditions, to the Special Court of the Protectorate. The Proclamation further defines the constitution of each tribunal, laying down that it shall have a limited membership appointed by specified tribal authorities, provides for the keeping, in all cases tried, of written records open to inspection by the District Commissioner, severely curtails the forms of punishment that may be imposed, and lays down various rules to govern procedure.

These Proclamations, first drafted in 1930, had been frequently and fully discussed by the Administration with the chiefs and their tribes. The necessity for them had become more and more evident. As the old chiefs died, they were succeeded by young men educated for the most part in schools outside the Protectorate, and so cut off from adequate first-hand experience of tribal government and jurisdiction. Instances multiplied of drunkenness and irresponsibility, neglect of duty, misappropriation of hut-tax and other tribal moneys, and of serious internal disputes, all calling for stronger Administrative control; while increasing educational, veterinary, and agricultural development made it still more desirable to define clearly the relations between the Administration and the tribes. Tshekedi opposed the Proclamations from the beginning, and even after their promulgation did not put them into force. Finally, in December, 1935, he and Bathoen, Chief of the Ngwaketse, took legal action against the High Commissioner. They claimed that the Proclamations were of no legal force and effect, because in them the High Commissioner *inter alia* both altered certain Native laws and customs, thus exceeding the powers conferred upon him, and violated treaty rights reserved to their respective tribes. The case was heard in the Special Court in July, 1936. Judgement was reserved and delivered in November. The court found in favour of the High Commissioner, holding that, while the Proclamations undoubtedly altered existing Native law and custom, he had acted within his powers; while on the question of treaty rights a ruling by the Secretary of State, that the power of the Crown in Bechuanaland Protectorate 'is not limited by Treaty or Agreement', was taken as conclusive. The Proclamations have therefore become binding upon the Ngwato, and Tshekedi has now begun to apply them. It is too soon yet to determine in detail how they affect the tribal administration, but some attempt will be made below to indicate their main tendencies.

III. Powers and Authority of the Chief

The general effect of the Proclamations, and of previous developments, is that although the chief and his councils still administer the affairs of the tribe, the supreme political and judicial authority in the Reserve is now the Administration, acting through the District Commissioner. Nevertheless, the chief, as head of the tribe, is always treated by his subjects with a good deal of outward respect. His installation and marriage are occasions of great public festivity, and his death evokes universal mourning. His household is usually far larger and more elaborate than those of ordinary tribesmen. In the olden days he always had many wives, retainers, and serfs, and even to-day the number of his direct dependants is very great. He receives various forms of tribute from his people, imposes levies upon them, and claims free labour from them for personal as well as tribal purposes. He has the first choice of land for his home, fields, and cattle-posts; he and his family formerly took precedence in the tribe in matters of ritual; and he alone has the right to convene full tribal meetings, create new regiments, arrange tribal ceremonies, and, in the olden days, impose the supreme penalties of death and banishment. Failure to comply with his orders is a penal offence. All other offences against him are generally punished more severely than if committed against ordinary tribesmen. Disloyalty and revolt against his authority are major crimes, punished as a rule, in the olden days, by death and the confiscation of the culprit's property, and nowadays by banishment or some other penalty inflicted directly by the Administration.

Despite the curtailment of his traditional rights and powers, the chief still plays a very prominent part in the government of the tribe. He decides upon questions of tribal policy, and can make regulations binding upon his subjects.[1] He determines upon and arranges for the execution of all important public works. He supervises the conduct of his subordinate authorities, and in case of extreme incompetence or abuse of office can replace his district governor by some other man, or depose the hereditary head of a ward or community, whose duties then fall to the man next in line of succession. Much of his time is spent daily in his *kgotla* (council-place), where he listens to news, petitions, and complaints from all over the tribe, and gives orders for whatever action may be necessary. He must protect the rights of his subjects, provide justice for the injured and oppressed, and punish wrongdoers. Before the establishment of the Protectorate, he was the supreme judge of the tribe. This function has been taken over by the Administration, but his court is still the highest Native tribunal, to which a right of appeal lies from the verdicts of the others. In the olden days, such serious offences as treason, homicide, assault, rape, and sorcery could be punished only by him and his court. They have now been removed to the jurisdiction of the European authorities, but he still adjudicates over all other breaches of tribal law and has greater punitive powers

---

[1] Legislation of this sort does not seem to have played a conspicuous part in the old tribal life, the chiefs being more concerned to maintain the existing law than to alter it. In more recent times, owing to the new conditions created by contact with Europeans, legislation by the chief has become a frequent occurrence. Kgama introduced so many changes that the people themselves sometimes distinguish between 'traditional Native law' and 'Kgama's law', although both are equally binding upon them. Among other things, he accepted Christianity as the official religion of the tribe; abolished *bogadi* (bride-wealth), and discouraged polygamy among the Ngwato proper, although not among his subject communities; abolished most of the old tribal ceremonies; prohibited the sale, manufacture, and drinking of Kafir beer and other intoxicating liquors throughout his Reserve; regulated the sale of corn and breeding-cattle to European traders; modified the customary rules of inheritance, so that daughters should also inherit cattle; prohibited the movement of wagons through the villages on Sunday; and officially protected certain big game animals.

than the judges of the lesser courts. He controls the distribution and use of the tribal land, organizes large collective hunts, and regulates trade relations with outsiders and the time for sowing and harvesting crops.

With the extension of European control, the chief's administrative duties have greatly increased. He is responsible to the Administration for maintaining law and order in the tribe, preventing crime, and collecting hut-tax and other dues. He must carry out all orders and instructions issued to him, and render any assistance required from him, by responsible officers of the Government; and he is expected to co-operate with the District Commissioner and other members of the Administration in all sorts of political, economic, social, and educational schemes and developments. His formerly undivided control over every aspect of public life has thus been diffused through various Government departments with superior authority. He must, further, deal with the traders, missionaries, would-be concessionaires, and other Europeans living in his Reserve, visiting him, or writing to him; and must issue to his subjects receipts for tax payments, permits for the sale of cattle and corn, and passes to leave the Reserve on visits to the Union or in search of work. The complaint sometimes made against Tshekedi that he is an 'office chief' rather than a 'kgotla chief' indicates sufficiently the change in administrative methods that all this has entailed.

Formerly the chief was also the head of the tribal army. He organized military expeditions, often accompanying them himself, performed the necessary war magic, and disposed of the prisoners and loot. With the abolition of inter-tribal warfare under European government, all this has disappeared. Formerly he also organized the great tribal ceremonies upon which the welfare of his people was held to depend. But Kgama, from the time he was converted, fought against these 'heathen' practices, and after he became chief deliberately ceased to observe them. Since they could not be celebrated without his authority and participation, they have altogether died away, and with them his functions of tribal priest and magician. The Ngwato are now officially a Christian tribe, acknowledging the ritual leadership of the local missionary. The latter is therefore to some extent a rival authority, whose claim to the allegiance of the faithful has at times brought him into conflict with the chief. The monopoly given by Kgama to the London Missionary Society in his Reserve has also been a source of subsequent trouble with immigrant communities professing some other variety of Christian faith.

On all questions of tribal policy the chief is expected to consult with his immediate paternal relatives. The sectional headmen and other prominent local leaders are also held to be among his rightful advisers. When any matter of outstanding importance arises, he further summons a general meeting of headmen, and so obtains the views of all the important men in the tribe before taking any action. Except for such meetings, held very infrequently, the chief's advisers were until recently not organized into a definite body with limited membership. He consulted them, severally or collectively, whenever he wished, and varied them according to the issues involved. He relied only upon the men whom he could trust, and ignored others, however important their standing, who were openly hostile to him or whom he regarded with suspicion.

In November, 1925, however, immediately after the death of Sekgoma II, the tribe, at the suggestion of the Resident Commissioner, elected a Council of thirteen to assist the temporary acting chief (Gorewang, son of Kgama's brother, Kgamane). The Council was not at all popular, the people feeling that it was an Administrative device to undermine the chief's power by limiting his freedom of action; and Tshekedi, when he returned from school in February, 1926, to take over from Gorewang, successfully insisted upon its abolition. The Native Administration Proclamation has now reintroduced the idea of a well-defined Tribal Council. It requires the chief to nominate publicly, and with the approval of the tribe, the men entitled to advise him as councillors, and directs him to consult with them in the exercise of his functions. A councillor's tenure of office is subject to the discretion of the Resident Commissioner, and not of the chief, whose powers are thus limited in another direction. This was one of the features in the Proclamation against which Tshekedi most strenuously protested, maintaining that such a limited body as it proposed to set up was alien to the tribal system; and the court, in giving judgement, found that it was undoubtedly a departure from the traditional method of government.

This is not the only change that has taken place. During and since the time of Kgama, the chief has come to rely upon European advisers apart from Government officials. He often consults the local missionaries on many aspects of tribal life remote from religion, seeks advice from traders on matters of finance, and frequently employs the special services of lawyers in Mafeking and Cape Town. Tribal policy is therefore no longer determined merely by the chief and his traditional Native advisers; it is moulded also in some degree with the aid of various interested European personalities, not always regarded with favour by the Administration.

All matters of tribal policy are dealt with finally before a general assembly of the adult men in the chief's *kgotla* (council-place). Such meetings are very frequently held, at times almost weekly. Normally only the men present in Serowe attend them, any decisions reached being communicated to those in other parts of the Reserve through the district governors and other local authorities. But on important occasions the people of the districts are also summoned, and the question at issue is debated by the tribe as a whole. Among the topics discussed in this way are tribal disputes, quarrels between the chief and his relatives, the imposition of new levies, the undertaking of new public works, the promulgation of new decrees by the chief, and the relations between the tribe and the Administration. The decisions made are generally the same as those previously reached by the chief and his personal advisers, who as leaders of the tribe can sway public opinion; but it is not unknown for the tribal assembly to overrule the wishes of the chief. Since anybody may speak, these meetings enable him to ascertain the feelings of the people generally, and provide the latter with an opportunity of stating their grievances. If the occasion calls for it, he and his advisers may be taken severely to task, for the people are seldom afraid to speak openly and frankly. The Administration has contributed greatly towards the retention and present vigour of these assemblies, by making a practice of getting its officers to discuss with the tribe in *kgotla* developmental schemes, new or projected laws, and other matters affecting the relations between the two bodies.

In his judicial and administrative capacities, the chief again relies primarily upon his personal advisers. They help him hear and judge cases at his court, although, as we have seen, any other member of the tribe may attend and take part in the proceedings. They also act as his state messengers on important occasions. he selects his district governors from among them, and he may delegate them to try cases on his behalf, supervise the execution of his verdicts, and undertake other duties of a similar kind. If he is ill, or away from head-quarters, his heir, if old enough, or else some other very close paternal relative, acts as his deputy. For such minor tasks as carrying ordinary messages, he uses any tribesman at hand, and he also has a few official policemen of his own, who see that his decrees are enforced and act as messengers of his court on most routine occasions. Within recent years he has also begun to employ paid secretaries and other assistants to handle his correspondence, collect tax, issue passes and receipts, and attend to other routine business of the same kind. The chief's principal secretary, owing to his access to all confidential documents and the close association in which he works with the chief, has become one of the strategic men in the tribal administration; and many royal headmen regard with resentment Tshekedi's employment of a Kalaka headman in this capacity, whereas Kgama and Sekgoma II both relied upon very close relatives.

Major enterprises are organized through the system of age-regiments (*mephato*) into which the whole tribe is divided. A regiment consists of people of the same sex and of about the same age, and every adult in the tribe must belong to one. The regiments are formed at intervals of several years apart, when all the eligible boys or girls, as the case may be, are grouped together into a single body. In the olden days they simultaneously went through an elaborate series of initiation ceremonies, but nowadays they are simply called together and told the name of the new regiment to which they henceforth belong. Each regiment of men is commanded by a member of the chief's own family (his brother, son, or fraternal nephew); while each group of men in it belonging to the same section, district, community, village, or ward is led by some similarly close relative of the appropriate headman. The headman himself leads the men of his group in his own regiment. The heir to the chieftainship commands his own regiment during the lifetime of his father, but on succeeding to office ceases to do so, the effective leadership passing to the member of the royal family next in rank. The women's regiments are organized along similar lines.

The men's regiments originally constituted the tribal army in the event of war, and were used at other times as a labour force.

Their former function has now disappeared, but the latter has been greatly intensified owing to the new forms of activity resulting from the introduction of Western civilization. They can be called up, whenever the chief wishes, for such tasks as making dams, rounding up stray cattle, building schools and churches, hunting beasts of prey, cutting down bushes in the chief's fields, building his huts and cattle-kraals, making roads and aerodromes, cutting boundary paths, preparing agricultural showgrounds, rounding up offenders against the law, and escorting distinguished visitors. The women's regiments, again, are employed to put up the walls and thatch the roofs of the chief's huts, draw water for any royal or tribal work, get wood for the chief's wife, clean the village, fetch earth and smear the walls and floors of the chief's homestead, and weed his wife's fields. Only the chief can mobilize a whole regiment for work, but district governors and other headmen may summon their own followers by regiments to perform purely local tasks of a similar nature.

Regimental labour is both compulsory and unpaid, and failure to answer a summons to work can be punished by a fine or thrashing. Within recent years, with the spread of education, on the one hand, and the increased burden of work, on the other, complaints have become common about the brutal methods sometimes use1 for rounding up defaulters and stragglers, and about the hardships and losses imposed by such calls upon people engaged in work of their own. These were among the grievances mentioned in a petition lodged against Tshekedi in 1930 by eight members of the tribe, and largely substantiated in the Administrative inquiry that followed. As a result of such abuses, present also in other tribes, the Native Administration Proclamation has made it illegal for the chief to exact free labour from his people except for certain clearly specified purposes.

IV. Rights and Responsibilities of Chieftainship

The authority of the chief is derived in the first place from his birthright. The chieftainship is hereditary in the male line, passing normally from father to son. In the days when polygamy was practised, the rightful heir was always the eldest son of the 'great' wife, i.e. of the woman first betrothed to the chief. Failing a son in her 'house', the eldest son of the wife next in rank succeeded. Sometimes, however, there were disputes regarding the relative status of a chief's wives, with the result that there would be more than one claimant to the succession. Sometimes, too, a regent acting for a minor chief would attempt to usurp the chieftainship permanently, or an ambitious prince would revolt against an unpopular ruler. But in every instance the rival claimant was himself of royal birth. No man who was not a senior member of the ruling family could ever hope to become recognized as chief. '*Kgosi ke kgosi ka a tsetswe*', say the Ngwato ('A chief is chief because he is born (to it)'). Since, as we have seen, the whole social system of the tribe emphasizes the principle of hereditary rank, since every local authority (except the district governor, a relatively recent creation) owes his position to the fact that he is the legitimate heir of his predecessor, the chief's status as head of the leading family in the tribe is sufficient in itself to secure for him the respect and obedience of his people.

Under the European Administration, hereditary succession to the chieftainship still prevails, but with certain modifications. It was early laid down that no chief could exercise jurisdiction over his tribe unless he had been recognized by the High Commissioner and confirmed by the Secretary of State. In effect, this made no difference to the succession, as among the Ngwato the rightful heir was always accepted by the Administration as chief. Under the new Proclamations, however, the Administration has assumed the right of refusing to recognize or confirm the heir as chief, if he appears, after public inquiry, 'not to be a fit and proper person to exercise the functions of the chieftainship'. So far no occasion has occurred for such refusal. But the possibility it embodies of passing over the legitimate successor in favour of a junior member of the royal family introduces a principle foreign to Ngwato law. Formerly such an event could only occur as the result of deliberate usurpation, resulting probably in civil war.

By virtue of his descent, the chief was formerly the link between his people and the spirits governing their welfare. His dead ancestors were held to afford supernatural protection and assistance to the people they had once ruled, and on all important occasions he would sacrifice and pray to them on behalf of the tribe. The role he thus played as tribal priest, a role which only he, as senior descendant of the ancestral gods, could fill, helps to explain the great reverence in which he was always held by his people.

Kgama's acceptance of Christianity, however, deprived the chief-tainship of almost all its ritual significance, and so of a powerful sanction for its authority. The whole tribe is by no means firmly attached to Christianity, and many of the old practices are still carried on more or less surreptitiously, especially among the subject communities. But the people no longer look to the chief for spiritual benefits, and certainly do not accord him the same pious reverence which contemporary observers show that Sekgoma I received as tribal priest and magician.

The chief's hold over his people was formerly also strengthened by marriage. His own wives were drawn mostly from the families of his close relatives, other influential headmen, and the chiefs of neighbouring tribes. Since in the Tswana social system a man's maternal relatives are expected to be among his strongest sup-porters, the chief made sure in this way that his sons, particularly the heir, should always have a powerful backing. At the same time, the practice of polygamy gave ample scope for intrigue. The rela-tives of each wife watched jealously over her interests, and did their utmost to further the fortunes of her sons. As a result many feuds arose which still play their part in tribal politics. Kgama's aban-donment of polygamy did away with these sources of possible conflict, but also deprived the chief of the political advantages he could obtain by judiciously selecting his wives. He is, however, still able to consolidate his hold over the tribe by marrying off his sisters and daughters to headmen with large followings. Kgama carried this policy into effect by marrying three of his daughters to the local chieftains of the Khurutshe, Kaa and Talaote respec-tively, and three others to prominent royal headmen, two of whom were important enough to be appointed district governors.

The chief's power is further dependent upon the uses to which he puts his wealth. As head of the tribe, he formerly received tribute from his subjects in corn, cattle, wild animal skins, ivory and ostrich feathers, retained most of the cattle looted in war, and kept all unclaimed stray cattle and part of the fines imposed in his court, especially for cases of assault. He could also confiscate the entire property of tribesmen conspiring against him or banished for any other serious offence. In addition, he could through the regimental system command the services of his people for personal as well as tribal purposes. He further had a large number of servants directly attached to him and doing most of his domestic work. Foremost among them were the *batlhanka* (common head-men) whom, as already noted, he put in charge of his cattle and other servants. The latter were drawn mainly from the ranks of the Kgalagadi and especially the Sarwa, who occupied the position of serfs. At first they merely hunted for him, the skins and other spoils they gave him forming an important part of his income; but under Kgama they were gradually taught to herd cattle also and to carry out menial household tasks.

Owing to the wealth he thus accumulated, the chief was always the richest man in the tribe. He was, however, expected to use his property, not only for his own benefit, but also for the tribe as a whole. He had to provide beer and meat for people visiting him, assisting at his *kgotla*, or summoned to work for him; reward with gifts of cattle and other valuables the services of his advisers, headmen, warriors and retainers; and, in times of famine, supply the tribe with food. '*Kgosi ke mosadi wa morafe*', it was said ('The chief is the wife of the tribe', i.e. he provided the people with sustenance). One quality always required of him was generosity, and much of his popularity depended upon the manner in which he displayed it. Kgama is still gratefully remembered as an extremely liberal chief, who not only imported corn for his people in times of scarcity—on one occasion to the value of between £2,000 and £3,000—but also bought many wagons, ploughs, guns, and horses, which he distributed among them, while in several instances he paid large sums of money to free some of them from debt.

In this connexion, the relationship between the chief and his *batlhanka* deserves special mention. These men, as we have seen, were placed as common headmen in charge of the chief's cattle-posts. The cattle entrusted to them were the hereditary property of the chieftainship, so that the *batlhanka* were always attached to the ruling chief himself. Each *motlhanka* was required to provide the chief's household with milk and meat from the cattle under his care, and to come with his followers to perform such other work as might be demanded of him. In return, he could use the cattle as he pleased: he kept the rest of their milk, slaughtered a beast whenever he wished, paid *bogadi* (bride-wealth) for his sons out of them, and exchanged them for other commodities, while on his death they passed to his children. He was also given the Sarwa inhabiting the region where the cattle grazed, and kept most of their hunting tribute for himself. The chief, however, had the ultimate claim not only to these cattle (known as *kgamêlô*, 'milk-pail', cattle), but to everything else acquired by the *motlhanka*. The entire property of a *motlhanka* was regarded as *kgamêlô*; and since the chief could withdraw his *kgamêlô* whenever he wished, he could at any time ruin the holder.

This system obviously bound the common headmen very closely to the chief. They were dependent upon him for their entire subsistence, and therefore of necessity were among his most loyal adherents. They were looked upon as and proved themselves his strong supporters against the intrigues of his uncles and brothers, and, since they could never be potential rivals for the chieftain-ship, he came to rely more and more upon them, until in time they became the most influential group assisting him to govern the tribe. The chief's own relatives, it may be added, were never entrusted with *kgamêlô* cattle, although he was expected to provide them also with cattle and servants of their own.

To-day the chief no longer receives most of the tribute formerly paid to him, Kgama having abandoned its collection. Cattle-raiding, at one time an important source of wealth, disappeared with the abolition of inter-tribal warfare. A still more drastic change occurred about 1900, when, as a result of disputes with his son Sekgoma regarding the ownership of *kgamêlô* cattle, Kgama declared that henceforth all such cattle would be regarded as the private property of their holders, and that he as chief renounced all rights over them. On the other hand, the coming of Western civilization provided him with new sources of income, such as the annual subsidy until very recently paid for mining concessions in the Reserve, the annual commission paid by the Administration on the amount of hut-tax collected from his people, and the cash levies he imposed at various times to finance public undertakings and to pay his debts. All this money was formerly controlled and used by him as he pleased. The present tendency, quite recently initiated by the Administration, is to divert the money and other revenue raised from tax, court fines, levies, and similar sources into a tribal fund kept apart from the chief's personal income. He and his assistants are paid annual salaries out of the fund, the rest of the money being used for specifically tribal purposes. As a result of these limitations of his income, coupled with the rela-tively expensive standard of living he must nowadays maintain, the chief has been deprived to a great extent of his traditional role of repository of wealth and dispenser of gifts, and so of yet another important sanction for his authority.

In the last resort, the power of the chief rests upon his personal character. Political life is so organized that effective government can result only from harmonious co-operation between him and his people. '*Kgosi ke kgosi ka morafe*', says the proverb ('The chief is chief by grace of the tribe'). Even in the olden days, despite the fact that control over almost every aspect of tribal life was concentrated in his hands, and that his power was in consequence very considerable, he was seldom absolute ruler and autocratic despot. In order to get anything done, he must first gain the support of his advisers and other headmen, who thus played an important part in restraining his more arbitrary impulses. Any attempt to act without them would lead to obstruction, if not to open revolt. A forceful and energetic man like Kgama could succeed in dominating his subjects and ruling in effect as a dictator—but at the cost of some painful disputes with his closest relatives. On the other hand, a weak chief like his son, Sekgoma II, became the virtual puppet of certain royal headmen, whose influence over him created an opposition which led to much subsequent trouble.

Tribal politics is in fact made up to a considerable extent of quarrels between the chief and his near relatives, and of their intrigues against one another to command his favour. As we have seen, they are entitled by custom to advise and assist him in his conduct of public affairs, and they actively resent any failure on his part to give them what they regard as their due. Since the time when Kgama, as a newly converted Christian, incurred the active hostility of his father (Sekgoma I), the tribe has been rent with dissensions in the royal family. Kgama, after expelling his father from the chieftainship, quarrelled successively with his own brother, Kgamane, his half-brothers, Mphoeng and Rraditladi, and his son, Sekgoma, all of whom were banished from the Reserve with their followers; while his increasing reliance first upon his son-in-law, Ratshosa, and then upon the latter's sons, John and Simon, alienated other royal headmen. Sekgoma, restored to favour after twenty years, became Chief in 1923; and soon, instigated mainly by the Ratshosa group, banished Phethu, son of Mphoeng. Phethu was pardoned shortly afterwards, and on his return began plotting against the Ratshosas. Tshekedi's accession in February, 1926, gave him his opportunity, and a series of steps was taken against the Ratshosas which led to their attempt, in April, to kill Tshekedi. For this they were imprisoned by the Administration and banished from the Reserve, but they have continued through their local partisans to be a disturbing factor in tribal life. Meanwhile, Tshekedi had trouble with his half-sisters, whom he also had to banish. This was followed by a conspiracy to claim the chieftainship for an illegitimate son of Sekgoma II, by a petition against Tshekedi's rule organized by several of the royal headmen, and finally by his open breach with the Rraditladi family, who are alleged to have been implicated in most of the preceding intrigues. All these disputes split the tribe into factions whose continuous agitations against one another obviously made the Chief's position very difficult. It is evident enough that the success of a chief's reign is determined in no small measure by his personal relations with his near kinsmen.

Formerly the chief's power was to some extent limited also by tribal law. If he committed an offence against one of his subjects, the victim could get some prominent man to intervene; the chief was then expected to make amends for the wrong he had done. But so great was the reverence attached to him by virtue of his birth and ritual position that the people would put up with much from him that would never be tolerated in one of lesser rank; and often enough, in practice, the victim had no real remedy except to leave the tribe and transfer his allegiance to some other chief. It was only under extreme provocation that drastic action would be taken. If the chief flagrantly misruled the tribe, or in other ways incurred the hostility of the people, the leading headmen would withdraw their support and publicly attack him at tribal gatherings; or there might be a split leading to wholesale migration. Given sufficient provocation, the people might even begin to plot against him, in the hope that he would be overthrown and one of his more popular relatives take his place; or, as a last resort, an attempt would be made to assassinate him. Instances of all these forms of revolt have occurred often enough in the past history of the tribe, and they did not always meet with failure.

The imposition of European rule deprived the people of the principal remedies they formerly possessed against oppression and abuse. The Administration has intervened more and more in local disputes, and tried to adjust peaceably troubles which would formerly have culminated in bloodshed. But since the official policy was to rule as much as possible through the chief, the Administration tended in most cases to uphold his authority, without inquiring too closely into the merits of the trouble. Freed, in consequence, from fear of the sanctions formerly restraining him, he became more arbitrary in action and jealous of any challenge to his authority. Kgama was a man of exceptional ability and enterprise, who through sheer force of personality was able to do much for the material advancement of his people; but he was also firmly insistent on his rights as chief, and brooked no opposition. The right of appeal from the chief's verdicts established in 1919 did little to help, since, by an astonishing arrangement, the appeal court consisted of the District Commissioner and the chief himself!

The Native Administration Proclamation has at last provided more effective machinery for controlling the chief and protecting the tribe against oppression or maladministration. While making it a statutory offence for any tribesman to 'conspire against or subvert or attempt to subvert' the authority of the chief, the Proclamation specifically states that this provision does not apply to *bona fide* criticism of his rule. On the other hand, should the chief (or any other tribal authority) fail to carry out the duties imposed upon him, he can be tried by the District Commissioner and, if convicted, fined or imprisoned. Moreover, if he at any time 'neglects or fails to discharge properly his duties as chief, or becomes physically incapable of carrying them out properly, or abuses his authority and oppresses his people, or otherwise proves to be a bad chief', he can, after having been given an opportunity of defending himself, be suspended from the exercise of his duties as chief; and until his suspension has been withdrawn, some one else, appointed either by the tribe or by the Administration, will act in his place. If the tribe so desires, but only then, the chief may even be deposed permanently. If necessary, he may also be ordered, after suspension or deposal, to leave the Reserve, and not to enter it again until given permission to do so.

As an institution, the chieftainship is still greatly honoured and respected, and the people still look primarily to the chief as their ruler and guide. But his loss of many old ritual and economic functions, the presence of a rival leader in the form of the missionary, and, above all, his subjection to the Administration, have inevitably deprived him of much of his authority. Moreover, educational advancement, and the possibility of escape created by labour migration, have made the people more openly critical of his conduct, and they no longer respond so readily to the many demands he makes upon their services. There is no tendency as yet to advocate abolition of the chieftainship, but the stricter measures introduced by the Administration to keep the chief under control and to protect the tribe from abuse have been generally welcomed, especially by his more literate subjects, who apparently hanker after a 'constitutional monarchy' of the kind they have learned to know from their school-books.

At the same time, the chief himself is in a by no means happy position. His people look to him to protect their interests, and often enough his actions are inspired by genuinely patriotic rather than purely selfish motives. The Administration, again, on the one hand holds him responsible for the maintenance of peace, order, and good government, and on the other expects him to see that the laws it imposes and the instructions it issues are duly carried out. It has already happened that a situation may arise in which the chief must choose between his duty to the Administration and what he regards as his duty to the tribe. If he attempts to enforce the wishes of the Administration, he is only increasing his own difficulties by arousing the hostility of the people; if he disobeys the Administration, he is liable to punishment and even suspension. These and some of the other problems nowadays confronting the chief were recently discussed in an article by Tshekedi,[1] which shows how far removed the modern system of administration is from the day, little over forty years ago, when Kgama was told in London by the Secretary of State that he would be allowed to continue ruling his people 'much as at present'.

[1] 'Chieftainship under Indirect Rule', *J. R. Afr. Soc.*, vol. xxv (1936), pp. 251-61.

THE POLITICAL SYSTEM OF THE BEMBA TRIBE— NORTH-EASTERN RHODESIA

By Audrey I. Richards

I. Bantu Political Organization—Some General Features

THE political systems of most of the Bantu peoples known to us show certain striking similarities, particularly as far as South and Central Africa are concerned. We are apparently dealing in each case with a tribal organization that is an outgrowth of a smaller lineage group, either split off from a parent stem in search of independence and new territory, or scattered by the onslaught of an enemy. In South, Central, and to a lesser extent East Africa most of the ethnic groups now known as tribes have a surprisingly short history of occupation of their present habitat —rarely more than 200 years and sometimes as little as 50 to 100. For this reason the original kinship structure of the immigrant people can still be recognized as the framework of their political system. Authority is almost invariably based on descent, whether within the family, the village, the district, or the nation, and the chief of the tribe combines executive, ritual, and judicial functions according to the pattern of leadership in each constituent kinship unit. Like the family head, he is a priest of an ancestral cult, believed in many cases to have a mystic power over the land, and he invariably claims rights over his people's labour and produce. The hierarchy of Bantu society allows only one type of authority, one basis of power, and one set of attributes in its leaders in most of the tribes so far described.

Besides this personal relationship established by tradition between the Bantu subject and his chief, yet another feature of the political organization depends on facts of kinship, emotional, legal, and ritual. Political power and prerogatives tend to become concentrated in the hands of descendants of the original lineage group, of which the chief is the living representative, and in many areas tribal cohesion seems very largely to depend on the predominance of this ruling line, whether the latter is to be reckoned as the first Bantu people to occupy the particular territory, or whether it conquered the earlier inhabitants and subsequently built up a new state. We find tribes called after the name of the original leader of the nuclear community[1] (e.g. the Zulu, or the lineage groups of North Basutoland loosely described as Bamoheng, or Bamoketela): and others called after his clan (e.g. Kwena, Mangwato). The descendants of the first chief's clan may form a ruling caste (e.g. Zulu, Swazi, Bemba), and the total number of clans in the tribe may be arranged in order of precedence based on the tradition of the original migration into the area, or else the degree of relationship with the descent group of the chief.[2] The next of kin of the chief may play a definite part in the political organization, may claim rights to territorial chieftainships or villages, membership of tribal councils or smaller advisory bodies (e.g. the council formed by the chief's brother, sister, and near relatives among the Venda), or they may act as a regency council at the chief's death (e.g. Venda, Tswana, Swazi).

These then seem to be common features of Bantu political organization—the position of the chief as head of a community held together by bonds, real or fictitious, of kinship and as priest of an ancestral cult, and a political structure based on the dominance of a leading family line or clan. It is the differences in the machinery of government and in the incidence of tribal authority within this common pattern that make the interest of a comparative work like the present. In examining a particular case, there are a number of different conditioning factors which seem to account for these variations in political structure. Of these the most obvious appear to be the following: (a) the length of time the tribe has inhabited its present territory; (b) the type of immigration, whether by peaceful penetration, ejection of other units or their amalgamation;[3] (c) the emphasis placed on different prin-

[1] Schapera uses this term to describe a ruling group which has conquered and finally amalgamated other peoples often of foreign stock (cf. p. 57).

[2] cf. the heirarchy of Ganda clans: the precedence observed in tasting first-fruits in order of clan seniority among the Sotho peoples, and the respect still accorded to the Zulu and Swazi clans that have split off from the original royal stock, when it became necessary to contract marriages between members of one house.

[3] Compare the differences in size and homogeneity between single tribes largely of one stock with a single paramount chief (Swazi, Bemba); the congeries of small autonomous tribelets with similar cultural features but no supreme head (the swamp peoples of north-eastern Rhodesia or the low-veld tribes of northern Transvaal); or the amalgamation of a number of different ethnic groups into one empire by conquest or absorption (the old Luba Empire of the Congo, or that of the Zulu under Shaka or the Basotho under Moshesh).

ciples of social grouping such as descent, age, sex differences, or
local ties by which the tribe may be integrated and the incidence
of authority determined; (d) the economic bases of the people's
activities which affect their degree of dispersal, the form of leadership required, and the economic values associated with political
prerogatives; (e) the type of foreign rule to which the tribe is
subject and the European elements that are effecting its political
development, i.e. variations in policy from the administrative
system known as Indirect Rule in Tanganyika, Northern Rhodesia,
Uganda, to the more direct government by the white man in South
Africa or the attempts made to create new political institutions
for Natives, such as the Bunga system of the Transkei.

All these factors will be found to account for differences in
political organization among a number of the kindred peoples
known as the Bantu, and I shall try to analyse the Bemba system
along these lines.

II. The Bemba Tribe

(a) *Tribal Composition.* The Bemba tribe at present inhabits
the Tanganyika plateau of north-eastern Rhodesia, between the
four great lakes—Tanganyika to the north-east, Nyassa to the
east, and Mweru and Bangweolu to the north-west and west
respectively. They number to-day about 140,000, very sparsely
scattered over the country at a density of an average 3·75 per
square mile.

The Bemba trace their origin to the area now known as the
Belgian Congo and declare that they were originally an offshoot
from the great Luba people which inhabits the Kasai district.
The fact that the first ancestor of the Bemba is known as Citi
Muluba ('Citi the Luban') substantiates this tradition, together
with the cultural similarities still noted between the two peoples
and the fact that Luban words, no longer understood by the
Bemba commoner, are still used as part of the religious ritual at
the paramount chief's court. The legends of immigration are
numerous and circumstantial. The first arrivals apparently crossed
the Lualaba River, which forms the western boundary of their
present territory, about the middle of the eighteenth century, and
travelled north and east until they established their first head-
quarters near Kasama, the present administrative centre of the
Bemba country. From the sociological point of view, their history

dates from this period, since the composition of the invading group still determines the title to chieftainships, rank, succession to various offices, and the order of precedence of a number of the older clans.

The Bemba are to all intents and purposes a homogeneous group. They form a quite distinct political unit from the Bisa, Lala, Lunda, and other neighbouring tribes with similar traditions of origin and marked cultural and linguistic affinities. The Bemba declare that their forefathers found the country empty on their arrival, and, whether this is true or not, there seems to have been no strong opposition from whatever groups occupied the territory. The war-like habits of this tribe seem to have developed later, when they spread into the surrounding districts, pushing back their neighbours, such as the Lungu to the north-west, the Bisa and the Lala to the west and south respectively, and the Cewa to the east. The dominance of the Bemba chiefs was still more effectively enforced by the import of Arab guns in the nineteenth century. Where they did not dislodge the occupants of the surrounding country, their chiefs appointed members of the royal family or specially faithful subjects to hold the district for him (*ukulashika*) and to collect tribute of ivory tusks, grain, ironwork, salt, or other goods. The empire of the Bemba extended at one time right up into the Congo and to the shores of Lake Tanganyika, and they exerted influence over most of the present Bisa and Lala country to the south. With the coming of the white man at the end of the nineteenth century, their authority over the surrounding tribes collapsed, and though Bemba chiefs still rule over Bisa villages, e.g. in the Chinsali and Luwingu districts, it is rather a case of tribal admixture on the borders than a large-scale incorporation of foreign elements such as has occurred in the history of some of the Southern Bantu states. For the purposes of the present inquiry, we can reckon the Bemba as a homogeneous tribe with a history of settled occupation of their present territory lasting about 200 years.

The distinctive marks of tribal membership are the following: (*a*) The common name *Babemba*, still uttered with a good deal of pride in such phrases as '*Fwe Babemba*' ('We, the Bemba'), used to preface bragging references to the exploits of the tribe as compared to those of surrounding peoples, who are still sometimes referred to contemptuously as slaves (*bashya*). (*b*) The common language (*Cibemba*), which forms a distinct dialect in native eyes, although it does not differ very considerably from the neighbouring *Cibisa* or *Cilala*. (*c*) The tribal mark, a vertical cut on each temple about 1 in. long behind the eyes. (*d*) The common historical traditions of the people—even young men at the present day speak with pride of the coming of their fathers from Lubaland, and take delight in describing the military exploits of their ancestors and the ferocity of the old chiefs. (*e*) Their allegiance to a common paramount chief, the Citimukulu, whose overlordship of the Bemba territory is unquestioned.

(*b*) *Social Grouping*. (1) *Kinship*. The Bemba are a matrilineal tribe practising matrilocal marriage. Descent is reckoned through the mother and a man is legally identified with a group of relatives composed of his maternal grandmother and her brothers and sisters, his mother and her brothers and sisters, and his own brothers and sisters. His membership of this group determines his succession to different offices and his status in the community, although in a matrilocal society it only occasionally determines his residence. He also belongs to a wider descent group, the clan (*umukoa*, plur. *imikoa*) which is also traced in the woman's line. Each *umukoa* is distinguished by the name of an animal, plant, or natural phenomenon, such as rain. It has a legend of origin usually describing the split-off of the clan ancestors from the original lineage group, and an honorific title or form of greeting. Clans are in effect exogamous, since a man may not marry a woman he calls 'mother', 'sister', or 'daughter', and these terms are extended to the limits of clan membership on the maternal side. Through his clan affiliation, a man traces his descent, rank —if he belongs to the royal clan—rights to succeed to certain offices, such as hereditary councillorship (cf. pp. 100, 108), and claims to his relatives' help and hospitality.

Some clans have a higher status than others, according to whether their original ancestors arrived in the country as part of the following of the first Citimukulu, or alternatively, split off as a separate descent group later. Thus the crocodile clan (*Bena ŋandu*) is the *umukoa* of the first immigrant chief and stands highest in status (cf. 'Rank'), while various others, such as the fish clan, millet clan, &c., are said to be of similar antiquity. The hereditary councillors described later belong to these clans. All the *imikoa* are paired with opposite clans that perform reciprocal ritual duties for each other, but this form of social grouping does not seem to affect the political organization at all at the present day.[1]

Within the clan, smaller lineage groups are recognized. These have no distinct name; though the Bemba often refer to them as 'houses' (*amaianda*, sing. *iŋanda*) of the same clan. Such a house consists of the direct descendants of one particular ancestress traced back to three or four generations—five at the most. Within this smaller descent group, succession to office is usually limited, and chieftainships tend to become hereditary within three or four generations in such lines.[2] Social replacement of one man for another, either as an heir, an officiant in a religious ceremony, in fulfilment of a marriage contract (in the case of a woman), or in compensation for blood guilt in the old days, tends and tended to take place within the 'house' and not the clan, though members of the *umukoa* do replace each other if there is no one more nearly related within the *iŋanda* to do so.

It is the smaller descent-group which is important in considering the influence of the ancestral spirits (*imipashi*, sing. *umupashi*) over the living, either as affecting the welfare of their descendants in general or as entering the wombs of pregnant women of that descent-group to act as guardian spirits to the children as yet unborn.

Apart from the descent-group that determines his status, there is the body of kinsmen with whom a Bemba co-operates actively in daily life. These are the people with whom he may choose to live, and who gather together at any important event in his life, such as marriage, the birth of a child, illness, or a death. This group is known by a distinct term, the *ulupwa*. It has a bilateral basis, since it is composed of the near relatives on both sides of the family and also relatives in law. The balance between the powers of the maternal and paternal relatives is a very even one in Bemba society, in spite of the legal emphasis on the matrilineal side, and the ties uniting the members of the *ulupwa* are very strong.[3] Though it is

[1] cf. my 'Reciprocal Clan Relationships among the Bemba of North-Eastern Rhodesia', *Man*, December, 1937.

[2] The late Nkula, Bwalya Cangala, claimed, in the course of a succession dispute, that his near relatives, the children of his grandmother, Nakasafye, must now be considered as a separate 'house', as distinct from the children and grandchildren of her sister, Mukukamfumu II (cf. chart on p. 102).

[3] cf. my 'Mother-right in Central Africa' in *Essays presented to C. G. Seligman* (1934).

more usual to live with kinsmen on the matrilineal side, the grand-father or the mother's brother, yet a man may choose to live with his father's people by preference, and they play an important part at all the great ceremonial occasions in his life. The strength of the bilateral *ulupwa* is in fact one of the distinguishing features of the Bemba kinship system as compared with the strongly patrilineal societies of South Africa to my mind. It affects the political system in two ways. First, it allows for a much greater variety in the composition of the village, and more possibilities of change in its membership; and, secondly, we find in the case of the chief's relatives that the *ulupwa* of a ruler is an important unit in the whole political machine. A ruler's sons receive positions and office as well as his heirs, the maternal nephews; and his father's relatives and those related to him by marriage are also favoured, so that his grip over the country is a strong one.

(2) *Local Grouping.* The local unit in Bemba society is the village (*umushi*, plur. *imishi*). It contains on an average thirty to fifty huts, and is a kinship unit first and foremost. A village comes into being when a middle-aged or elderly man has acquired a big enough following of relatives to justify his applying to the chief for permission to set up a community on his own. He usually builds near other relatives, but land is so plentiful that it is perfectly possible for him to settle almost where he pleases within the chief's domain. The core of the village consists in the first place of the headman's own matrilocal family group, i.e. his married daughters with their husbands and children, and probably members of his matrilineal descent-group, i.e. his sisters and their children. Polygamy is rare. A chief will have a number of wives, say ten to fifteen, but commoners do not often have more than one.

A successful headman will be able to attract more distant rela-tives to him, both on the patrilineal and matrilineal side. On his death he may be succeeded by his heir, and such a local com-munity may continue in existence with frequent changes in its composition, for two, three, or even more generations. Indeed, the village of the hereditary officials of the paramount chief (*bakabilo*, cf. pp. 100, 108) remain permanently fixed in one village. Thus in every district there are a number of new villages brought into existence by the chief's favour (*ukupokelafye kuli mfumu*) and therefore specially dependent on his support. These include com-munities newly gathered together by commoner headmen, as described, as well as existing villagers which have been given, with or without the inhabitants' goodwill, to a relative of the chief. Besides these new headmanships, there are those founded in the chief's predecessors' reigns and described as such, and on the whole less dependent on the present ruler. The proportion of new to old villages in Citimukulu's district in 1933 was as follows:

On 160 *villages*:

	per cent.
New villages	28
Villages with one previous holder of the headmanship	16
Villages with two previous holders of the headmanship	10
Villages with three or more holders of the headmanship	40
Villages constituted from remnants of two old villages	6

The skill with which he allots headmanships, and the positions in which he places his own relatives, contribute greatly to a chief's power.

In spite of the provisions for inheritance of headmanships, the Bemba village is an impermanent community from many points of view. It moves every four or five years, in keeping with the practice of shifting cultivation, and is liable to disruption at the death of an important member or at any loss of popularity by the headman. The plentiful supply of land and the many alternative possibilities of kinship grouping provide ample opportunities for a man to change from one village to another if he pleases, and in any case he is almost bound to live in a series of communities during his lifetime, e.g. the village of his birth, that to which he moves when he marries, any other village he may go to when he acquires the right to move his wife and family from her people's care, and lastly, in some cases, a community of which he may acquire the headmanship through succession to his maternal uncle. Hence, although a man's companions and fellow workers are those of his *umushi* and he speaks with some affection of the village of his birth or of his mother's people (*icifulo*), yet the bonds of kinship are much stronger than those of the impermanent local group. A Bemba is a member of a *ulupwa* and may move as he pleases to live with any of the relatives composing it, and he is the subject of a chief and may obtain permission to live in any part of the latter's territory, but his ties to a given locality are not necessarily strong.[1]

---

[1] cf. my *Land, Labour and Diet in Northern Rhodesia* (1939), chap. vii.

A chief's village (*umusumba*) is very much larger than that of a commoner. Inhabitants of the capital are composed of relatives of the chief, his followers, and also a number of families which moved there originally to win royal favour and have become accustomed to court life.[1] Since a chief's reputation depends largely on the size of his capital, and his councillors, courtiers, and administrative officers were drawn largely from his villagers, the *umusumba* is an important unit in the political machine. The late Nkula's village had about 400 huts when I visited it in 1931, that of the Citimukulu 150 in 1938. The capitals of pre-European days were evidently very much larger. These communities were divided into sections (*ifitente*, sing. *icitente*) and though nowadays there are nine *ifitente* at the paramount's village, there were formerly thirty to forty, according to native accounts.

The whole Bemba territory is divided into districts (*ifyalo*, sing. *icalo*). The *icalo* is a geographical unit with a fixed boundary and a name dating from historical times, e.g. the district of the Citimukulu is known as Lubemba, the country of the Bemba, and that of Mwamba, Ituna. These districts are territories originally allotted to members of the royal family, but once so divided they have never been sub-divided to provide smaller chieftainships for a new generation of princes as has happened in some parts of South Africa.

But the *icalo* is also a political unit. It is the district ruled over by a chief with a fixed title—the name of the first ruler to be appointed over each particular strip of land, always a close relative of one of the earlier Citimukulus. There are several types of chief, the paramount, who has his own *icalo*, as well as being overlord of the whole Bemba territory; the territorial chiefs, five or more in number, who have under them sub-chiefs who may rule over very small tracts of country or, rather, over a few villages.[2]

Each of these chiefs is known by the same title *mfumu* and each *icalo* is a more or less self-contained unit, a replica of the social structure of the other. Each capital has its own court, however small. Each chief has rights over the labour of his own villages. They work for him only and not for the paramount as happens among

---

[1] The phrase '*umwino musumba*' ('inhabitant of the capital') is used to indicate a 'chief's man' or a person of specially polished manners and knowledge of affairs.

[2] Mwamba has as a sub-chief, the Munkonge, and the Nkula has Shimwalule, Mwaba, Mukuikile, Nkweto, &c.

the Zulu, Swazi and other tribes with the regiment system. The *icalo* is also a ritual unit. At each capital are the sacred relics (*babenye*) of the first holders of the chiefly title and their ancestral spirits are thought to act as tutelary deities of the district, and are worshipped at the *umusumba*, at village shrines, and old hut sites throughout the country, and are also commonly supposed to act as guardian spirits to children born within the *icalo*.[1] Naturally the ritual and political organization of the paramount's capital is more elaborate than that of his inferiors, but even the smallest sub-chief maintains his miniature court and tries to ape the state of those above him, while the bigger territorial chiefs sometimes rivalled the power of the Citimukulu in the old days.

The territorial chieftainships are arranged in order of precedence, according to their nearness to the centre of the country—Lubemba—and the antiquity of their office. To the most important of these chiefdoms—the Mwambaship, the Nkulaship, the Nkolemfumuship, and the Mpepoship, for instances—the Citimukulu appoints his nearest relatives, the one succeeding the other in order of seniority. Thus the present Citimukulu, Kanyanta, has acted in turn as the Nkolemfumu, and the Mwamba before succeeding to the paramountcy (cf. chart on p. 102). On the other hand, the sub-chieftainships have tended to become concentrated in local branches of the royal family, and the paramount's strong grip over the country and his intimate knowledge of affairs at the courts of his fellow chiefs is certainly weaker in these outlying districts than in the case of chiefdoms ruled by his close relatives.

To the commoner, membership of an *icalo* means his allegiance to the chief of that territory. He will describe himself as an inhabitant of a district, such as *Icinga*, i.e. *mwine Icinga* or, alternatively, as the subject of its chief, Nkula, i.e. *mwine Nkula*, and both terms are synonymous. He may move from village to village within the *icalo*, but he remains his chief's man. The latter, in his turn, reckons his assets, not in terms of the size of his territory or its natural resources, but rather by the number of his people and in particular the villages he has under his rule.

(3) *Rank*. Rank is a marked feature of Bemba society. It is based on kinship, real or fictitious, with the chief. All members of the royal crocodile clan (*Bena ŋandu*) are entitled to special respect, precedence on ritual and social occasions, and sometimes

[1] Hence the great preponderance of one or two birth-names in each district.

to claims on the people's services. The potential heirs of a chief within his own branch of the family—that is to say, his brothers, maternal nephews, or maternal grandsons—are treated with particular deference. The former two categories are described as chiefs and addressed by the title *mfumu*, while the latter, only slightly lower in status, are referred to by a special name *beshikulu ba mfumu* ('grandchildren of the chiefs') and have their own ritual and social prerogatives.

Women of the royal line, the mothers, sisters, maternal nieces, and granddaughters of the chiefs are called *banamfumu* and are treated with much the same deference as are the men of the family. The mother of the paramount is highly honoured, succeeds to a fixed title—the *Candamukulu*—takes part in tribal councils, and has several villages of her own. The sisters of chiefs are privileged persons, protected and supported by their royal brothers, and usually granted one or more villages to rule. They are above the law in matters of sex morality, and a princess is allowed to have as many lovers as she pleases, provided she produces many children as potential heirs to the throne.

Not only members of the royal clan, but also persons who merely belong to the *ulupwa* of the chief, can claim high rank, i.e. his relatives on his paternal side, and his own sons. Some fathers of chiefs were nobodies and were quickly forgotten, but some have been famous men, honoured by their sons when the latter succeeded to the throne. The children of chiefs, though not members of his clan, and therefore not heirs, are also entitled to special privileges, and the *bana bamfumu* ('children of the chief') form a class of their own. They are brought up at the court, where they are treated in many ways more favourably than the heirs themselves and are able to claim headmanships and even chieftainships.[1] Even the half-brothers of chiefs, through other fathers (*bakaulu*), have rights to special treatment at court.

Added to this, already numerous class of royal personages are the descendants of close relatives of dead chiefs. Roughly speaking, any person who can claim to be maternal nephew, grandson, or son of a chief is succeeded by a man who continues to hold the same rank by the *ukupyanika* system described on p. 98. He is then addressed as 'chief' or 'son of chief'. The descendants of

---

[1] A few chieftainships are definitely handed on to 'sons of chiefs' instead of to 'chiefs', e.g. the Makassaship, the Lucembeship, or the Munkongeship.

royal princesses are also entitled to honour, as well as those of
wives of chiefs and even consorts of princesses. It will be seen,
therefore, that the royal rank is a very large one. Any one who can
possibly claim connexion of any sort with any chief, dead or
living, does so, although the perquisites of rank are in most cases
honour only and the possible favours of the chief, rather than any
material assets. Every one outside the royal clan, or *ulupwa*, is an
umupabi, or 'ordinary person', and in old days there was a slave
class below—men and women captured in battle or enslaved to
their own people for some crime. These individuals were known
as *bashya*. The term is now used as an opprobrious epithet
especially for foreigners—often assumed to have been enslaved by
the Bemba formerly. Slavery itself no longer exists.

(4) *Other Principles of Social Grouping*. Age is not a principle
of social grouping among the Bemba. Precedence is reckoned on
the basis of seniority, as in most Bantu societies, and there are
special terms used to describe the different stages of life, suckling,
infant, child, adolescent, unmarried, married, old, &c. But there
are no regiments based on age, as in South and parts of East
Africa, and the boys initiation ceremonies so often found associated
with such institutions do not exist among this group of the
Central Bantu.

There are no occupational groups, with the exception of certain
specialist fishing communities on the banks of the big rivers, and
in the old days there were specialist hunters of big game. Secret
societies, such as the *ubutwa*, which is common among neighbouring tribes over the Congo border, and has been adopted by the
Bisa of the swamps, do not seem to have been introduced among
the Bemba.

To conclude, Bemba society is as yet undifferentiated to any
large extent. The tribe is an outgrowth of a lineage-group which
has occupied its present territory for 200 to 300 years, and has
remained more or less homogeneous. The original kinship structure is still apparent. All the social groups to which a man
belongs are ultimately based on kinship—whether it is his household village or descent group, and there are no other forms of
association such as age-sets to cut across this original grouping by
descent. Rank consists of membership of the clan of the first
immigrants to enter the land.

(c) *Economic Background*. The Bemba are an agricultural people like most of the Central Bantu group to which they belong. They keep no cattle. Tsetse-fly at present prevents their keeping stock over most of the country, but in any case they seem to have no pastoral traditions, whatever they may have had formerly. Thus they have no means of storing wealth as have the Southern Bantu. Their marriage contracts are fulfilled by service and not by the passage of cattle. In the old days military glory and the extraction of tribute from conquered peoples seems to have been the dominant ambition of the Bemba chiefs, and their wealth consisted in the size of their following and the amount of service they were able to command. This fact profoundly influences their position at the present day (cf. p. 116).

The soil of most of this district is poor and it has not attracted white settlement. The staple crop is finger millet (*eleusine corecana*), while some kafir corn, a little maize, legumes, and pumpkins are also grown. The people practise shifting cultivation of a primitive type, and the plentiful supply of land and the lack of any localized natural resources which might attract the inhabitants to settle in one area rather than another all affect the political system. As has been shown, they decrease the strength of local ties as against political or kinship affiliations, and they account for the fact that the power to distribute land is not an important prerogative of leadership in distinction to conditions in most Southern Bantu tribes.

Hunting and fishing contribute a small share of the food-supply only. Organized marketing does not exist, and under modern conditions no cash crop has been found for this area. This fact, together with the absence of opportunities for local employment, forces the adult male population to look for work outside the tribal area, with resultant effects, as will be seen, on the political system of the tribe.

(*d*) *White Administration*. The type of white administration introduced in this area is described on pp. 112–20.

III. Bases of Authority

The positions of leadership in Bemba society consist of the following offices: (*a*) *territorial rulers* (chiefs and headmen); (*b*) *administrative officers and councillors;* (*c*) *priests, guardians of sacred shrines, and magic specialists with economic functions;* (*d*) *army leaders* in the old days. Succession to all these offices is based on descent in nearly every case. Chieftainships were limited to one clan, as we have seen; some of the councillorships (i.e. the *bakabilo*) are confined to a few of the older clans; and head-manships, though they may be won through the chiefs favour, tend to become hereditary in their turn. All priestly offices are hereditary without exception, as is natural where an ancestral cult of this type is practised. Magico-economic specialists, particularly those in charge of fishing villages, usually acquire their powers by descent also, as do some of the doctors and diviners (*ŋanga*). In each case the supernatural powers almost invariably correlated with political authority in this area are conferred by a rite, of great complexity, in the case of the succession of a chief, known as *ukupyanika*. For these reasons it is essential to study the dogma of descent by which these powers are believed to be transferred from one generation to another, and the legal rules of succession by which status and office are passed from one man to another.

(*a*) *The Dogma of Descent*. By dogma of descent I mean, first, those theories of procreation[1] which express a people's beliefs as to the physical contribution of the father and mother to the formation of the child, and hence the traditional conception of the physical continuity between one generation and the next; and next their beliefs as to the influence of the dead members of each social group over the living, and hence the social identification[2] of a man with the line of his dead ancestors.

Among the Bemba it is believed that a child is made from the blood of a woman which she is able to transmit to her male and female children. A man can possess this blood in his veins, but cannot pass it on to his children, who belong to a different clan. Physiological paternity is recognized. Children are often described as being like their fathers, and are expected to give the latter affection and respect although they have no legal obligations to them under the matrilineal system. 'We take our fathers' presents because they begot us,' they say. But it is nevertheless the physical

[1] This term was first introduced by Malinowski, who showed how the rules of matrilineal descent among the Trobriand islanders are buttressed by beliefs that the father makes no physical contribution to the birth of his child. Similar material published by Rattray from the Ashanti area shows a belief in a double contribution of blood from the mother and spirit from the father correlated with a bilateral emphasis on descent.

[2] To use a term employed in a very stimulating manner by Radcliffe Browne.

continuity of the mother's line of ancestors which is the basis of legal identification with her descent group.[1] A royal princess might even produce an heir by a slave father in the old days without lowering her child's prestige. The relationship between brother and sister, which is a very close one, legally and ritually, is based on the fact that the two were born from one womb, and in the case of the royal family it appears to be equally strong when the two are children of different fathers. These theories of procreation account, not only for the matrilineal descent of the Bemba, on which succession to chieftainship is based, but also for the rank accorded to the royal princesses as mothers of chiefs, and the headmanships and other positions of authority given them.

The Bemba dogma as to the influence of the dead over the living is also of the utmost importance as a basis for political authority. The spirit of a dead man (*umupashi*, plur. *imipashi*) is thought to survive as a guardian presence associated with the land or village site formerly inhabited, and as a spiritual protector of different individuals born in the same lineage group and called by the same name. The *imipashi* of dead chiefs become tutelary deities of the land they ruled over, and responsible for its fertility and the welfare of its inhabitants. They can be approached by the successor to the chieftainship at various sacred spots in the territory and at the sacred relic shrines (*babenye*) in his own village. A chief is said to be powerful because he 'has great *imipashi*!' It is for this reason he is described as the *umwine calo*, 'owner of the land', and it is important to note that in every case the most important *imipashi* and the most sacred relics are those of the first chiefs to enter the land, or the first occupants of a chieftainship.

This dogma as to the influence of the dead over the living inhabitants of a district, or the members of a descent group, is very similar to the general Bantu pattern. But the Bemba belief in the social identification between the dead man and his appointed successor seems to me to be particularly complete. It is the basis of the belief as to the supernatural influence exerted by the chief in his own person as distinct from his direct approach to the spirits

[1] The patrilineal tribes on the Nyassaland border consider the Bemba theory of procreation as entirely ridiculous. One Ngoni expressed his contempt, thus: 'If I have a bag and put money in it, the money belongs to me and not to the bag. But the Bemba say a man puts semen into a woman and yet the child belongs to her and not to him!'

in prayer. When a man or woman dies, his or her social personality must be immediately perpetuated by a successor who passes through a special ritual (*ukupyanika*) and thus acquires the name, the symbols of succession (a bow for a man and a girdle for the woman), and the *umupashi* of the dead man. By this social identification, a man assumes the latter's position in the kinship-group, uses the same kinship terms and, in the case of a chief, it is almost impossible to tell when a man is describing incidents which took place in his own life or those of an ancestor two or three generations dead. So important is this social perpetuation of the dead considered that immediately after a death, before the successor has finally been appointed, a small boy or girl, usually a maternal grandchild, is chosen to inherit the name of the deceased temporarily (*ukunwa menshi*, 'to drink the water'). He or she is given some small piece of the latter's property and thereafter addressed as grandfather or grandmother, or whatever the right kinship term may be.

In the same way, a chief, once he has succeeded to the name, the spirit, and the sacred relics of his predecessor, has magic influence over the productive capacity of his whole territory. His ill health or death, his pleasure or displeasure, his blessings or curses, can affect the prosperity of the people, and even his sex life reacts on the state of the community.[1] For a chief to break a sex taboo is an act which may cause calamity to the whole people, and the rites by which he is purified after sexual contacts form one of the most important elements in the politico-religious ceremonial requiring the participation of thirty or forty hereditary officials (*bakabilo*) in the case of the paramount. Conversely, legitimate sex intercourse, especially as prescribed on certain ritual occasions, may actually be a health-giving influence. Any headman has a certain degree of supernatural influence in his own village as the successor to his predecessor's *umupashi*, but a chief has considerably more. For all these reasons, ritual precautions guard the sacred person of a chief. Special taboos must be kept to preserve the ritual purity of the ruler's sacred fire, and his sacred

[1] There are rumours that chiefs were throttled by their hereditary councillors when they were obviously sick unto death, for fear they took 'the land' into the grave with them. This information was sent me by Mr. T. Fox-Pitt after I had left the country and was afterwards checked by Mr. Godfrey Wilson. In fact it is probable that in the old days the Bemba chiefs would fall under Frazer's definition of a 'divine king'.

food, and to protect his person and that of the sacred relics from the contagion of illness, death, or sex defilement.[1]

The ritual by which a successor to the chieftainship is converted from an ordinary individual to a ruler with almost divine powers, has a good deal of political importance. It confers authority on the priests—in this case hereditary officials (*bakabilo*) who carry it out—and gives them, as we shall see, considerable power to check the chief himself. The complete ritual by which the *umupashi* of a dead ruler is liberated to guard the land he governed, and the new heir is installed, is too complex to describe here and now. Briefly speaking, it consists of the desiccation of the body during a period of a year, from one kafir-corn harvest to the next; its burial in a special grove (with human sacrifices in the old days); and the building of a shrine on the site of the deserted capital. To make the new chief, *bakabilo* must preside at the installation of a new great wife, arrange for the sexual purification of the royal pair, and the lighting of their new sacred fire.[2] They must hand over to the heir the heirlooms (*babenye*) of which they have been in charge during the interregnum, and must finally found a new village and build again the sacred huts in which the relics are to be kept. Such a ceremonial may take eighteen months to two years and the participation of all the *bakabilo* and hereditary buriers (*bafingo*) in the case of the paramount; a lesser time and very many fewer priestly dignitaries in the case of the territorial chiefs. The secrecy and awe surrounding these ceremonies is, I believe, one of the ways by which the people's reverence for their chiefs is maintained.

(*b*) *Legal Rules of Descent and Succession.* Against this background of beliefs as to the continuity between one generation and another, the nature of descent and succession is defined exactly by legal rule. Descent in the royal family is reckoned to the time of first occupation of the country, and twenty-five to thirty Citimukulus are remembered. In the case of a territorial chief, the line of ancestors is not so long, and most are described as having been 'born in the country'. Most of the names honoured are those of men but some are those of women, and it seems that

---

[1] cf. my *Land, Labour and Diet in Northern Rhodesia* (1939), chap. xvii.
[2] Hence the importance of the great wife of the chief (*umukolo ua calo*) in the political life of the tribe and the belief that her behaviour also influences the welfare of the land.

the first ancestress to inhabit a new chiefdom, or one who was a mother of numerous powerful sons and was thus able to found a new branch, could claim to be so respected.[1] But it is to the men holders of titles that most shrines are built.

The hereditary officials (*bakabilo*) also trace their descent to the first arrival for the most part, and tell stories which account for their right to the ritual offices they hold to-day, e.g. the *bafingo* who now bury the chief, claim to be the descendants of those who buried the first Citimukulus when on the march. This reckoning of descent to a definite epoch in history very clearly remembered is of service in maintaining the myth of absolute continuity of the chiefly lines. In actual fact, the present Citimukulu is a descendant of one Cileshye, who seized the throne from the occupier, Cincinta, only four generations back. This branch of usurpers is able to claim descent from the first Citimukulu all the same. The first ancestors are remembered very accurately and their sacred relics kept. The ensuing vagueness in the chain seems to be of no account.

In most types of succession whether to the name and spirit of a dead man or to his office, there are usually two or three potential heirs, and although there are certain rules of priority, it is practically never the case that there is one child known as heir to the chieftainship from birth and brought up as such, as occurs in those South African tribes in which the eldest son of the great wife must always succeed. A Bemba chief, or commoner, is succeeded by his brothers in order of age, next by his sister's children, and, failing them, by his maternal grandsons. Difficulties arise when there is a choice between an older classificatory 'brother', not a sibling, but possibly a mother's sister's son, or an even more distant 'brother' still, and a young man, a maternal nephew who is the child of the deceased's own sister, with whom, as we have seen, his ties are very close. Here the principles of primogeniture conflict with that of propinquity of kinship, in the case of a branch of a family that has been in existence for three or four generations, and it is probable that in these cases the nearest heir is appointed unless he is manifestly unsuitable, when the more distant 'brother'

---

[1] e.g. Bwalya Cabala, the first ancestress said to have been fetched from Lubaland by her brothers when the latter had occupied what is now Bembaland; or the Nakasafye, grandmother of the present Nkula, who is described as having started a new line, and was evidently a woman of great character as well as the mother of many sons.

or 'maternal nephew' is selected. I never heard of a regent being appointed for a young man as is commonly done in those Bantu tribes where the heir to the throne is known from his time of birth.

The situation is more complicated in the case of succession to chieftainships, since through the custom of inheriting one big territorial chieftainship after another within the paramount's immediate family, a tradition has grown up that, e.g., the holder of the Mwambaship should always succeed to the Citimukuluship, whatever the priority of kinship. This claim was put forward in the last succession dispute (1925) and is commonly supported by Government officials who naturally prefer a fixed system of succession to the discussion of rival candidates' rights that seems to have been the older procedure. There is also a tendency becoming more and more evident for certain of these bigger chieftainships to be confined to sub-branches of the main royal line, as distinct from sub-chieftainships which are nearly always given to descendants of local branches of the crocodile clan (e.g. the Mwabaship). This constant growth and separation of different sub-lines or houses of the royal clan seems to have been continuous in the past. The chart of the present central branch of the *Bena ɲandu* should make the situation clear. It will be seen that the first and second Citimukulus in this line were siblings, and were succeeded by another pair of own brothers—Citimukulu III and IV, the sons of the first ruler's eldest sister, Candamukulu. The paramountcy then passed to the line of a younger sister, Bwalya Cabala, tradition stating that the eldest maternal nephew of Citimukulu III and IV, then holding office as Mwamba, refused to succeed to the office for various reasons. The title then passed to another pair of brothers in succession, Citimukulu VI and VII, the sons of a younger daughter of Candamukulu—Nakasafye. Hence the famous dispute of 1925 just referred to, between Kanyanta, now Citimukulu, and his mother's mother's sister's grandchild, Bwalya Cangala, then holding the Nkulaship, and reckoned as Kanyanta's classificatory brother. Bwalya claimed that he was own maternal nephew of the dead chief, Ponde, and Kanyanta that he came of an older line and that it had now become established that the Mwambas always succeeded the Citimukulus. The Government supported the latter claimant, but there seems to have been very little to choose between the

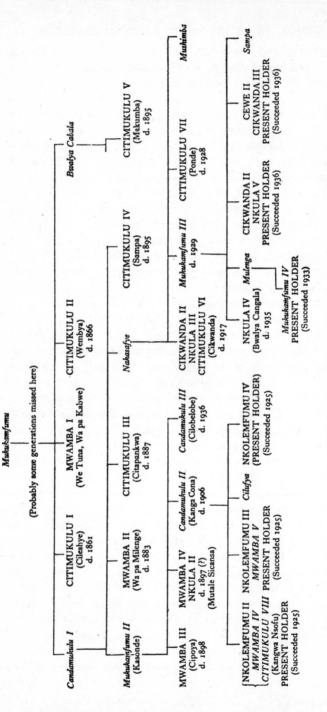

Chart showing succession in central branch of the royal family (taken from a table made by E. B. H. Goodall and kept at the Government Office, Kasama)

Men shown thus: CITIMUKULU   Women shown thus: *Candamukulu*

NOTE—(1) Two or more titles means the successive holding of two or more chieftaincies.   (2) Citumukulu I designates the first Paramount
in *this particular lineage group.*

legal rights of the two rivals, and the rather complex machinery of tribal deliberation on such matters (cf. p. 109) was not called into motion.

The chart also shows clearly the way in which certain chieftain-ships have also tended to become fixed in different family lines of this main branch of the *Bena ŋandu* even during the last four generations, i.e. the Mwambaship, the Nkolemfumuship, the Mpepoship in the line of the chieftainess Mukukamfumu, and the Nkulaship, the Cikwandaship, and the Ceweship in the line of Nakasafye. The separation between these two branches will probably become wider and wider with time. In the case of the outlying sub-chieftainships, this separation off of local family lines of the royal clan has proceeded even further. To conclude, there are definite rules of succession according to Bemba kinship but the type of matrilineal succession usually provides two or three pos-sible heirs, and in the case of the bigger chieftainships there are a number of different factors, such as the paramount's control over the more important *ifyalo*, the traditional order of succession to different offices, local feeling in the case of sub-chieftainships, and last, but not by any means a negligible point, the personal qualities of the candidates themselves.

IV. Functions and Prerogatives of Leadership

The functions of the territorial heads, i.e. chiefs and headmen, seem to be derived from two sources—the position of the leader as head of a kinship group and his role as the representative of a line of dead ancestors in a particular district. In the case of a headman, these two aspects are indistinguishable, while the latter predominates where a chief is concerned.

(a) *The Headman.* Bemba headmen are described as looking after, keeping, or actually 'herding the people' (*ukuteka bantu*). As senior kinsman of most of the villagers, a headman is responsible for the discipline of the children and young people; he hears cases informally and directs some economic activities. There are few activities carried out by the whole community in common except fishing and hunting, but besides organizing these latter pursuits a good headman initiates each new agricultural process and encourages and criticizes the younger men and women. Land is not often a matter of dispute in this area. The headman does not allot individual plots, but listens to cases should any arise. He is said to 'feed his people' and actually does so if they are in need, besides dispensing hospitality to strangers.

The head of the village acts as its ritual head. In the old days, he put up one village shrine to his own ancestors and one or more others to the dead chiefs of the land. This is still done in out-of-the-way parts of the country and in most places, I think, prayers are offered to these tutelary deities, whether shrines are built to them or no. The headman, like the chief, also influences the life of the community through his own person. He must 'warm the bush' (*ukukafye mpanga*) by an act of ritual intercourse with his wife before the huts of a new village are occupied. He blesses seeds for sowing, axes for tree-cutting, and first-fruits. His fire stands for the life of the community as a whole and must be ritually lighted when occasion demands. He presides over the special divination rites connected with village activities, such as the founding of a new community or the death of a member, and blesses new babies or individuals who are sick.

In the political hierarchy, the headman has his definite place. No Bemba may cultivate land except as a member of a village group, and the headman is responsible for organizing the supply of tribute and labour which must be paid to a chief by the community as a whole. He accompanies his villagers to court when they have cases to present and often speaks for them. He transmits the orders of a chief to his people and nowadays those of the Government. His prerogatives are few in number. As head of a kinship-group, he can command personal service from his younger relatives and should be able to exact one day's work from his people on the first day of tree-cutting and sowing. He is always given tribute of beer or meat. But probably, apart from these few economic privileges, the Bemba headman values most his position of authority, his small following, and the favour of his chief.

The sanctions for his authority nowadays are mainly his popularity, together with the strength of kinship feeling, and the belief of the Bemba that it is dangerous to allow an older relative to die injured. His supernatural powers were a source of strength in the old days, but to a very small extent now, and it must be admitted that the forces which keep a village together are not very strong. It is a constant fear to a headman that his people will melt away.

(*b*) *The Chief*. The functions of the different types of chief differ only in degree. All are said to look after their people, to 'work the land', and, with reference to their supernatural powers, to 'spit blessings over the land' (*ukufunga mate*). Their political duties consist in the administration of their capitals and also of their territories as a whole. A large *umusumba* means plenty of coming and going, enough workers for joint enterprises, a large panel of advisers for court cases, many messengers to keep in touch with the surrounding villages—in short, the possibility of keeping the tribal machine running. To maintain and even augment such a community by his popularity and his reputation for generosity is one of the chief's important political tasks. He has also to keep contact with the people widely dispersed over his *icalo* and to appoint new headmen, amalgamate old villages, and decide as to the selection of heirs to old titles. On his success in these last duties the integration of his people as a political unit largely depends.

As a judicial authority, the chief presides over his court with advisers selected from his village, and in the old days he alone could hear charges of witchcraft and, in the case of the greater territorial chiefs, put the accused to the poison ordeal (*mwafi*). In the economic sphere, he initiates agricultural activities by performing the customary ceremony before each begins; he makes big gardens with the aid of tribute labour from which he is able to fill large granaries and thus find the wherewithal to feed his following; he controls directly certain fishing and hunting enterprises: and he criticizes and directs the gardening work of his own villagers.[1]

The ritual duties of a chief consist in the observation of the taboos for the protection of his own person and the safety of the sacred relics at his disposal, and the carrying out of a number of rites for the sake of his whole *icalo*—in the case of the paramount, for the whole tribe. These last consist of economic rites, tree-cutting, sowing, and first-fruit ceremonies, those performed in case of national calamity, and for success in war in the old days. He was formerly bound to protect the people from witches and used to employ a special doctor at his court to destroy, by burning, the bodies of those found guilty of this offence.

In the old days the chief organized military expeditions,

[1] cf. my *Land, Labour, and Diet in Northern Rhodesia* (1939), chap. xiii, for a full account of the chief's economic powers.

E

although he did not necessarily take part in the fighting. As one chief put it, 'If we were killed, the whole *icalo* would fall to pieces'. The ruler had certain military captains in his following, could call up men to fight, direct their operations from afar, and arrange for the performance of war magic for success before battle and for purification from the stain of blood after it.

The prerogatives of a chief consist in rights over the labour of his people, who are required to do a few days' tribute labour each year and to answer sudden calls for help if made; and also claims to tribute in kind, usually paid in the form of an annual present of beer and/or grain, and portions of animals killed in the hunt.[1] It is through this tribute that he is able to pay his advisers, servants, labourers—and soldiers in the old days. Formerly, he maintained rights to certain monopolies, such as ivory tusks, salt from the big inland deposits at Mpika, and guns and cloth traded from Arabs. Slaves or booty captured by the army were brought to him, and he had a number of his own people enslaved for various offences. Besides these economic prerogatives, he commanded great, one might almost say abject deference, and had the satisfaction of seeing his following grow, his authority increased, and his power over life and death over his subjects recognized.

The sanctions for a chief's authority are numerous, and they were still greater in the old days. The most important of these has already been described as the people's belief in their rulers descent from a long line of ancestors and the supernatural powers thought to be so conferred. Besides this, a reputation for generosity and a system by which advancement could only be attained through royal favour naturally bound people to him. Much of his power also rested in the old days on force. A chief practised savage mutilations on those who offended him, injured his interests, laughed at him or members of his family, or stole his wives. A number of these mutilated men and women still survive in Bemba country to-day. Command over the army and over the supply of guns also lay in the chief's hands and there is no doubt that the greatness of the *Bena ŋandu* rested to a large extent on fear. The people explain that the royal family were named after the crocodile because 'they are like crocodiles that seize hold of the common people and tear them to bits with their teeth'.

---

[1] All these dues are very much harder to exact nowadays (cf. p. 116).

V. The Machinery of Government

Within each district there are a series of officials, messengers, &c., who carry out the activities of government and the different forms of ritual on which the chief's power depends. Some of these are personal followers of the chief promoted by him for their special loyalty (e.g. the *bafilolo*, *basano*), while others are hereditary officials who are more independent of their ruler's favour (e.g. *bafilolo* and *bafingo*). All these different dignitaries can be classed under various functional heads, i.e.:

(*a*) *Administrative.* These include the executive officials in charge of business in the *umusumba* and those responsible for carrying out the chief's orders in the *icalo* at large. Within the capital the most important are the heads of divisions (*bafilolo*), who are appointed from among the chief's personal friends. These are charged with keeping the peace of the village, organizing the tribute labour from the capital, allotting land for cultivation, which is often necessary in the bigger settlements, arranging hospitality for visitors—an important task at the capital—and acting as a panel of advisers on all occasions (cf. 'Judicial', below). Besides these elder men, there are at the *umusumba* a number of courtiers and in the old days young men (*bakalume ba mfumu*). Young boys, often members of the royal clan, were, and still occasionally are, sent to court to be educated there, and some families remain as courtiers for several generations apparently. All these act as messengers, attendants, and in the old days took duty as executioners.

As regards the country at large, the main difficulty was keeping in touch with the scattered villages. The Bemba have no general meeting like the *pitso* of the Sotho peoples or the *libandla* of the Nguni. For the chief's orders to be conveyed to his villages, messengers have to go to and fro. Other officers are required to recruit the tribute labourers and to demand beer or produce for the chief, and to apprehend criminals. Since some villages are sixty miles or so from the capital, an enormous amount of time is spent in coming and going in this way and even with the introduction of the bicycle a great many messengers of one sort or another are still required. In the old days courtiers and younger relatives of the chief acted in this capacity. Nowadays they have anything from four to twelve uniformed messengers, *kapasus*, and for the rest they go short of service.

(b) *Military*. There was no general military organization in this tribe, but attached to each big court were one or two captains (*bashika*). Some of these were hereditary, with ritual functions connected with war magic, and others appointed at the chief's will. They now act as specially trusted messengers.

(c) *Judicial*. There is no fixed composition to a Bemba court, although its procedure is laid down by custom. At a small chief's court, the elderly men of the village attend, while the *bafilolo* act as advisers at the big *imisumba*. Cases go on appeal from sub-chief to chief, chief to paramount, and in the event of a case of extreme difficulty presenting itself, the Citimukulu can summon from their villages some of his hereditary priests or councillors, the *bakabilo* (cf. below). Witnesses are brought by each party to a case and are marshalled by the *bafilolo*. The senior man present claps as each point is made to mark the recognition of the court, and the chief himself finally sums up and gives judgement. The advisers speak when asked a point of precedent or law, and influence the chief's final decision by black looks or alternatively enthusiastic clappings of the hand.

(d) *Advisory*. There is no council or meeting of all the adult men of the tribe for special occasions, as among many Southern Bantu. Sub-chiefs have a panel of village elders and relatives to advise them, while the biggest territorial chiefs have hereditary officials who combine political and judicial with ritual functions. In the case of the paramount, these officials—the *bakabilo*—number between thirty-five and forty and form an advisory council on special matters of State. The *bakabilo* have been described as having descent as long as that of the chief himself in many cases and possess sacred relics in their own rights. The power of these relics is so strong that the Citimukulu is not permitted to pass through their villages for fear that one chieftainship should harm the other. *Bakabilo* are immune from tribute, wore special feather head-dresses in the old days, and even now claim special respect equal to that given to a chief when travelling about the country. They call themselves *Fwe Babemba* ('We, the Babemba'), may not leave the central territory (Lubemba) for long, must be buried within the royal district, and keep sex taboos similar to those of the chiefs. They succeed by a special accession ceremony and are buried according to particular rites. They are divided into groups according to the order of their ancestors arrival in the country, and each has a special office based on the privileges of his original ancestor, e.g. the care of the royal drum, the right to sit on a stool in the chief's presence, or the duty to call him in the morning by clapping outside his door.

The main duties of the *bakabilo* in native eyes are ritual, as has been described. They are in charge of the ceremonies at the sacred relic shrines and take possession of the *babenye* when the chief dies. They alone can purify the chief from the defilement of sex intercourse so that he is able to enter his relic shrine and perform the necessary rites there. They are in complete charge of the accession ceremonies of the paramount and the bigger territorial chiefs, and some of their number are described as *bafingo*, or hereditary buriers of the chief. Besides this, each individual *mukabilo* has his own small ritual duty or privilege, such as lighting the sacred fire, or forging the blade of the hoe that is to dig the foundations of the new capital.

Besides their priestly duties, the *bakabilo* acted as regents at the death or absence of the chief, and any question of succession or other matter of tribal importance is placed before the *bakabilo*, and the big ceremonies I witnessed at the chief's capital were all made occasions of such discussions. The procedure is complex, but an effective method of deliberation. The paramount sends two special hereditary messengers, also *bakabilo*, to place the matter before the council. The senior members speak and if a difficulty arises they refer the matter to the head priest of the land, the Cimba, who sits apart with his own following, and gives decisions on matters of tribal precedent or suggests rewording decisions to be carried to the chief. Some of the discussion is carried on in archaic *cibemba*.

The importance of the *bakabilo's* council is the check it holds over the paramount's power. These are hereditary officials and therefore cannot be removed at will. Two or three of the *bakabilo* have been chased out of the country in the past for overweening pride, according to tradition, and the Cimba was removed from office in 1934, but only after the tribe had suffered for many years from the results of a species of megalomania to which he seemed to be subject. Otherwise the *bakabilo* are immune from the chief's anger and exert a salutary influence over him by refusing

to perform the ritual functions that are necessary to the chief's
state.[1]

Other advisory officials consist of the near relatives of the chief
himself. These do not attend discussions as to succession to
chieftainships, but are constantly informed of the progress of
affairs. The paramount's mother and the Makassa (the eldest
'son of the chief') play an important part in this way. In the past
senior members of the royal family seem to have intervened
occasionally when some chief was behaving too outrageously, as,
for instance, in the case of a sub-chief, Fyanifyani, apparently
attacked by a sort of blood-lust. This man was removed from
his office, according to history.

In brief, the Bemba system of government is not a democratic
one in our sense of the word. The elder commoner has fewer
rights to speak on tribal matters than have the Zulu, Swazi, or
even some of the Sotho peoples. The affairs of the icalo are in
the hands of a body of hereditary councillors whose offices and
most of whose deliberations are secret. But I was impressed by
the sense of tribal welfare which these bakabilo showed, and they
were quite able to discuss and shrewdly adapt some old tribal
precedent to modern conditions. Their strength, as regards tribal
government at the present day, is their esprit de corps and sense
of responsibility; their weakness, the fact that in the eyes of the
people and the Government their function is mainly a ritual one.

VI. The Integration of the Tribe

The integration of the tribe depends chiefly on the sentiment
of tribal cohesion and loyalty to the paramount, and the means
by which the activities of the different districts are brought under
one control in this widely dispersed group. The dogmas of kinship have been shown again and again to be the basis of tribal
feeling and of the allegiance given to the territorial and paramount
chiefs. In other Bantu tribes there is some tribe-wide organization such as the Nguni regiment system, that seems to act as an
integrating force. There are also forms of public ceremonial at
which all the adult men of the tribe are gathered, or all the warrior
classes. The first-fruit ceremonies of the Swazi or of the Zulu in

[1] During 1934 I found the paramount living in grass huts. He was unable
to build his new village because the bakabilo, indignant at his behaviour, refused
to perform the foundation ceremony for the new community.

the old days are an example. The big tribal councils of most of the African peoples described as being attended by 'every one' and in reality very large meetings, must also act as occasions when the loyalty of the tribe is fostered. Among the Bemba much of the tribal ritual is secret, as has been shown, and the advisory council is composed of what might be called an aristocratic caste. If the *bakabilo* meet in sitting on the open ground in the capital, as I have seen happen, they use archaic language on purpose, so that the common people cannot understand. It is no occasion for high-flown oratory or any of the demagogue's arts. On the other hand, the Bemba chiefs were formerly considered very nearly divine, and the belief in their supernatural powers is still strong enough to integrate the tribe. The sacredness of the royal ceremonial largely depends on its secrecy and the fact that only persons of the right descent can take their part in the ritual. The ordinary people do not attend the ceremonies except in the case of some inhabitants of the capital, but they value their secret nature and speak contemptuously of the Bisa and neighbouring tribes with less complex rites. The number of the *bakabilo*, each scattered through the chief's *icalo* and each with his own ritual function, sometimes secret from his own fellows, also adds to the strength of the whole ceremonial system. Each is insistent that *his* part is absolutely essential to the welfare of the tribe, and his own village is convinced to that effect, too. Another integrating factor is the belief in royal descent and presence in the society of such a large number of men and women who claim chiefly rank. These are dispersed all over the country, generally in charge of villages, and they naturally support the chiefs from whom they derive their power.

As regards the activities of the different *ifyalo*, it has been seen that these are self-contained units and there is no regular provision for regular meetings of *icalo* heads. They are linked by the over-lordship of the paramount, who acts as judge of their court of appeal, and the different tiny states are bound together because of the close relationship between their different chiefs. Messengers constantly go from one court to another to inquire after family matters, the children of one chief are sent to be brought up at the capital of another, the chiefs themselves take office first in one *icalo* and then another, and even the Citimukulu takes no important step, ritual or political, without consulting his 'brothers', the big territorial heads.

But here again ritual is one of the big integrating forces. The Citimukulu can initiate a series of sacrifices (*ulupepo lukalamba*), which start at his relic houses and spread to all the shrines throughout the land. The *bakabilo* are sent from Lubemba to bury any of the bigger territorial chiefs who die in their distant *ifyalo* and to install the new heir. The paramount prays for rain on the rare occasions when it is required, on behalf of the whole tribe. Thus for ritual purposes, in spite of the quarrels and jealousies between different lines of the royal family, the whole Bemba country can be said to act as a whole and to be conscious of its unity. If the paramount chief were to turn Christian before the political institutions of this tribe have been considerably adapted, tribal cohesion would, I think, be very much weakened, whether temporarily or permanently.

VII. Post-European Changes

The advent of British rule in Northern Rhodesia changed at once the position of the Bemba chief and his political machinery, and it continues to do so in an increasing variety of ways. Some of these changes are due to the actual introduction of new authorities into the area—whether Government officials, missionaries, or other Europeans—who have either replaced the old Bemba officials, divided the spheres of authority with them, or introduced entirely new conceptions of the functions of government itself. Others seem to be mainly the result of changed economic conditions, particularly the introduction of money, the institution of wage labour, and the provision of opportunities for money-making in industrial undertakings outside the territory. Such factors, over which the Administration has often little direct control, have inevitably affected the position of the Bemba chief. They have altered the people's conception of authority, destroyed the whole basis of labour on which the powers of the chief depended, and the old correlation between political authority, economic privilege, and military strength.

The total effects of white domination on the Bemba political organization have not yet proceeded to their full length, but it will be well to indicate some of the changes produced by the introduction of a new machinery of government, e.g. the alteration in the balance of the old tribal system, and the resultant weakening of the personal relationship between subject and chief upon which the whole structure of authority depended. To do so, it will be simplest to try to indicate the position when the Europeans first took over the administration of the country, and to compare this with the situation produced by the introduction of a modified system of Indirect Rule in 1929.

(*a*) *New Authorities Introduced.* In 1900 north-eastern Rhodesia was placed under the control of the British South Africa Company by an Order-in-Council after its officials had established posts in or near the Bemba country at Kasama, the present administrative centre of the northern province of Northern Rhodesia, in 1899 and at Mirongo, near the present Chinsali, in 1896. This administration continued until 1924, when the Colonial Office assumed control. To the Bemba, considered a particularly fierce and warlike tribe before the arrival of the white man, the superior force of the new administration must have been immediately apparent. The officials of the British South Africa Company were better armed. They at once intervened in a case of disputed succession over the Mwambaship which had then fallen vacant, and appointed their own nominee instead of his maternal uncle, who was endeavouring to take the title by force. One by one the functions of the old chiefs were taken over by the new authorities. New courts of law were introduced, and though some Native customary law was administered by the white officials, yet here as elsewhere customs considered 'repugnant to natural justice and morality' were prohibited, this category was such a large one[1] that to the natives it must have seemed like the introduction of a new code. Certain totally new offences were also created, e.g. the killing of elephants and a number of other forms of game, the digging of game-pits, and the use of primitive iron-smelteries. The penalties for legal offences were changed too. For mutilation at the hands of the chief, enslavement, and compensation paid to the injured party was substituted imprisonment, beating, fines paid to the Government, and the death sentence. New demands on natives' goods and services were also made, such as the hut-tax of 3*s*. 6*d*., afterwards changed to a poll-tax, which now stands at 7*s*. 6*d*., and the enrolment of natives as carriers, road-builders, &c., in Government pay. The B.S.A. administration recognized the Bemba chiefs and in 1916 defined their authority more

[1] e.g. accusations of witchcraft, murders for ritual purposes, the use of the ordeal in determining guilt, &c.

exactly,[1] but they were used in the main as executive officials and shorn of most of their authority and their privileges, such as the owning of slaves, the possession of arms, the right of mutilation, the power of administering the poison test, and the collection of the ivory tusks.

The sanctions for the power of the new administration were, in native eyes I think, its military strength and the fact that it had overcome the once powerful Bemba chiefs, and later, as new economic values were acquired, its apparently endless wealth.[2] But when talking with elder natives one is aware how largely the pattern of fear and personal allegiance accorded to the old chiefs was transferred with little modification to the new authorities. The same terms are used for both: there is the same assumption that the tax, game-laws, and even the paid employment of natives are all dues demanded by the Government for its own aggrandisement, as was the tribute of the chiefs in the old days.[3] There is much the same belief in the ruler's complete omnipotence, and a similar expectation of sudden arbitrary action, even as I noticed, when the most good-natured and reasonable officials appeared to be concerned. It is no exaggeration to state that each Government station is in effect a native capital or *umusumba*. Each has its district officer, an authority like the chief with a following to whom allegiance may mean advance, and who is regarded with mingled fear and loyalty. Each has its force of messengers and police, employs its own labour.

The missionary bodies in the country must also be regarded as new authorities set up in the tribe. The White Fathers entered the Bemba country just ahead of the B.S.A. administration and set up their first post near Kasama, in the heart of the Bemba country. They can still be said to dominate this central district, although the Church of Scotland Mission and the London Missionary Society also operate elsewhere. Each different mission station must also be regarded as an *umusumba*. Many

[1] cf. Report of the Commission appointed to inquire into the financial and economic position of Northern Rhodesia (1938), p. 179.

[2] Older natives seemed to me to comment most on the ferocity of the Government officials (*ubukali*), and the younger to speak of the wealth of the Administration.

[3] It is common for old men and women to refer to their sons who have either been recruited or else gone voluntarily to the mines as having been 'seized by the Government', and to speak of opportunities arranged for the sale of their grain as having their food 'seized' by the native commissioner.

are big establishments, with enormous and impressive cathedrals. They own and cultivate ground, attract a following, have villages on their estates regarded as 'mission people,' just as the *bena musumba* are considered to be the personal following of a chief. Each society, again, has introduced what is, in native eyes, its own new code of laws, often differing from those of the Government and those of the chiefs, e.g. most missions prohibit polygamy, some divorce, others beer-drinking, dancing, or religious ceremonial of different kinds. In native eyes at present there are certain well-known rules binding on the Christian members of the community, sometimes even bringing them into conflict with the other authorities of the society, the district official and the chief, and a new category of offence known as *fya busenshi* ('things of heathendom'), or *fya kale* ('things of the past') believed to be strongly condemned.[1]

Besides their own villagers, the missionary societies exert authority over Christians scattered in nearly every community in the territory, and their grip over these distant 'subjects' must in some cases be just as strong as those of the chiefs of old days. At the Roman Catholic missions at any rate, each baby of Christian parents is registered and summoned at the right time for instruction, however far away he or she lives. Each village is constantly visited by travelling native teachers and evangelists, and by the white missionaries themselves.

The sanctions of the missionaries' authority are many. On the positive side, their teaching and their way of living command a new allegiance and a new opportunity for advance and their personalities very often inspire admiration, affection, and personal loyalty. On the negative side, there is the introduction of a new supernatural sanction quite as powerful as those that supported the chief's authority,[2] and the threat to withdraw the Christian members of a community in which the Christian law is being flouted by a headman or prominent member. This acts as a powerful deterrent in the case of many Roman Catholic villages,

---

[1] This last is, of course, an injustice to the modern missionary, who is often one of the first to try to encourage interest in and respect for native custom.

[2] The fear of hell-fire, and, in the case of the older and less educated natives, the fear of curses seriously believed to be uttered by missionaries, evidently on the strength of some such statement as 'God will punish you if you behave like that'—such a belief being almost inevitable in an area where chiefs were thought to have power to curse.

since the break-up of the whole settlement may become inevitable in such circumstances.

There are no other organized bodies of Europeans in this area —no big bodies of farmers or settlers, for instance. But it may be said that all Europeans are in a sense in a position of authority. They all have the sanction of wealth and the power of employing a following. All have the high social status that enables them to talk to a chief as an equal, or more usually as an inferior, and all are believed by the natives to be backed, whether right or wrong, by the administrative officers of the district however unjustifiably.

Besides these new authorities introduced into the political arena, the power of the Bemba chief is inevitably reduced by his economic position, which must have grown increasingly bad since the first days of European occupation. The Bemba rulers were never rich compared to a number of African potentates. Theirs is a poor country. They possess no cattle which could be converted to money under modern conditions; the ivory of their country no longer belongs to them, nor their mineral rights. Land has no financial value as yet, and the salaries given to chiefs have always been low compared to the income, say, of the paramount chief of the Barotse.[1] Added to this, the service on which the Bemba chiefs depended is cut down by half or more by the absence of men at the mines, and what remains is often given unwillingly. These chiefs never apparently exacted court fines as a regular thing, after the fashion of the cattle-owning Bantu, and have not yet put a levy on the earnings of men away at the mines, as has been done in some parts of South Africa.

In view of these facts, it may be asked how the power of the *Bena ŋandu* survived at all up till 1929, when a determined effort was made to restore it. Partly because of their closely knit kinship structure, but also, I think, because of the strength of the supernatural beliefs on which their authority was so largely based. These were certainly weakened by the introduction of Christianity and the prevention or discouragement of many tribal rites, but it is impossible to treat them as mere survivals at the present day. Even young men are affected by such beliefs. For much the same reasons, the chiefs' courts continued to function alongside of the

---

[1] The Barotse chief receives an annual subsidy of £1,700, together with £850 from the British South Africa Company and £1,500 from the Zambesi saw-mills, as compared to the £60 a year of the Bemba paramount.

District Commissioner's courts in spite of thirty years or so of non-recognition. Natives took there the cases they believed the European magistrates did not understand, i.e. ritual matters, affairs with their roots in past history, and certain civil actions. Thus there were still some functions which the people believed the Bemba chief could perform better than all the new white authorities in the territory, besides the great historic tradition behind his authority.

Effects of the 1929 *Ordinances.* By the Native Authority and Native Courts Ordinances of 1929 a form of Indirect Rule was introduced into Northern Rhodesia, the power of the authorities then instituted being still further extended and more closely defined by a subsequent Ordinance of 1936. Chiefs, and in some cases councils of chiefs, were constituted as native authorities by these measures. They were given jurisdiction over definite territories, and encouraged to issue orders on matters of hygiene, bush-burning, the movement of natives, the constitution of villages, &c. Native courts were also recognized and given jurisdiction over all cases except witchcraft, murder, issues involving Europeans, &c. The chiefs were given salaries, small in actual fact and quite inadequate to the needs of an administrator at the present time,[1] yet in the eyes of natives, who are unaccustomed to see large sums of money at any one time, they were substantial marks of Government favour and often described as such. Clerks and *kapasus* (messengers), at exceedingly low salaries, were also attached to the courts. No financial control was given until recently (1936), when native treasuries were set up.[2]

As far as I could judge,[3] this new policy certainly did much to restore the personal prestige of the chiefs. The loss of an authority which was largely based on ritual was compensated for to some extent by the evident support of the Government. Most Bemba realize clearly that their chiefs are still merely servants of the Administration and note the fact that they cannot imprison or try the most important cases, and that their judgements are liable to be reversed, but they often commented to me on what seemed to

---

[1] Citimukulu receives £60 per annum, Mwamba £50, and the other chiefs less in proportion. For details showing the inadequacy of these amounts cf. my 'Tribal Government in Transition', *Journ. African Society*, vol. xxxiv, 1935.

[2] The Bemba Treasury had a balance of £143 in 1938 on a sum of £1,303 to be divided between six districts. See *Report* cited on p. 114.

[3] I arrived in the country the year after the introduction of these measures.

them evident signs of favour bestowed by the new policy on their rulers. As we saw, the judicial machinery of the Bemba never really disappeared with the institution of white courts, but the legal recognition of the chiefs' courts by the 1929 Ordinance certainly increased the latter's status tremendously. Successive Government reports have described the new native courts as functioning well, while few charges of excessive fines or hearing fees have been made against the chiefs. Such complaints as I heard seemed to come mainly from educated natives belonging to other areas, particularly from Nyasaland, who found themselves subject for the first time to Bemba law. In the legislative field, determined efforts were made by the district officials to restore the self-confidence of the native authorities and to encourage them, not only to resume functions of government they had lost, but also to take on new tasks, such as the issue of orders as to hygiene, &c. In fact, as regards the personal position of the Bemba chiefs, it may be said that there was a gradual increase in status due to Government support, added to a respect and fear which had never been entirely lost. Their power is in many ways surprising, in view of their poverty, their lack of means to enforce any decisions taken, and the presence in their territories of other authorities in command of their subjects and in particular of large numbers of Christians bound by codes that are not recognized in the chiefs' courts.[1]

Apart from the chief's own position, it is necessary to review the political system as a whole. How far was the old machinery of Government re-established by the introduction of the 1929 Ordinances? And, more important still, is such a machinery adapted to the new needs of the tribe? The answer to the first question is a decided, 'No'. The whole balance of authority has been altered, partly by the changed economic position of the chief and partly by lack of Government recognition. We saw that the executive and judicial officials on whom the chief relied were kept together by hope of rewards and food and in some cases in virtue of their religious functions. Nowadays the chief is less able to feed his councillors, principally owing to the decay of the tribute labour system. He does not consider himself obliged to distribute

---

[1] Some missionary societies have followed the Government policy and have invited chiefs to take a part in school education committees, &c.; others have viewed any increase in the chief's authority as a retrograde step.

money in the same way as food, and in any case has not sufficient to enable him to reward his people adequately. So that at a time when he is asked to take on new functions of administration his following is becoming smaller and smaller. I have seen Citimukulu hearing cases alone with his paid clerk and watched the *bakabilo* melting away during the midst of the discussion of important matters owing to want of food. This makes an impossible situation which may be changed for the better by the greater measure of financial control which the Government has recently granted to the native authorities,[1] though the sums now allotted to native treasuries are small, and lack of funds has always prevented the compensation of chiefs for the lack of their tribute labour and other perquisites that has occurred in Nigeria, Barotseland, and elsewhere.

Government recognition of the political organization of the tribe and its purposeful adaptation to modern conditions is also essential at the present time. Apart from the economic breakdown at the chiefs' courts which has just been indicated, much of the trouble has been due to the fact that no serious investigation of the judicial, executive, and advisory machinery of Government was made in the first instance. Chiefs were constituted as authorities with little study of the way in which their orders were to be enforced. They were listed as 'members of court', but, though headmen and council were mentioned as eligible to sit on such courts, the presence of the latter was not apparently compulsory. The *bakabilo's* important advisory functions as a tribal council and a potential regency council were not recognized until anthropological research in the area had been made.[1] The unfortunate result was that the chief felt free to act without this former check on his power and openly expressed to me his delight in the fact. The councillors, on the other hand, felt discouraged, and declared: 'The Government likes the chiefs. It does not listen to us, the *Babemba*.' Hence a political system that could never have been described as democratic now provides less check than ever on the chief's authority.

The difficulty from an administrative point of view is evident. Here is a system of political authority based largely on hereditary ritual privilege. To abandon the *bakabilo* council is to do without a body of men with strong traditions of government and a sense of

[1] Twenty-five of the *bakabilo* are now given £1 a year (see *Report* cited, p. 144).

the public weal; to rely on them without at the same time training them in new functions, and adding to them other elements, especially for the more educated members of the tribe, is to build on a foundation that cannot endure, and to deny to the commoner the experience of administration he will require to have in the future. Similarly, the co-ordination of the activities of each of the smaller political units known as *ifyalo* is at present one which is based on the intimate relationship between the chiefs ruling each, and the ritual which unites them. There is no official representation of each district on the Paramount Council, since all the *bakabilo* are drawn from his own territory, however much they consider themselves responsible for the affairs of the whole tribe. Ritual prohibitions still prevent the frequent meetings of the big territorial chiefs themselves, though they do occasionally come together at Government *ndabas* outside their own capitals. Hence, if it ever became necessary to provide for closer co-ordination of the different districts or for local representation, it appears that a general tribal council of the type of the National Council of the Basuto or the *libandla* of the Swazi would have to be constituted in this tribe.

THE KINGDOM OF ANKOLE IN UGANDA

By K. OBERG

I. Traditional and Historical Background

ANKOLE is but one of a series of small Native kingdoms stretching from north to south along the western borders of Uganda Protectorate. Both geographically and anthropologically, this is an interesting region. Bounded on the east by the great barrier of Lake Victoria and on the west by the mountain mass of Ruwenzori, and a chain of lakes extending from Lake Albert to Lake Tanganyika, it forms a corridor leading from the broad grasslands of the Upper Nile to the plateaus of Belgian Ruanda and Tanganyika Territory. Geographically this corridor is typical African savanna with its rolling grass-covered hills and sparse acacia scrub.

Some time in the dim past this region was occupied by Bantu-speaking, agricultural Negroes. The rainfall, though scanty, was sufficient to permit a fairly even distribution of the population over the country, scattered thinly in the drier plains of the east, but more densely in the hilly regions of the west. Later in the history of Africa this same corridor provided a pathway over which waves of Hamitic or Hamiticized Negro cattle people migrated southward. These pastoralists, with their vast herds of long-horned cattle, are believed to have been crowded southward from southern Abyssinia and many believe them to be of Galla origin. Whatever be the exact location of their original home or their specific tribal connexion or the reasons for their migration, there is no doubt that these people are closely linked to the Hamites in blood and in certain customs concerning cattle. What is more important, however, is the fact that whenever these pastoralists settled upon territory already occupied by the Bantu agriculturists they made a uniform adjustment, they conquered the agriculturalists, and established themselves as a ruling class. Thus when the British took over the management of Uganda, some forty years ago, they found everywhere in this corridor the pastoralists as rulers and the agriculturalists as serfs. The pastoralists calling themselves variously as Bahima or Bahuma and the agriculturalists as Bairu or

Bahera. Although it is said that the Bahima were once united and held sway over a great empire called Kitara, in historic times this territory was split up into kingdoms stretching from Bunyoro through Toro and Ankole to Ruanda in Belgian territory. The kingdom of Buganda also belongs to this classification, but, owing to the greater percentage of the agricultural population, sharp racial differences soon disappeared, the royal family alone stressing its foreign descent.

This upland corridor, then, is the stage upon which Bahima and Bairu have for centuries played their political drama. Intriguing and heroic as the opening scenes of this drama undoubtedly were, the story as historical fact is lost to us for ever. But to every Muhima this past is a living, fascinating reality. Whether it be embodied in song, recitation or fireside tale, the theme is the same. It is of raiding, of wandering, of battle between clans and kings, of famine and disease, of sorcery and sacrifice. Through this vast body of myth and legend, we are able to grasp something of the epic nature of the struggle which took place on the plains of western Uganda and which, in one instance, gave rise to the kingdom of Ankole.

Long ago, these legends say, there were Bahima and Bairu in the land. The Bahima lived in eastern Ankole with their cattle while the Bairu tilled the soil in the west. In those days the Bahima had neither king nor chiefs, but important men in the clans settled disputes. Among the rich men the following are still remembered: Nyawera lived in Kashari and belonged to the Abaitera clan; Rwazigami lived in Rugondo and belonged to the Abasite clan; Ishemurindwa of the Abaishekatwa clan lived in Masha; Karara of the Abakoboza clan lived in Ruanda; Rwanyakizha of the Abarami lived in Nshara; while Mariza of the Abararira clan lived in Bukanga. There were other clans as well, too numerous to mention here. These Bahima are spoken of to-day as being the first Bahima of Ankole. There are no stories of how they got there. Other clans came into Ankole later from the neighbouring countries.

The Bairu lived in Rwanpara, Shema, Buhwezhu, and Igara. It is not known whether they had clans or whether they were organized under chiefs. There were no wars between the Bahima and the Bairu in those days, each living in his own section of the land and trading beer and millet for milk and butter.

Then very suddenly a strange people appeared. They were

called the Abachwezi. From the cycle of songs and legends, these Abachwezi seem to be the same figures who played such an important role in the past of the Banyoro, Baganda, Batoro, Abakaragwe, and, at least certain groups, among the Banyanruanda. While statements as to their origin and disappearance differ, there is at bottom a fundamental agreement about their character, doings, and direction of their movements. All legends point out the fact, for instance, that the Abachwezi came from the north, that they were not very numerous, that they conquered the people in their way and then disappeared southward finally vanishing into lakes or craters.

According to legend, these Abachwezi were wonderful people. 'They were like the Bahima, but more brilliant. One could not look them in the face because their eyes were so bright that it hurt one's own eyes to look at them. It was like looking at the sun. They wore bark cloth and went about in cow-hide sandals. Their women covered their faces in public and were guarded by eunuchs. The important Abachwezi built large grass houses and had their kraals near by. They had many cattle and lived on milk, meat, and beer, especially beer mixed with honey. They were great hunters and magicians.' This description of the Abachwezi is the most matter-of-fact. Most accounts deal with their superhuman feats, their terrible strength, their power of making themselves invisible, their wealth in cattle, the beauty of their women, and the ruthless domination of all whom they conquered.

Most stories agree in stating that Ndahura was the great conqueror, the leading Omuchwezi. In Ankole, Ndahura is not as well known as in Toro and Bunyoro, where he is considered as the first Abachwezi king. He is there considered the son of a former king and a woman called Nyinyamwiru (mother of Mwiru) and it was he who is said to have consolidated the Kitara Empire. After the conquest he reorganized his kingdom into districts, appointing his sons and henchmen as rulers. To Ankole he sent Wamara, who is there considered the first Abachwezi king. The word 'Wamara' comes from the verb *okumara*, to finish or to complete. Many Banyankole explained that he finished what his father began— namely, the conquest of an empire. Wamara lived at Bwera, which was then a part of greater Ankole, and ruled over Ankole, Karagwe, and a part of southern Buganda. Wamara was said to be kind to his henchmen and always ready to help them out of difficulties. When their cattle died, he gave them cows from his own herd and helped to pay their marriage-prices. By means of his magical powers, he could make rain, make barren women bear children, and prevent disease among cattle. Wamara had many sons and relatives, who are all described in song and legend. There was Murindwa, the eldest son of Wamara, who was noted for his wisdom; there was Mugenyi, who herded his cows at Bwera and is said to have built the earthworks at Biggo; Kazoba was another son, 'beautiful as a berry and as timid as a marsh antelope'; Ibona was a diviner; Riangombe, a hunter; Kagoro, a conqueror of new pasture lands, foremost in all wars; Mugasha was the maker of water holes for cattle.

The Abachwezi, then, lived in Ankole, ruling the country, herding their cattle and performing miracles, but they did not remain long. Misfortune came to them. First, the people began to disobey the Abachwezi and even their wives turned against them. Then the cows began to die and the people to sicken of a new disease. When the cow Bihogo and the leading bull died, the Abachwezi became worried and wanted to move on. The final catastrophe was the murder of Murindwa by the members of the Abasingo clan. He was said to have been thrown into a pit and to have died there. But before leaving, Kagoro avenged the death of his brother by killing many of the Abasingos, and Wamara cursed the clan and to this day the curse is maintained in Ankole. The Abachwezi then moved on into Karagwe with what cattle they had left. Mugasha is the tragic hero of this retreat. On being forced to leave Ankole, he became very sad and tried to commit suicide. The other Abachwezi, however, prevented him from accomplishing this by magic. Instead of disappearing into Lake Kyaikambara, like the other Abachwezi, Mugasha went to the Sesse Islands in Lake Victoria and he is said to be there still.

While the Abachwezi were fleeing from Ankole, Katuku, a Mwiru headman, overtook them and persuaded Ruhinda, one of the younger Abachwezi, and his mother, Nzhunwakyi, to return to Ankole with him. There was a long debate before Ruhinda finally assented. He is then said to have been hidden along with the royal drum, *Bagyendanwa*, by Katuku and his followers for some time. When peace once again ruled over Ankole, Ruhinda came out of hiding and established himself as ruler of the Bahima and the Bairu, and thus he became the founder of the Abahinda dynasty, which rules Ankole to this day. Many Banyankole to-day firmly believe that the Abachwezi did not die, but disappeared and that they will return again to rule over them. In the meantime, the spirits of the Abachwezi still rule over the land and a cult has grown up, the members of which make periodic offerings to the Abachwezi spirits. This Abachwezi spirit worship is to-day known as the Emandwa cult. Furthermore, in Ankole there are many places and relics connected with the Abachwezi. These places have become sacred to the Banyankole and are avoided by them, and the relics have become symbols of kingship. So impressed were the Banyankole with the Abachwezi that when the white men came to Ankole they believed them to be the Abachwezi returned. The Europeans were different, more powerful, able to do unaccountable things. The Europeans, like the Abachwezi, are able to travel in the air, to make a fire without leaving ashes, and to travel over the country with great speed. Another tale has it that the Europeans are not really the Abachwezi, but their servants sent to punish the Banyankole for their ill treatment of their former rulers.

The cycle of Abachwezi legends, then, is the Muhima's version of his cultural history, particularly as it relates to the origin of his political institutions. We cannot, of course, consider this version as exact history. Yet its sociological significance is far-reaching. It describes Ankole as first occupied by the agricultural Bairu and a few pastoral Bahima, living in relative isolation and without a developed political organization. It describes subsequent Bahima migrations, a period of struggle, and a final subjugation of the Bairu by the Bahima and the establishment of a kingdom. But even more than this, it provides the political structure with a traditional legendary background which lends to it a traditional sanctity and a foundation of absolutism and permanence.

But we do not need to go to native legends in order to account for the origin of the Banyankole kingdom. Evidence lies before the student on every hand. Even to-day we can observe the environmental and social forces which gave rise to the particular complexion of Banyankole society and its political institutions.

The role of the environmental factors of climate and topography in bringing the pastoral Bahima and the agricultural Bairu into contact cannot be underestimated. Ankole, as we have seen, is a section of a long and narrow belt of savanna country stretching along the eastern side of the western Rift Valley from Lake Albert in the Sudan to Lake Kivu in Ruanda. It is fairly well established that Hamiticized negro peoples migrated southward along this route and that in time this belt of grassland was filled with cattle-keepers. Similarly, climatic conditions made possible the settlement of this area by relatively dense agricultural populations.

But contact due to environmental conditions alone does not account for permanent subjugation, the payment of tribute, and a state structure. Isolation, segregation, and extermination were alternative ways of adjustment. Isolation was not possible, due to the nature of the country and the density of the population. All the Bairu could not move into the relatively small hilly areas. On the other hand, as we have shown, legends relate a stage of segregation before the pressure of Bahima population brought about a general settlement of Ankole by the pastoralists. Extermination was perhaps possible, but the Bahima chose to dominate the Bairu because it paid to dominate. Although the agricultural technique of the Bairu did not produce a great surplus, it could produce, under pressure, enough beer and millet to make domination profitable. In this connexion, we must always remember that the Bairu had to supply a population only one-tenth its own size. Had the numbers been reversed, exploitation would not, perhaps, have been successful. On the other hand, agricultural production was not such that it could have supported the Bahima entirely. The Bahima, then as now, lived upon their cattle and forced their serfs to give them as much beer, millet, and labour as possible without destroying their source of supply. In this connexion, it might be illuminating to contrast the situation in which the Masai found themselves. As they swept down in the extensive plains of the eastern Rift Valley region, they found there only a few wandering Wanderobo hunters who neither interfered with the pastoral habits of the Masai nor offered possibilities for economic exploitation. Exchange relationships were established, but exploitation leading to political domination through a state organization did not arise.

Bahima domination of the Bairu arose not only because these racially and economically different people were brought into contact in large numbers by environmental conditions and because it was economically profitable, but also because the Bahima were able to dominate. Bahima herdsmen, accustomed to protecting their herds from animal and human enemies, were individually superior fighting men. Constant raiding and counter-raiding developed a military discipline which could be expanded and put to political uses. The organization of the Bahima kraal was a larger collective enterprise than the Bairu homestead. The unilateral *ekyika* or lineage offered wider political and military co-operation than the relatively smaller Bairu *oruganda* or extended family. Thus, even without a further development of the political organization, the Bahima had the advantage in fighting experience and co-operation.

Once the Bahima of Ankole had conquered the Bairu and had imposed their will through a state organization, they were faced by a new situation, they had to defend their country, their cattle and the Bairu subjects from external attack. Defence forces and counter-raiding were not a guarantee of security. The most satisfactory method of preventing aggression lay in the permanent subjugation of raiders. Conquest of other cattle people, less strongly organized, became a necessary feature of state defence. Here again we can contrast the situation in which the Bahima found themselves with that met by the Masai. The Masai were pre-eminently cattle-raiders, making sudden attacks upon the villages and homesteads of their settled neighbours, taking what cattle and goods they could find, and then retreating to their plains. They did not invade the territory of their neighbours, for they did not require expansion of their pasture lands, nor was the land of their neighbours, like that of the Kikuyu and the Kavirondo, ideal cattle country. Furthermore, the Masai were not subjected to permanent pressure by the surrounding tribes. They were primarily attackers and not attacked.

While conquest of surrounding cattle people was imposed by the needs of defence, it had its aspect of economic profit. It paid to dominate these weaker groups, for tribute in cattle could be extracted from them. Conquered cattle people came under the rule of a king's representative, who undertook the collection of tribute and its presentation to the king. An interesting feature of these conquered cattle people was that, being Bahima, they soon amalgamated with their conquerors. The Bahima of Empororo, who were formerly independent, were conquered and for a time paid regular tribute, but, with the increase of pressure from Ruanda, they fought along with their conquerors and were subsequently given equal political and legal status with the Bahima of Ankole.

Exactly how the Bahima of Ankole were organized into a State and how they created the political society of the Banyankole kingdom we cannot now tell. But the elements of the situation as we have enumerated them are observable. There were external conditions to which the Bahima adjusted themselves and by the detailed analysis of the processes of adjustment these conditions became evident. This adjustment process corresponds to the functions of the Bahima State. First among these functions was the domination of the Bairu, expressed by inferior legal status and the obligation of tribute payment; and along with inferior legal status went inferior social status amounting essentially to a caste difference. Secondly, the State defended the territory and the people of Ankole from external raiders and conquerors. Thirdly, the State embarked upon a programme of conquest which was limited only by similar ventures on the part of neighbouring kingdoms.

II. Political Status

What is political action but the creation and destruction of forms of social organization through the exercise of organized power? No sooner were the ethnically different Bahima and Bairu brought into contact by the environmental and social forces already described than they were forced to define not only their relationships to one another, but also to modify the relationships binding the members of each group to one another.

No longer were the Bahima cattle men free agents, united in extended families and loosely knit lineages and clans; they were now also members of a political group. If the Bahima were going to further their interests as Bahima, they had to organize and act together as Bahima. At bottom this new relationship was based on Bahimaship—upon race and cattle-ownership. But this special political bond had to be created, had to be consciously entered into. It involved leadership, co-operation, submission to authority. It gave rise to kingship and the dynastic principle, the organization of military forces and chieftainship. In short, it welded the Bahima into a State, the nucleus of the Banyankole kingdom.

This new political relationship was established through *okutoizha*, or clientship. A Muhima cattle-owner would go before the Mugabe, or king, and swear to follow him in war and would undertake to give the Mugabe a number of cattle periodically to keep this relationship alive. On the other hand, clientship could be broken by the *omutoizha*, or client, refusing to pay homage. This was a perfectly recognized way of breaking off the relationship, and it was only when a number of Bahima banded together in order to defy the king more effectively that this act was considered rebellion. Even then, if the rebellious people resumed homage payments, they would be pardoned by the king. If, however, a Muhima induced others to pay homage to himself and raided cattle without giving the Mugabe a share, he could be accused of treason and the Mugabe would move his forces to suppress him.

Clientship involved a number of obligations on the part of the client towards the Mugabe. Foremost among these duties was military service. Every Muhima, even if he were not a member of a military band, had to go to war when called upon. Any cattle which a Muhima acquired through a private raid were claimed by the Mugabe and a part of them had to be handed over to him. Clientship obliged every Muhima to make periodic visits to the Mugabe's *orurembo* (kraal), with homage payments. He was also obliged to assent to the giving of cattle to the Mugabe's collector when the king was in need of cattle. Whenever a Muhima died, his heir had to report to the Mugabe and renew the bond of clientship by giving a 'cow of burial'.

In return for military service and the payment of homage, the client received protection. First, the Mugabe undertook to shield the cattle of his client from cattle-raiders and to retaliate when his client had suffered from raids. If a client had lost all of his cattle through raid or disease, the Mugabe was obliged to help the man start a new herd. Secondly, the Mugabe maintained peace between his clients. No client was permitted to raid or steal the cattle of another client or to do harm to his person or dependants. If breaches of the peace occurred, the transgressor was accused and tried before the Mugabe. In cases of murder, the Mugabe granted the kinsmen the right of blood revenge. Finally, the Mugabe was instrumental in enabling his clients to enlarge their herds and pasturage by raids and conquest.

To sum up, then, the Bahima State consisted of the cattle-owning freemen and their leader, the Mugabe. The specific tie which bound the herdsmen to their leader was in the nature of clientage, *obutoizha*. The Bahima alone were politically organized in that they combined to create and maintain the particular system of differential relationships which existed in the kingdom. The fundamental force which the State exercised in maintaining these relationships was military power. Now let us examine the ties which bound the subject peoples to the king.

To the Bahima, the word 'Bairu' signifies serfdom, a legal status inferior to that existing between themselves. The index of Bairu status was race and the dependence upon agriculture for a livelihood. The difference in status is perhaps best expressed by a statement of the limitations of Bairu rights.

The Bairu were not permitted to own productive cows. For services rendered to the Bahima, they were sometimes given barren cows and bull calves. These cattle the Bairu either kept for making marriage payments or slaughtered for food. If a Mwiru did have productive cows in his possession, any Muhima could take them away from him. There is a story among the Bairu that long ago they owned cattle, but that these cattle were taken from them by the invading Bahima. Some veterinary officers in western Uganda believe that this is true and that the cattle which the Bairu owned were of a different breed from the present-day Ankole longhorn. This belief they base upon the existence of shorter horned stock upon the fringes of Bahima country, as, for instance, the cattle of the Bakiga of Kigezi.

The social distinction between the Bahima and the Bairu was maintained by a strict prohibition of marriage. No Mwiru could marry a Muhima woman. The Bahima, when questioned upon this matter, laugh and say that such a marriage is quite unthinkable. Not only is the idea of such a marriage repugnant to the Bahima, but the validation impossible, as the Bairu, in former times, did not possess the cattle necessary for the bride-price. Bahima men did not marry Bairu women, for it was illegal to give the Bairu cattle, which alone legitimized marriage and offspring. On the other hand, however, Bahima men took concubines from among Bairu girls. These women had no status as married women and were usually described as servant girls. Bairu concubines were especially common among Bahima chiefs and gave rise to a class of half-castes known as *Abambari*. From the point of view of legal status, the *Abambari* were classed as Bairu, but personal consideration often modified the strict rigour of the rule. A Muhima chief or cattle-owner without sons by a Muhima marriage would make an illegitimate son his heir. In time entire lineages were formed from such unions. These half-caste sub-clans the Bahima distinguished by calling them the people of a certain man instead of the children of a certain man, which is the name given to a sub-clan of pure Bahima stock. The effect of concubinage is quite noticeable when one compares the physical types of the chiefly class with those of the ordinary herdsman of districts more remote from the agricultural sections. One finds a markedly larger percentage of dark Bantu types among the chiefly class.

The military organization, we have seen, was in the hands of the Mugabe, who instructed certain chiefs to form warrior bands for the protection of the borders. No band could be formed without the express wishes of the king. While every Muhima was liable for military service, the Bairu were, on the contrary, barred from serving in these bands. The Bairu thus lacked the military training and discipline necessary for effecting any change in their status.

High official positions were likewise barred to the Bairu. No Mwiru, for instance, could become an *enganzi* or an *omugaragwe*. The *abakungu*, however, appointed Bairu assistants who aided them in the collection of tribute in the various districts. These assistants were also called *abakungu* and were considered by the Bairu as district chiefs. The Bahima, however, claim that these individuals never had chiefly status.

Perhaps the most outstanding characteristic of Bairu serfdom was the rule that under no circumstance could a Mwiru kill a Muhima. The right of blood revenge which was exercised by the extended families of the Bairu among themselves could not be extended to the Bahima. If a Muhima killed a Mwiru, the extended family of the murdered man could not claim blood revenge, although it sometimes was able to exact compensation through the agency of the Mugabe. The Bahima, on the other hand, could avenge the death of a kinsman if he were murdered by a Mwiru without consulting the Mugabe.

The Bairu had no political status. They had no recognized means by which they could alter the inferior legal rank imposed upon them. The exploitation of the Bairu by the Bahima took the form of tribute payment in food and labour, and for this purpose the Bahima endeavoured to keep them in subjection. But the Bairu were not outside of the law, inferior as their status was to that of the Bahima. Within its own sphere, this status had its positive aspects. Tribute gathering was so organized that only chiefs could exercise it at will. Small cattle-owners had no legal right to exact tribute from the Bairu.

This does not mean, however, that the chiefs alone benefited from the tribute collected. It was a common practice for Bahima herdsmen to visit their chiefs, sometimes remaining for several days at the chiefs' kraals. It was a chief's duty to provide these men with beer and millet porridge. Thus food that came to the chief's kraal in the form of tribute was later distributed among the Bahima as a whole. Every chief had a number of Bairu craftsmen who made spears, milkpots, and watering pails. These articles, too, were obtained by the ordinary Bahima from the chiefs. Herdsmen, of course, could obtain these articles direct from the Bairu through barter and they did so to a limited extent. But organized tribute and its distribution checked exchanges which would otherwise have been quite extensive.

Unauthorized tribute collection was considered robbery and was punished by the Mugabe. Any Mwiru could go before the Mugabe or one of his chiefs and complain of ill treatment and could claim compensation for damages. To make his claim more effective, a Mwiru would take special gifts to the Mugabe and thus claim protection. In other words, although the Bairu system of rights was narrower and more restricted than the fuller status of the Bahima, this system was still protected by the Bahima State.

Another class which formed a part of the Banyankole kingdom consisted of conquered Bahima *Abatoro* who had formerly constituted chieftainships or parts of other kingdoms. Over these people the Mugabe would appoint an overlord who forced them to pay tribute in cattle and who put down any attempts at rebellion. These people being of the same race and economic status would, in time, amalgamate with the Bahima of Ankole. An *Omutoro* could become the Mugabe's client by paying *obutoizha*, after which he enjoyed the full rights of a Muhima.

The *Abatoro*, although not having equal status with the *Abatoizha* or clients, fared better than the Bairu serfs. There was no bar to intermarriage and blood revenge could be exacted, this right being derived from the underlying racial similarity and clan rights. The breaking up of the *Abatoro* as a class was gradual and went through a process of individual shift of allegiance to the Mugabe. On the other hand, the Mugabe's representative in these districts sometimes endeavoured to establish himself as an independent chief by rebelling against the Mugabe. Repeated rebellion often meant the complete confiscation of the cattle of the *Abatoro* and the killing off of the cattle-owners, the women and children of these cattle-owners being taken and distributed by the Mugabe among his followers.

The *Abahuku*, or slaves, were another class of subject people in the Banyankole kingdom. Very little could be learned about slavery in Ankole. Slaves were owned by the Mugabe, the leading chiefs, and the wealthier cattle-owners, and they consisted entirely of Bairu captured in raids made upon neighbouring kingdoms. Slaves had their ears cut off so that if they ran away they could be recognized and recaptured. Slaves were used as hewers of wood, drawers of water, and as butchers. There is nothing to indicate that slaves were sold or exchanged, although chiefs gave each other slaves as presents. While the slaves performed menial tasks, it cannot be said that their lot was any harder than that of the Bairu craftsmen who formed a part of every chief's household. Being a prisoner of war, the slave had no legal status in the community and was the private property of the person who owned him and who had the right to do as he pleased with him.

From all accounts, slavery was restricted to the very wealthy and slaves were restricted in numbers. Only those individuals who had sufficient surplus wealth could afford to keep slaves. When the Bahima are asked why they did not keep slaves as herdsmen, they answer that they could not trust them and that they would have had to accompany them while herding. Slaves, they say, were used only to clean the kraals and to bring wood and water. In agriculture, with Bairu tools and techniques, slavery would not pay. Neither agricultural technique nor craft specialization had developed far enough to make slavery on a large-scale economically profitable.

Although supreme political and judicial authority was invested in the Mugabe as the representative of the politically organized Bahima, a certain amount of judicial and political power was left to both the Bahima and Bairu extended families. The function

of the Mugabe and his chiefs lay more in giving judgements than
in meting out punishments. Moreover, there was no police
organization to guard life and property. How then did members
of the community guard themselves against criminal actions and
aid in the carrying out of sentences passed by the Mugabe? It is
just here that the extended family fulfilled its important role. As
a political unit, it discouraged attacks upon its members by individual malefactors. Once a crime had been committed, the head
of the extended family took the matter before the Mugabe. In
cases of murder, the Mugabe would grant the right of blood
revenge, which, however, had to be carried out by the members
of the injured extended family. In lesser offences the judgement
of the Mugabe was generally sufficient to settle a dispute. The
extended family, therefore, guaranteed the rights of its members
in the community against the attacks of individual offenders of
customary law and practice. In matters concerning an extended
family alone, judicial authority was left almost entirely in the
hands of the head of this group. Murder within the extended
family was not a matter for the Mugabe to decide, but was settled
by the *nyinyeka*, or head of the extended family.

In summary, we might say that from the standpoint of political
and legal status the members of the Banyankole kingdom did not
form a homogeneous mass, but were distinguished by a wide
range of rights and prohibitions, resulting in a stratification of
society into classes. At the top was the Bahima State with its
governing nucleus centring around the Mugabe. Below were the
subject classes of the Bairu, the *Abatoro* and the *Abahuku*. The
caste nature of this stratification was pronounced, resting ultimately on racial and economic differences.

The complex working of this political society becomes intel-
ligible, not only by determining the roles played by the various
parts, but by observing the genetic relationship of these parts.
The status of the Bairu, for instance, as a subject class, is not fully
explained by stating that they paid tribute and were prohibited
from possessing cattle, but by showing that this status was imposed
and maintained by the Bahima as a militarily organized group.
The Bahima-Bairu relationship was a Bahima invention. If we
contrast this class difference with the political relationship existing
among the Bahima, the distinction becomes clear. The politically
organized Bahima State was an association of free men expressing

their unity in terms of clientship, this unity arising as a spontaneous response to well-defined external conditions. Clientship, as has been shown, can be described by its functions. Clientship as a system of co-operation carried out such collective enterprises as raiding, conquest, and domination, and served as a system of mutual insurance against the risks inherent in a raiding community. Exchanges of cattle among the Bahima were free exchanges depending upon the mutual interests of the parties concerned. The Bairu-Bahima relationship, or Bairu serfdom, on the contrary, was not a system of co-operation of this kind. The Bahima and the Bairu did not co-operate in collective activities, economic or political, nor can tribute payment be termed 'free exchange'. We might contest that the Bairu received protection for the services which they rendered to their masters, the Bahima. Yet if we carefully analyse this protection, it appears to be no different from that which the Bahima provided for their cattle, land, chattels, and slaves. And, moreover, the Bairu had to be protected from the Bahima of neighbouring kingdoms and not from other Bairu.

On the other hand, the distinction should not be pressed too hard, for serfdom is not slavery. The Bairu had well-defined rights which the slaves did not possess. Furthermore, Banyankole society was not static. The sharp differences between the Bahima and the Bairu which have been stressed in the preceding analysis were subjected to a steady pressure of social forces making for their obliteration. In spite of the prohibition of intermarriage, miscegenation took place. A class of half-castes arose known as *Abambari*, whose status, although not clearly defined, was not always that of the Bairu. An *omwambari* whose father was a chief often came into the possession of cattle and was recognized as a man of importance, if of uncertain status. In our description of the kinship organization, we had occasion to refer to a number of Bahima sub-clans of pure descent. It is also said that the present Mugabe's father established a Bairu band of warriors in order to counteract the determined effort of the Banyanruanda to conquer Ankole. From reports given to me by the natives of Toro and from Roscoe's account of the Bakitara, it appears that the Bairu-Bahima amalgamation had proceeded much farther in these kingdoms than in Ankole. In spite of these forces making for uniformity, the traditional political structure of the Banyankole kingdom was essentially stratified, depending upon the Bahima as a dominating power.

III. The King and the Royal Kraal

So far we have stressed the forces which brought the ethnically different Bahima and Bairu together and the resulting social stratification with its formalization into strictly defined political relationships. The king, or Mugabe, we observed, formed the centre of this system of relationships. The exercise of power demanded still further developments. A system of government grew up round the king's person, consisting of office holders, the military bands, and the host of servants and specialists to uphold the king's dignity and authority and to carry out his orders as the leader of the politically organized Bahima ruling caste.

The position of the Mugabe was exalted, his authority supreme, his leadership all-embracing. As high status was sanctioned, in the first place, by his descent from Ruhinda, the originator of the Abaninda dynasty, and, in the second place, by his possession of the symbols of kingship—the royal drum, Bagyendanwa, and the beaded veil, Rutare. Both descent and the symbols of kingship are said to date from the times of the semi-mythical Abachwezi kings. The word 'Mugabe' is derived from the verb okugaba, to give, and seems to imply that the Mugabe was a giver, although many Banyankole describe the Mugabe as one to whom the Mugabeship was given by the Abachwezi. The power of the Mugabe extended over the free, cattle-owning herdsmen of Ankole who were bound to him by mutual ties of defence and aggression, over conquered herdsmen who paid him tribute, and over any Bairu peasants who lived upon the tribal territory. Even to-day, when kingship in Ankole has lost its essential purpose and much of its colour, its original form is revealed to us by countless songs and stories which are sung and told around firesides in Bahima kraals.

Physical, magical, and religious powers were invested in the king's person. In song and in address he was called the 'lion', the fiercest and most courageous of animal cattle-raiders. He was called the 'leading bull', for cattle increased through him by raid and gift. He was called the 'territory of Ankole' for he had 'eaten' the pastoral lands at his accession and defended them against aggression. He was called the 'drum', for like the drum he maintained the unity of the men under his power. He was called the 'moon', for through the moon he had power to drive away evil and bring fortune to the tribe. Power, then, both physical and spiritual, was the inherent quality of kingship. And when the physical powers of the king waned, through approaching age, these kingly powers were believed to wane with them. No king, therefore, was permitted to age or weaken. When sickness or age brought on debility, the Mugabe took poison, which was prepared for him by his magicians, and died, making way for a new, virile king who could maintain the unity of the kingdom and wage successful wars against external enemies.

The legal status of the Mugabe gave him the highest political authority. Appointments to office were ultimately in his hands, as was the decision for war or peace. From among his relatives, the Mugabe appointed the leaders of his military bands and his favourite chief, or *enganzi*. Even those functionaries which custom decreed should be selected from certain clans, as his drum-keepers and personal servants, the Mugabe could refuse to recognize. In other words, while the clan held the office, the Mugabe selected the individual who was to fill that office. Moreover, the Mugabe could demand the services of any individual in his kingdom as he could demand any woman for his wife or could claim any cattle he wished. As one would suspect, the Mugabe could dismiss office-holders for incompetency, personal incompatibility, or because they brought him bad luck.

The Mugabe's legal status gave him also the position of supreme judicial authority. He had the right to punish individuals by death, exile, beating, torture, and cursing. He could confiscate the cattle of any of his subjects. He could prevent the execution of his people by his chiefs for criminal offences and could override the judicial decisions of the kinship-groups. In disputes involving two lineages, the Mugabe alone could grant the right of blood revenge. Excepting among rebellious subjects, the Mugabe did not initiate legal action. All other cases had to be brought before him.

Although the political and judicial powers of the Mugabe were great, they were in the last analysis circumscribed powers. The Mugabe, like all individuals in his kingdom, with the exception, perhaps, of slaves, was bound by custom. It was his duty to defend the cattle and lives of his subjects, to perform certain magical and religious rites, to offer economic help to people in distress and to pay, like any one else, a bride-price to the father of any woman he wished to marry. He acknowledged the rights of clans to certain offices and took the advice of his supporters in political affairs. In judicial matters, his mother and sister could veto his decisions. No man, it is said, could be executed by the Mugabe until the consent of these two women had first been obtained.

We must be careful to note, on the other hand, that while the Mugabe was bound by custom, he was, strictly speaking, above the law. No man could take legal action against him, for there was no authority higher than the Mugabe before which he could be accused, tried, and sentenced. Political action could be and was taken against him. The legal relationship which bound subjects to the Mugabe could be broken by the subjects moving to another kingdom or by refusing to pay homage until the king fulfilled his obligations.

While the Mugabe was the unquestioned head of the State, he did not stand alone. He was supported in his kingly duties by a large number of individuals, who, together with the king, formed what might be called an effective government. Among these individuals, the king's mother and sister were the most important. They lived in separate kraals and maintained establishments almost as elaborate as that of the Mugabe. Next in rank came the Enganzi, or favourite chief, who lived with the Mugabe and acted as his adviser. Then there was a large group of individuals known as the *abagaragwa*, or king's relatives, who had a variety of duties to perform in the king's kraal. Finally, there were the executive chiefs, or *abakungu*, comprising war leaders and tribute collectors.

We shall for the moment postpone the discussion of the mother and sister of the Mugabe and deal with the dignitaries who derive their positions through royal selection. The Enganzi has been variously called the 'prime minister', the 'head chief', the 'beloved one' and the 'favoured one', but we shall here call him the 'favourite chief'. When during the new moon the Bahima see the new moon and the evening star together in the western sky they say that the Mugabe and the Enganzi are in conference, the moon representing the Mugabe and the evening star the Enganzi. When relations between the Mugabe and the Enganzi are strained, the people are afraid, for they say 'power and wisdom' are quarrelling. The Enganzi is selected by the Mugabe with the advice and consent of

his mother and sister. The first act of the Enganzi after the accession war is the establishment of the new Mugabe. In this sense he
is a king-maker. Although the Enganzi was a rich and powerful
man, he was always selected from a clan other than the *Abahinda*
and, therefore, could not lay claim to the Mugabeship himself.
The Enganzi was the chief military adviser and with his advice
every new Mugabe selected the leader of his military bands.
During war the strategical movements of these bands were
decided by the Enganzi. After a successful cattle-raid, the
Enganzi was responsible for the first distribution of cattle. After
the death of the Mugabe, the Enganzi would support the favourite
son of the Mugabe in the struggle for the Mugabeship. In this
struggle, his power would often turn the scales against the other
sons. The Enganzi then often formed a link between the two reigns
and was thus instrumental in checking the worst excesses of the
accession war.

In the Mugabe's kraal there was a group of young men collectively known as the *abagaragwa*, or king's relatives. These men
were selected from among the sons of the prominent men in the
kingdom and followed the Mugabe in all his movements from one
part of the country to another. It was from among these young
men that the future Enganzi and the future *abakunga* were
selected. The younger men were known as *abashongore*, or singers.
They sang praise songs to the Mugabe, amused him by wrestling,
and accompanied him when he went hunting. Men older than
these youths were known as the *abakazhwarangwe*, or warriors, who
accompanied the Mugabe on cattle-raids, acting as his body-guard
and as messengers. Older men who had not received official positions from the king were known as the *emikyeka*, or councillors.
They attended the meetings of the Mugabe and the Enganzi. They
were at once respected and feared by the executive chiefs, respected
because they had great influence with the Mugabe and feared
because any failure was at once reported to the Mugabe by them.
The carrying out of the Mugabe's orders was in the hands of a
number of chiefs known as the *abakungu*, or prominent men. The
majority of these *abakungu* were *abatware*, leaders of military
bands. It was their duty to guard the borders of Ankole against
raiders; they were almost constantly away from the Mugabe's
kraal. Each *omutware* gathered a band of warriors around him
who lived with their cattle near his quarters. The *abatware* were

men of power and importance and would sometimes rebel against the king. Another class of *abakungu* consisted of *entuma*, or tribute collectors. Whenever the Mugabe needed extra cattle, it was the duty of the *entuma* to go to every cattle-owner, select a number of cattle and take them to the Mugabe's kraal. The Bairu do not make distinctions between the *abatware* and the *entuma*, but call them all *abakungu*, the reason being that all the Mugabe's officers were just tax collectors to the peasants.

Another important class of individuals involved in the management of the State was the king's relatives known as the *abanyi-gyinye*. As will become clear later, these relatives were almost always relatives of his mother's side. The king's mother's brothers, who helped the king to secure the Mugabeship, were later given positions as military leaders, and the sons of these men became members of the *abagaragwa*. The king's *barimi* (mother's brothers) had the same status in the State as the king's mother and sister. They were permitted to collect tribute from the Bairu and to demand cattle from the Bahima without the king's permission. The members of the king's *ekyika* (sub-clan) were given special status, if they had supported the Mugabe in the accession war; otherwise they were treated as ordinary Bahima. One of our nearest neighbours was the son of the present Mugabe's brother, who claims that he was too young to be involved in the accession war. To-day he is just an ordinary herdsman in possession of a small herd and in no way distinguishable from the average Muhima kraalsman. He stated that he had no right to demand chieftainship or other offices and privileges, as his relatives had not supported the Mugabe at the time of his accession. On the other hand, the Mugabe supported the wives of his father's brothers and those of his own brothers after these men had been either killed or driven into exile.

Besides these individuals who were directly concerned with the management of the State, the Mugabe had a large following of wives, guards, magicians, and servants, who formed the permanent membership of his kraal. This kraal or residence was known as the *orurembo* and was made up of a number of enclosures. Like other Bahima, the Mugabe moved about the country. His movements were partly determined by the needs of his herd and partly by magical considerations. If he were in poor health, the diviners might decide that he must go to one or other of the sacred places in

Ankole to offer to his *emandwa* spirits, in which case the whole *orurembo* would move. Moreover, as the Banyankole were almost constantly on a war footing, the *orurembo* had to be ever ready to move to places of shelter.

The *orurembo* consisted of the *ekyikari*, Mugabe's private enclosure, and the *amachumbi* kraals, in which lived the *abagaragwa* or retainers, his private military band, and the *abahuku*, his Bairu servants. Of these kraals, the *ekyikari* was the largest and formed the centre of the *orurembo*. It was made of the same materials and in the same way as the ordinary Bahima kraals, the only difference being that the walls of the enclosure were higher and the huts were larger. The main entrance to this enclosure was called the *mugaba* and was guarded night and day by the *abarizi*, gate-keepers. Inside the kraal and to left of the gateway there was the *ekyikomi*, main fireplace. All visitors, messengers, and litigants had to remain here until their wishes were heard by the Enganzi. It was at the *ekyikomi* that the Mugabe received his men, tried cases, and held meetings of lesser importance. The *ekyikomi* was, therefore, the public part of the *ekyikari* and took up about one-fourth of the kraal space. The rest of the *ekyikari* was separated into five distinct enclosures. The most important of these enclosures was the *nyarubuga*, which housed the Mugabe's women. The *nyarubuga*, in turn, was divided into five lesser enclosures. Within the *ekyiniga* were the huts of the Mugabe's favourite wives. These women were known as the *enkundwakazi* and were waited upon by immature girls and guarded by the *ebishaku*, castrated Bairu servants. In another of these lesser enclosures within the *nyarubuga* was the *rwemhunda*, in which the Mugabe kept the immature girls, *enshorekye*, who were later to become his concubines or wives. The Mugabe had the right to take any girl in his kingdom if he wished. It was one of the duties of his retainers to inform the Mugabe of pretty girls in his kingdom and to bring them before him. If the Mugabe was pleased with the appearance of a girl and was assured that she was a virgin, he would include her with the *enshorekye*. Parents whose daughter was taken by the Mugabe in this manner did not deem it an outrage; on the contrary, they looked upon it as an honour. Many Bahima and even Bairu would offer their daughters to the Mugabe. Girls accepted or taken by the king were not always an economic loss to their parents, for if the Mugabe decided to make a girl his wife he would pay the girl's father the *enzhugano*, or bride-price, and, of course, there was always the chance that she would become the future Mugabe's mother. These girls were taken care of by the Mugabe's brothers' widows, who taught them to dance, sing, and play the harp. It was the custom of the Mugabe to spend his evenings in the *rwemhunda*, where the *enshorekye* entertained him.

When a girl became mature and pleased him, the Mugabe would select her as his next concubine. She was first, as was customary among the Bahima, put into a separate enclosure to be fattened. This enclosure, which formed part of the *nyaruhuga*, was known as the *wayetwoka*. Here one of the older women forced the girl to drink large quantities of milk. When she was so fat that she walked with difficulty she was considered fit to sleep with the Mugabe. She then became an *ekyinyashunzhu* and was quartered with the rest of the *ekyinyashunzhu* in the *kagyerekamwe*, the enclosure for the king's concubines. The *ekyinyashunzhu* were most closely guarded by Bairu eunuchs and were waited upon by the *enshorekye* girls. Any man caught in the quarters of the king's concubines was put to death instantly. From among the *ekyinyashunzhu* concubines, the Mugabe selected his wives. Any of the girls whom he did not wish to marry he gave as gifts to his friends and retainers. Older wives who were bringing up children lived in another enclosure which had no special name and which was not very closely guarded. The Mugabe did not neglect these women, however, for they had already produced children and one of them was destined to become the *nyamasore*, mother of the future *mugabe*; they were, therefore, already respected by the people. The Mugabe was anxious that his sons should grow up to be strong and capable men and took an active part in their training. No matter how intimate the Mugabe might have become with his wives and children, he never ate with them. His cooked food was prepared for him by a Mwiru and served to him by one of the *enshorekye* girls.

The next place of importance in the *ekyikari* was the large meeting hut, *nyarunzhu rweterekyero*. It was in this hut that all important meetings took place and before which the Mugabe entertained his special guests. Near the meeting hut there was a large beer-store and a number of smaller huts for visitors. When a large cattle-raid had been planned, the men who were going to take part in it gathered before the *nyarunzhu rweterekyero* and swore before the Mugabe to come back with cattle or to die in the attempt. It was before this hut that every new Mugabe was invested with office, before which cases of murder and treason were tried and punished, and where the peace ceremony was performed. All important meetings were accompanied by beer-drinking, the beer being served in individual calabashes by Bairu servants. The *ekyikomi* (great fireplace), we saw, was the common meeting place where minor cases were tried, where entertainment took place, and where every commoner had the opportunity to do homage to the Mugabe. The *nyarunzhu rweterekyero*, on the other hand, was the official centre of the Banyankole State, where only the leading men met to discuss and transact State business.

The Mugabe was never completely free from danger. Not only foreign enemies, but rebellious subjects threatened his position. Chiefs who had fared badly in a distribution of captured cattle or who had had their possessions and positions taken from them were ever ready to revenge themselves upon the king. In the accession war, it sometimes happened that one of the Mugabe's brothers would flee to another kingdom and later endeavour to return and slay the king. Against these external and internal enemies, the Mugabe maintained a strong guard, permanently quartered in the *orwekubwo*; this enclosure was built next to the women's quarters, the *nyarubuga*, and was the enclosure into which the Mugabe retreated when the alarm was sounded by the gate-keepers. In the *orwekubwo* there was a special hut for the spears which were made by the Mugabe's blacksmiths. As a rule, the command of the king's private guard was in the hands of the king's mother's brother, who owed his high rank to the king and was, therefore, believed to be loyal and trustworthy.

As we shall see later, religion played an important part in the Mugabe's life. Offerings had to be made to his ancestors and to his *emandwa*, not only for his bodily welfare, but also for the success of his enterprises and for the health of his cattle. A special enclosure, the *kagondo*, was set aside for this purpose. In this enclosure there were the *endaro*, spirit huts for the ancestral and *emandwa* spirits. These *endaro* were so large that the spirit wives of the Mugabe were able to live permanently in them. The *emandwa* huts were the same in form as those used by the commoners, i.e. they consisted of a sheaf of grass tied near one end and set up to form a conical hut into which a pot of milk or beer could be deposited. In the *kagondo* the *okubandwa* ritual for the *emandwa* spirits was performed and here cattle were killed that were to be used as offerings and to act as the leader in the *okubandwa* ritual. Also that part of the moon ritual which entailed *okubandwa* was performed in the *kagondo*.

The milk and the meat which the Mugabe personally consumed was obtained from his own herd. For this purpose, a considerable number of cattle were kept in the *ekyikari* in an enclosure called the *eka y'enkorogyi*. The word *enkorogyi* means the herd which remains with the owner and differentiates it from the *enshubi*, or herds which are dispersed throughout the land. These terms are used generally by all Bahima when speaking of their herds. The Mugabe's herd, like the herd of every Muhima, was made up of cattle, some of which were set aside for the ancestral and *emandwa* spirits and others which served purely economic purposes. The Mugabe's herds were noticeable for the fact that they contained many black and white cattle. As cattle of these colours were used for special ritual purposes, any Muhima bringing the Mugabe a black or white cow would be well received and rewarded with cattle of other colours. This special herd was kept in the *ekyikari*, the Mugabe's private enclosure, and was clearly separated from the large herd belonging to the Mugabe, which was kept in one of the numerous enclosures surrounding the royal kraal. The cattle of this large herd were used to support the Mugabe's retainers and were given away as gifts to visiting Bahima. It was constantly being replenished by cattle which were confiscated from rebellious subjects, came in as fines, payment for trying legal cases, or in the form of *okutoizha* (homage payments).

So far we have concerned ourselves with the internal form of the *ekyikari* (royal enclosure). Within it we found the *nyarubuga*, with all the various enclosures for the Mugabe's women, the *nyarunzhu rwetirekyere* (meeting hut, the guard quarters), *orwekubo* (the ritual enclosure), *kagondo*, and the *eka y'enkorogyi* (cattle enclosure). Just inside of the gateway, *mugaba*, there was the *ekyikomi*, or great fireplace, where the Mugabe's subjects gathered to ask favours and to pay him homage. The *ekyikari*, then, was the centre of the *orurembo* or royal place; around it were scattered the subsidiary kraals called the *amachumbi*.

In one of these *amachumbi* kraals lived the king's private warrior band consisting of several hundred men, commanded by a favourite retainer. These men had sworn to defend the Mugabe until death and were picked from among other warrior bands for their courage. This band was constantly near the *ekyikari* and its members had their wives and such cattle as they needed with them. They remained until age made them unfit for military duty. The Mugabe's private band was used only as a last line of defence when an enemy force invaded Ankole. When danger threatened they would move the Mugabe's cattle and people to a safe part of the country, scattering his cattle in small herds and taking special care to hide the royal drums and beaded veil, *Rutare*.

The king's magicians had a kraal to themselves. Most of these magicians (*abafumu*), were Bairu and were forced to serve the Mugabe during his lifetime. Any *omufumu* who had won fame might be called upon by the Mugabe to serve him. Not only were all departments represented, as divining, sorcery, white magic, and the smelling out of bad medicine, but each department had its own specialists. There were diviners who foretold the future, using the *entondo*, a small insect, others who read the signs in the entrails of a white cow or sheep, others, again, who divined with cowrie shells. There were sorcerers who practised with their horns filled with secret medicines; others who used the bow. There were practitioners in white magic who were experts in purifying, in casting spells against evil influences, or in making charms for use against disease and bad luck. Of particular importance was the *omutsiriki* (cattle magician). The Mugabe himself did not possess magical paraphernalia. Each magician procured his own medicines. In divining, however, it was sometimes necessary for the Mugabe to be present. While some of the Mugabe's magicians were busy from morning till night protecting the king's person from harm, it was during war-time that the majority were most busy.

IV. Tribute

The labour required for the upkeep of the royal establishment was considerable. Menial tasks such as wood-cutting, water-carrying, and butchering were performed by the *abahuku*. These men were slaves and had their ears cut off to prevent them from permanently escaping. They were said to be peasants who were taken for this purpose from the neighbouring kingdoms. They lived near the royal enclosure and worked under the supervision of a Mwiru headman. Besides these menials, the Mugabe had his expert craftsmen. The foremost of these were the king's blacksmiths, *abahesi*, who made spears, knives, axes, and ankle and arm bands out of iron. Important also were the carvers, who made milk-pots, drums, wooden spoons, and carved decorations out of wood, ivory, and bone. Then there were the skin-dressers, bark cloth-makers, sandal-makers, beer-brewers, and sanitary attendants. Some of these crafts were the special prerogative of certain clans. The king's sandals were made from the skin of a duiker by a man selected from the *abaigara* clan, who also grew and prepared the king's tobacco. A man of the *abasingo* clan had the duty of washing the Mugabe every morning, after which a man from the *abararira* clan gave the Mugabe a magical potion to drink. The Mugabe's musicians were men from the Koki district who had learned to play the Baganda flute. His hunters came from Buwhezhu and Bunyaruguru with their nets and dogs. The labour required by the Mugabe thus fell into two classes: slave labour and *oruharo*, or forced labour. The slaves were the property of the Mugabe and no payment was made to them. The craftsmen, magicians, and servants whom the Mugabe called to his service were rewarded by a form of payment known as the *engabirano*. This payment, however, was not made until a servant was given permission to leave. This permission was given on account of old age or if a servant left a son or some other trained person in his place. The *engabirano* consisted of barren cows, bullocks, sheep, and goats when the servants were Bairu and cows when the servants were Bahima. *Oruharo* was also used by the Bahima chiefs and wealthy cattle owners, but only with the sanction of the Mugabe.

　　Besides labour, the Mugabe required large quantities of food and beer, not only for the upkeep of the royal kraal, but also for feasting his chiefs and visitors and to help such followers and subjects who were in need. The essential foods, such as milk, meat, and blood, came from the private herds of the Mugabe and his principal chiefs. But other foods like millet and beer came from the Bairu peasants in the form of tribute. The duty of tribute collection for the royal kraal was placed upon the Enganzi (favourite chief), who appointed Bairu collectors, who, in turn, were responsible for the actual collection. These subsidiary collectors were called *abakungu*. Each *omukungu* appointed local collectors, who brought the necessary beer and millet to certain local centres ready for transportation to the King's kraal.

As tribute collection was exercised by the chiefs, there was, of necessity, a division of the country into areas. Every Muhima chief had, while in a given locality, the right to collect tribute, but part of his collection must be sent to the Mugabe. Besides the tribute sent in by the chiefs, the Mugabe levied tribute directly from the peasants in the Shema district. In this locality the Mugabe had two Bairu tribute collectors who collected by the moon. When the moon was on the increase, one man collected the tribute which was called *orubabo*. When the moon was waning another man collected it and this was called *ekyirabamu*. The quantity collected depended upon the needs of the Mugabe's establishment, the collectors being informed of the amounts necessary. Before and immediately after a cattle-raid, when feasting took place at the king's kraal, more tribute was necessary than during normal times. Failure on the part of the peasants to provide the necessary amount was followed by destruction of property and by beating. Persistent neglect of the tribute obligation often resulted in the execution of the rebellious peasant.

There was considerable variation in the quality of millet in Ankole and in the knowledge of beer-making. Whenever the Mugabe found a brew that was to his liking, he selected its makers as his private brewers. Such peasants had to take special pains over the Mugabe's beer and were forced to take it in person to the king. These private brewers often became favourites and were eventually rewarded with an *engabirano* payment.

It is difficult to-day to assess the amount of tribute gathered, the hardships which it brought to the Bairu, and the reaction of the Bairu to the tribute burden. The peasants are unanimous in stating that this burden was heavy, but 'it was better to pay the tribute than die'. The old men complain most about the collectors, who, they claim, exacted more than the Mugabe demanded, keeping the surplus for themselves. When the collectors became too bold, the peasants would complain to the Mugabe, who would then appoint new collectors. It is said that both the peasants and collectors practised sorcery upon one another and that a particularly evil collector would be speared to death. The Bairu, then, were more concerned with the abuses of tribute collection than with the existence of tribute itself. The payment of tribute, like the payment of poll-tax to-day, they accepted as part of the order of things. It was an admitted burden, but it had to be made in order that life could be carried on.

Okutoizha, or the payment of homage by the client to the Mugabe, was a source of considerable income. Here, again, the exact amount is beyond investigation. Every Muhima, upon becoming an *omutoizha*, or client, presented the Mugabe with from one to three head of stock, depending upon the size of his herd. Poor herdsmen who could not afford to give away cattle brought milk, butter, or calf-skins. The payment of *okutoizha* was made periodically and as long as a Muhima wished to be the Mugabe's client. *Okutoizha* differed from tribute in that it was freely given by the client, who believed that the protection received warranted the payment.

Although *okutoizha* was essentially a political instrument, a means for setting up the Mugabe-client relationship, we are here concerned with it as an economic measure, a specific institution for the maintenance of the State structure. As the cattle came to the Mugabe's kraal and were presented to him, they became his personal property; he knew the names and appearance of these cattle and knew also the increase which they constituted to his herd. The Mugabe, himself, however, did not use these cattle for his own food, but sent them to swell his herds distributed throughout the country of Ankole. For the purpose of keeping a tally upon his cattle, the Mugabe had special men called *entuma*, who knew exactly where every cow was stationed and from whom it had been received.

From the purely economic standpoint, cattle received through *okutoizha* formed a savings fund, a surplus upon which herdsmen in distress could draw. Any of the Mugabe's clients, when in need of cattle, could come to the Mugabe and explain his plight. After carefully hearing the matter, the Mugabe would present the man with a number of cattle in order that he could establish a new herd. The number of the cattle which the Mugabe would give to a client depended upon the man's former wealth and his relationship to the Mugabe. If the man had performed many services for the king, he would be given more help than if he were unknown. This differential treatment among the Mugabe's favourites was a source of ill will among the Bahima and often led to open rebellion on the part of dissatisfied herdsmen. It was the particular duty of the Enganzi, or favourite chief, to see that equal treatment was extended to all followers of his master.

The surplus fund of *okutoizha* cattle was also used by the Mugabe for making *engabirano* payments to servants, magicians, and other followers. Important chiefs like the war leaders (*abatware*), were given extensive herds by the Mugabe on their retirement. Exceptionally successful cattle-raiders were given great numbers of cattle as a reward for increasing the king's herds. The numerous marriages of the Mugabe demanded many cattle for the marriage-prices. Large feasts, before and after cattle raids, were supplied with meat from the Mugabe's herds. Finally, as hostile as the Mugabe's relations were with the neighbouring kings, there were times of peace in which the kings exchanged gifts of cattle, during which time they aided one another against other kings or rebellious subjects. The Bahima have a saying, 'Darkness makes the mountains touch', meaning that, unknown to the commoners, the kings have dealings with one another in which cattle pass from one monarch to another. *Okutoizha* cattle were not used for ritual purposes by the Mugabe. All cattle which he set aside for the spirits of his ancestors or to those of his *emandwa* or which he permitted to be used in divination came from his private herd, the *enkorogyi*.

Another form of economic income to the Mugabe, which was not, however, very extensive, was the payment of *okutoizha* by the Bairu. With the political aspects of this form of gift we shall deal later. Whenever a Mwiru visited the king's kraal, he would bring with him a goat or a sheep, millet, beer, maize, beans, &c., as presents. These articles the Mugabe used for making payments, especially to his Bairu diviners and sorcerers, and for feeding his large following of Bairu workmen and slaves. Any Mwiru, moreover, who had consistently visited the royal kraal and made payments of this kind to the Mugabe could claim his assistance if he found himself in economic distress.

We come finally to a form of income known as *ekyitoro*. As the name indicates, *ekyitoro* cattle were derived from the *Abatoro*, conquered herdsmen. The king's *entuma*, cattle collectors, went periodically among the herds of the *Abatoro* taking as many cattle as the king required. Very little attention was given to the needs of conquered herdsmen and very often a man's entire herd would be taken from him. The Bahima look upon the payment of *ekyitoro* as a terrible event and say that 'the *entuma* are like lions which attack at night when the men are drunk'. *Ekyitoro* was open to the worst phases of abuse in tribute collection. The *entuma* took what they wanted, keeping many cattle for themselves and if a cattle-owner threatened the collectors with exposure to the Mugabe he was simply speared to death. The Bahima also apply the word *ekyitoro* to a form of compulsory tax levied upon their cattle by the Mugabe. If through disease or raid the Mugabe had lost many of his cattle, he claimed the right, as supreme protector of all the cattle herds of Ankole, to send out his *entuma* to bring in as many cattle as were needed in the royal kraal. I have never heard the Bahima object to this levy. They claim that this right was seldom exercised by the Mugabe and was always practised with due consideration to the needs of the herdsmen. *Ekyitoro* was a royal privilege and was extended to the Mugabe's mother and sister and the mother's brothers. The greatest honour which the Mugabe could confer upon a chief was the right of *ekyitoro*. Very few men received this privilege for life but many able warriors were given the right temporarily. While a man had the right of *ekyitoro* he could take what cattle he wished within the kingdom, excepting only those of the king. Along with this privilege went the right to kill any one who resisted the confiscation of his cattle. The Bahima claim that any man who had been given this right used it to damage his enemies by taking their cattle and by killing any people who had formerly harmed him.

V. *The Cult of Bagyendanwa*

A visitor to the royal enclosure on Kamukuzi Hill, near Mbarara, to-day would be shown an old ramshackle, mud-walled, grass-roofed hut, the shrine of *Bagyendanwa*. If he were to enter into the dim, smoke-grimed interior of this shrine, he would see on a raised platform or altar a number of drums surrounded by milk-pots and partly covered with bark cloth robes. Before the drums he would see a number of bleary-eyed natives squatting beside a fire which, he would be told, is never permitted to go out except upon the death of a Mugabe. A European acquainted with the Banyankole would tell him that these drums are the royal drums of Ankole and would add that no white man has been able to solve their mystery. He would gain little, if any, insight into the true meaning of the drums to the Banyankole, the tremendous magical power which the natives attribute to *Bagyendanwa* and the part which it, along with other objects, plays in the life of the people.

Bagyendanwa is the tribal charm or fetish of the Banyankole. In the past, it is said, that at the accession ceremonies human sacrifices were made to it. 'So long as *Bagyendanwa* remains in Ankole,' the people say, 'so long will the country and the people prosper.' The Banyankole do not think of *Bagyendanwa* as a symbol of abstract unity, but as a concrete power capable of helping men in need. '*Bagyendanwa* is like the Mugabe, only greater. Ankole is the land of *Bagyendanwa* and we are the people of *Bagyendanwa*. The Mugabe is his servant', is the way in which a Munyankole describes the power of the drum over the king and the people.

It is difficult to understand the beliefs which the Banyankole hold about *Bagyendanwa*. They will deny that the drum has a soul like human beings, but will say that it can see and hear and that it knows what is going on in Ankole. The notions held about *Bagyendanwa* are akin to the beliefs which they hold about the magic horns of the magicians. Like these medicine-filled horns, *Bagyendanwa* has the power to perform acts, but, unlike these horns, the power in the drum is inherent and not due to the application of medicines. The Banyankole have no special word for this power, but describe it as a capacity to perform certain acts. This power or capacity, although inherent, can be reduced by the evil influences of men, things, and events, and the drum has, therefore, to be periodically purified and protected. Furthermore, the drum requires cattle, milk, meat, millet, and beer for its welfare. Although these offerings are given to the drum as offerings by individuals who require its help, the Banyankole believe that the drum must have food to remain strong. *Bagyendanwa* must be kept warm, so it is usually covered with a bark cloth and the fire is said to add to its comfort. *Bagyendanwa* is considered a male, and a female drum has been selected for him which is always kept by his side. Attendants must not speak loudly in the presence of the drum, as he is believed to punish such levity.

The Mugabe is a Muhima and has the interests of the Bahima at heart; the Bairu are his serfs. *Bagyendanwa* is impartial. He is as much interested in the Bairu as in the Bahima. The conquered herdsmen, *Abatoro*, also had the right to offer to *Bagyendanwa* and used this practice as a way of getting into the good graces of the Mugabe as a preliminary step towards clientship. Slaves who had no legal status were barred from worshipping the royal drum. While *Bagyendanwa* showered his blessings upon the Bahima and the Bairu alike, he still distinguished between them. The Banyankole say that, 'the Bahima are the cattle of Bagyendanwa and the Bairu are his goats'. 'The Bahima must offer cattle and the produce of their cattle and the Bairu must offer the produce of their gardens.' Thus, while *Bagyendanwa* was the tribal charm, it would be untrue to say that he considered his 'children' of equal status.

The power of the drum is apparent in the activities which it performed. When a chief decided to ask a favour, or to ask for advancement from the Mugabe, he would first go to the shrine of *Bagyendanwa* and offer a cow. He would take the beast in person before the drum and say, 'I have brought a cow; one of the Abachwezi, they who have gone before, may you take this cow, this red one of mine, one that I have herded, a clean one in the *orurembo* [kraal], so that the king will not refuse me, so that the king will not walk towards his *nyarubuga* [private quarters]'.

Once an offering had been made, a man felt encouraged to make his request. This does not mean, of course, that no other magic was resorted to, but that the offering to *Bagyendanwa* was an essential element in uncertain enterprises. If the request was granted, the chief would take another cow to *Bagyendanwa* as a thank-offering. 'I have brought you this one, my king, for you have heard me. The great ones have heard me; they shall have what I have.'

Similarly, any man undertaking a cattle raid, in the past, would always offer to *Bagyendanwa*, asking the drum to protect him from the spears of his enemies. 'We are making a raid for you. We are going to increase your herds. We are going to make your land strong', they would say. Not only in cattle raids would the Bahima ask for the help of the drum, but also if they were moving into another part of the country, digging a new water hole, or launching any enterprise in which there was great danger. The Bairu would also ask the drum for success when they moved to new parts, when going on a hunting trip, or beg for help when their crops failed or their children died. In the case of the Bairu, beer and millet would be offered, and if they were successful a second offering would be made to thank the drum for its solicitude.

Not only did *Bagyendanwa* help people in their endeavours, but he was also believed to punish evil-doers and to avenge wrongs. If a man felt that he had been wronged by some one, but could not prove his case before the Mugabe, he would go to the drum and beseech it to punish his enemy. The common occasions for thus appealing to the drum were theft, adultery, sorcery, and slander. The Bairu, it is claimed, sought justice more often from the drum than did the Bahima, for the Mugabe was 'often deaf to the complaints of his serfs'. *Bagyendanwa* punished people by making them ill, letting their cattle die and by causing wild animals to destroy their cattle and crops. If through divination a man found that the drum was punishing him because he had wronged some one, he would go to the person whom he had wronged and compensate him for the loss or damage he had incurred. Sometimes the two men who had come to terms thus would go to the shrine of *Bagyendanwa* and offer to him and swear by the drum not to harm each other again. Such men would continue to offer to the drum for some time afterwards, for, they said, 'he had brought peace where there had been hate'. For all requests and answers offerings had to be made.

Even though nothing had gone wrong, the people would sometimes take offerings to the drum in order to solicit protection against the evil devices of men and spirits and the malignant forces which every Munyankole believes to reside in the world at large and which are revealed to him through omens and signs. The wealthier a man is, the greater is the danger around him and the greater and more frequent must his offerings be to the drum. Wealthy chiefs who were envied by rivals were particularly careful to make large offerings of cattle in order that evil would not be spoken about them to the Mugabe.

Bagyendanwa is also said to induce fertility in barren women. In the past, women who had no children would take an offering to the drum and ask it to make them fertile. The Abaruru, clansmen who were the drum-keepers, also had the power to induce such fertility, and upon request supplied charms made from plant medicines which had been prepared in the shrine and which contained powers associated with the drum. Besides having the power to induce fertility, *Bagyendanwa* looked with favour upon marriages and showered gifts upon important people after their marriage feast. When the son of a chief married, he went with his bride to *Bagyendanwa*, where an *omururu* would show him the drum-stick, *omurisyo*, as a symbol of fertility and would give the groom bark cloth, milk pots, and millet. When a princess was married, the sacred spear, *nyamaringa*, was shown to the newly married couple and the groom would be given a cow called 'cow of the sacred spear'. Any couple who had a long and successful marriage with many children would go to the drum and thank it for its help and make an offering of beer and millet or a cow. Children who had been born to a couple through the goodwill of *Bagyendanwa* were called *bene Bagyendanwa*, or children of the drum. They were considered more fortunate than other children and certain to accumulate large herds and to be successful raiders.

Bagyendanwa, like the Mugabe, provided a certain amount of economic help to people in dire distress. Offerings of cattle and food accumulated at the shrine of the drum. Some of the food was consumed by the Abaruru drum-keepers and the slaves who fetched wood and water, but much of it found its way back to the people of Ankole. Cows were milked, bull calves were slaughtered, and the beer and millet accumulated in greater quantities than were needed to supply these attendants. At marriages food and cattle were given away, as we have seen. But more important than these gifts of the drum were the cattle which were given to Bahima who had lost their herds through raids or disease and the food which was given to Bairu who had suffered from crop-failure. The case of a person in distress was heard by the head drum-keeper, who decided whether the person had a just cause or not. It was said that no person was helped if he had rich relatives who could help or if he were a favourite of the Mugabe. Here, again, we see the power and importance of the Abaruru drum-keepers. They were believed to have, not only the magical power of *Bagyendanwa*, but also the capacity for justice and the discernment of human wrong and weakness. The shrine of *Bagyendanwa* provided a centre for the saving of surplus wealth and for the redistribution of it in times of economic stress.

It has been mentioned that the cult of *Bagyendanwa* acted as a unifying agent in the political organization of Ankole. How, specifically, did the drum cult perform this function? The particular teleological purposes carried out by the drum do not, in themselves, explain this integrative action. The drum, through its magical power, was believed to contribute to the welfare of the people as a whole, to enable individuals to rise in social position, to add to their strength in war and to the acquisition of material goods, to right wrongs and to punish evil-doers, to increase the fertility of women and cattle, and to protect men from evil powers resident in the world. But other spiritual and magical agents were also instrumental in furthering the interests and endeavours of men, such as the *emandwa* spirits, ghosts, sacred places, charms, and magical practices of various kinds. The power of *Bagyendanwa*, then, lay not so much in what the drum did, but rather in the fact that the drum did these things alone and for the entire tribe.

First of all, there was only one *Bagyendanwa*, while the spirit cults, the ancestor cult, magical charms, and shrines were very numerous and therefore differentiating influences. The beliefs and practices associated with these agents formed associations, it is true, but there was nothing about these groups which emphasized and supported the unity which the political structure represented. But *Bagyendanwa* was common to all men in Ankole— as common as the land of Ankole and the king of Ankole. Its shrine was the tribal centre, where individual and tribal interests were furthered through ritual performances, and *Bagyendanwa* was the focus of all those beliefs which made for the well-being of men. '*Bagyendanwa* is ours. We are the children of *Bagyendanwa*', the Banyankole say in expressing their common aspirations and allegiance to a unifying agent that is at once concrete and a source of power. In the second place, *Bagyendanwa* belongs to Ankole and to the Banyankole. It differentiates the kingdom of Ankole from all other kingdoms. 'Bunyoro', the people say, 'has its *Ruhuga*; Karagwe has its *Nyabatama*; Ruanda has its *Karinga*; but Ankole has *Bagyendanwa*.' Here, again, other cults are of little value as buttresses for political unity, for they extend beyond the borders of politically differentiated territories. The people of all these kingdoms had the ancestor cult, and the *emandwa* cult was common to Bunyoro, Toro, Karagwe, and Ruanda. Thus while, on the one hand, the cult of *Bagyendanwa* formed a common centre for belief and practice in Ankole, overriding sectional beliefs and rituals, it differentiated, on the other hand, the people of Ankole from the inhabitants of neighbouring kingdoms.

To say that the cult of *Bagyendanwa* supported the tribal unity is not enough in itself to show that this cult contributed to the maintenance of a particular form of political organization. Tribal cults emphasizing the unity of a group, by relating that group to its mythical origins, are common enough in Africa and elsewhere. The unity represented by *Bagyendanwa* was not of this general character. The drum cult was specifically a king cult. It sanctioned the particular complexion of political relationships which existed in Ankole by relating these relationships to their legendary origins, namely, to the Abachwezi. *Bagyendanwa* was the drum of the Abachwezi, and as such is concrete evidence that they once lived and founded the kingdom of Ankole. It does not matter whether the particular beliefs held about the Abachwezi are fact or fancy. The belief that the Abachwezi established the kingdom of Ankole a recognized number of generations back is to the Banyankole a fact and the belief upon which their political structure rests.

To the Banyankole, *Bagyendanwa* represents the Abachwezi; the Abachwezi, in turn, sum up the beliefs and values inherent in Ankole kingship. From what has been said about the functions of the drum, it has become clear that the drum performed the actions of an ideal king. Besides fulfilling the duties of leadership, the Mugabe has magical power which protects the people from evil. The drum has this same power to an even greater degree. Both king and drum derive this power from the same source, the king by being a member of the Abahinda dynasty which links kingship by descent to the Abachwezi, the drum by being a relic of those ancient times which represent the values embodied in Banyankole kingship.

To the Banyankole, *Bagyendanwa* is greater than the person of the king. 'The Mugabe dies, but *Bagyendanwa* is always with us', they say, stressing the permanence of the drum as compared with the temporary nature of the individual ruler. The Mugabe is also the 'servant of *Bagyendanwa*' in that he guards it and watches over it. In the succession rights, as we shall see, it is the drum which makes the successor a Mugabe, which gives the final stamp and seal. The accession war is for the possession of the royal drum, and many Banyankole claim that if a foreign king were able to capture the royal drum he would automatically become King of Ankole. In their tales of former wars, the

Banyankole constantly stressed the importance of hiding *Bagyen-danwa*, so that it would not be captured. Perhaps the most con-clusive evidence to the statement that *Bagyendanwa* is greater than the Mugabe is the power of the drum to provide sanctuary. If, after being condemned to death by the Mugabe, a Munyankole were able to dash to the shrine of *Bagyendanwa* and to touch the drum he would not be killed. The Mugabe would forgive him; he would be freed and given his former rights. This sanctuary was effective only in protecting a man from the death penalty and only when this sentence was passed by the Mugabe. When a father or head of a family passed such a sentence upon one of his subordinates. the drum provided no sanctuary.

VI. Succession

The emphasis which the Bahima placed upon the health, strength, and courage of the Mugabe was so extreme that it affected his tenure of office and the selection of his successor. This excessive concern about the physical virtues of the king's person is explained partly by his position as a permanent war leader, and partly by the magical powers attributed to him in his capacity as a protector of the tribe from evil influences. As has already been mentioned, no Mugabe was permitted to die of illness or of old age. As soon as his wives and followers observed signs of weakness, the Mugabe was given a poison which brought about his death. The Bahima compare the Mugabe to the leading bull in the herd. They say, 'The Mugabe is like the leading bull. When the *engundu* [leading bull] is beaten by a younger bull, we kill the *engundu* and let the strongest of the younger ones take his place'.

After the king's death a successor must be chosen. Two rules governed this choice. First, the new Mugabe must be in the royal line; second, he must be the strongest of the last king's sons. Patrilineal descent fulfilled the first requirement. The second depended upon some method by which the strength and courage of the Mugabe's sons could be tested. Primogeniture and favouritism, both important factors in the selection of a successor in the extended family of the commoners, also played their part in the royal family, but were overbalanced by the political and ritual demands of kingship. The Bahima demanded that the strongest of the king's sons should be their leader and that the

test should be one of war. The brothers must fight among themselves until one of them alone remained alive in Ankole to claim
the drum and the Mugabeship.

In the king's kraal the sons prepared to fight for the Mugabeship
and to find *Bagyendanwa*. In the meantime Ankole could not be
left without a king. After the mourning ceremonies, a mock battle
took place in the royal kraal between common herdsmen, and the
winner was chosen as mock king. He maintained a semblance of
order in the royal kraal until the accession war ended. This mock
king was called *ekyibumbe*. The word *ekyibumbe* has a variety of
meanings. In common usage, it describes a stupid, foolish person.
Sometimes it is used to indicate a person who is the butt of jokes
and tricks. A small, toothless baby, who must be taken away from
the kraal upon the death of its father, is also called an *ekyibumbe*.
The royal brothers watched this mock battle, but after the person
had been chosen they chose their own followers and went out to
look for *Bagyendanwa*. If they met on the way they fought and
each tried to kill the other. If one brother had fewer followers than
the other, he generally got killed or fled to another country. On the
other hand, strategy often made up for lack of followers. The
brothers spied upon one another in order to creep up during the
night and get the other unawares. They put poison in each other's
food or stabbed one in his sleep. Magic and the help of foreign
allies were both resorted to. Each son was aided by his mother
and sister, who practised magic against his enemies and protected
him from the spirits of his slain enemies.

During the accession war which might last for several months,
the country was in a state of chaos. Every man resorted to his
kinsmen for protection. It is said that there was much cattle
stealing and people who had a grievance took advantage of the
chaotic condition of the country to take revenge upon their
enemies. But the great chiefs who guarded the borders of Ankole
did not take part in the accession war. They endeavoured to keep
as much internal order as possible and to guard the country from
foreign invaders.

One by one, the princes were either killed or driven into exile
until only one remained. The hidden son then came out of his
hiding place and fought with the one remaining son for the
possession of *Bagyendanwa*. The late Mugabe's favourite son did
not always win, but he usually had the most powerful magicians

and a large following. When the accession war was finally over, the new king went back to the royal kraal with *Bagyendanwa*, his mother and sister, and the Enganzi, killed the *ekyibumbe*, and was finally proclaimed and accepted as the new Mugabe.

Several days later there was an accession ceremony, after which the king went on a long purification journey through the land. With him went a number of special magicians, a small herd of cattle, and a group of expert hunters. Upon his return to the royal enclosure, the most thoroughgoing changes took place among the office-holders immediately surrounding the king's person. A new group of retainers would be selected from among the king's friends. These were usually men who had fought for him in the accession war. In the selection of the most important function-aries, the old Enganzi acted as adviser along with the king's mother and sister. After the principal appointments had been made, the old Enganzi retired and was rewarded for his long service with many cattle. The king then selected a new Enganzi from among his followers and the governmental machinery was again complete. In the change from the old to the new reign, the strongest link was the old Enganzi. In a sense, he was the king-maker. During the accession rites, he was the one who announced the new king to the Bahima chiefs and who aided in the selection of the next governmental personnel. His retirement was due to a stipulation which said that 'the Enganzi [evening star] must set with the Mugabe [moon]'.

Succession in the Banyankole kingdom was regulated by a particular body of beliefs and practices, the general function of which was to maintain the continuity of kingship as an essential part of political co-operation and to eliminate, as far as possible, competition and discord as permanent elements of political leadership. The dynastic principle, by restricting kingship to the Abahinda clan, at once ruled out general competition. The dynasty found its source in the legendary past, in the person of Ruhinda, the descendant of the Abachwezi. Patrilineal descent further restricted the range of candidates. The accession war, which at first appears as chaos and anarchy, in the long run serves the purpose of eradicating likely rivals. After the accession war, the Mugabe stands alone in the kingly line. The accession war, therefore, is a way of defining the succession, similar in general function to the rule of primogeniture or the rule of the favourite son.

The particular features of the succession rites, like the accession war, elaborate purification, and the importance of the king's mother and sister, are understandable only in terms of the particular nature of Bahima political structure and Bahima magic. Once we grasp the importance, to the Bahima, of the king as a military leader, as a symbol of unity and magical power which is amply illustrated by the ritual surrounding his daily life, practised in order to enhance this magical power, and the belief that a physically weak or ailing king makes the people of Ankole weak, we can readily understand the special stress laid upon getting the strongest and ablest scion of the dynasty as king. Elimination through a trial of strength certainly provided a more practical method of choosing the best son than any specific rule of succession could have done. As far as I was able to discover, there is no myth sanctioning the accession war. The Abachwezi did not practise it, nor did Ruhinda, the only survivor of the Abachwezi in Ankole, need to establish a precedent, for he had no brothers and no rivals to the Mugabeship. In this case, we can scarcely say that the accession war, although formally and traditionally sanctioned, was a periodic re-enactment of any myth. But once we recognize the importance of the physical strength and the magical power of the king to the Banyankole, we can comprehend the purpose of the accession war as a means of obtaining the desired end.

As we might suspect, the accession war had far-reaching consequences on the family connexions of the Mugabe. In theory, if not always in practice, the king had no living brothers or father's brothers. The intimate religious, magical, and judicial duties generally performed by the father or the eldest brother in Banyankole society were performed for the king by his mother and sister. The king's mother and sister, in the past, had no special titles, but were called simply *nyinya omugabe*, king's mother, and *omunyana omugabe*, king's sister. Their status was practically equal to that of the Mugabe himself. They both had their private kraals with cattle, herdsmen and warriors, and they both had the right of levying *ekyitoro* on Bahima cattle. They also received a share of all cattle taken in raids. The principal duty of the king's mother was the making of offerings to the king's *emandwa* spirits and the practising of magic against the ghosts of men whom the king had killed. Although the king himself made offerings to his ancestors, his mother was said to have occasionally sent a white cow to Ishanzi

Forest as an offering to the dead Mugabe. In the kraal of the king's mother there was a shrine for the four *emandwa* of the king—namely, Wamara, Mugasha, Kagoro, and Nyakiriro—where during every new moon she made offerings of cattle and of meat. If the diviners said that it was necessary for the king to go through an *emandwa* ritual (*okubandwa*), he was said to have gone to his mother's kraal for the rite. Besides these ritual duties, the king's mother had judicial and administrative functions. No man could be executed without her consent. She sat beside the Mugabe at all important judical cases and helped in deciding questions of war and peace. If messengers came from foreign kings, they had first to go to the king's mother, her consent being necessary for an audience with her son. The function of the mother as a protector is in these cases a better indication of her status than any hypothetical assumption of a former matriarchate. But the fact that the mother assumed these duties seems to be correlated with the fact that the king had no living brothers nor father's brothers.

VII. Conclusion

In the brief analysis of the political organization of the Banyankole given above, I have tried, not only to describe the form of the kingdom of Ankole in its political aspect, but also to point out the underlying forces which contributed to its formation and maintenance. We can readily see that this kingdom falls into that larger class of political structures known as conquest states, wherein ethnically different groups come into contact, resulting in a stratified society and a mechanism for maintenance.

The political relationships of clientship, serfdom, and slavery may be classified on the basis of their origin, as contractual and compulsory, differing in this from the relationships based on kinship which formerly were predominant and still play a fundamental role in Banyankole society. As to their nature or constitution, we might say that clientship was a well-balanced relationship arising from the need for political co-operation. Serfdom and slavery, on the other hand, were unbalanced relationships and exploitational in nature.

In my treatment of the Abachwezi myths, the drum cult, and the succession rites as forms of political ideology and practice, I have stressed the fact that even their particular form is explicable in terms of the political situation and the age-old magical conceptions present in the culture. In other words, the political structure of the Banyankole is understandable only when we know the objective situation out of which it grew and the cultural material out of which it was created.

The imposition of British rule, of course, has brought about great changes. Clientship, serfdom, and slavery as political relationships have disappeared. The Mugabe, although still part of the picture, is no longer a political leader and magical power as of old. The effects of British rule have altered, not only the political relationships, but also the fundamental nature of the kinship relationships, besides introducing new relationships of a legal nature between the Native and the white man, on the one hand, and between the Native and the Indian, on the other. A significant discussion of these new bonds as they touch personal relationships, land, economic activities, and governmental machinery requires more space than this paper will allow.

THE COUNTRY OF THE KEDE

Kede settlements in capitals. Settlements of Downstream Kede in capitals underlined (e.g. OGUDU).
Non-Kede villages with Kede settlements underlined (e.g. Kacha). Twin-villages thus ∞.
(L) Indicates a Ledu village. —·—·— Boundary between Upperstream and Downstream Kede
settlements. —··— Boundary between Kede and Kakanda. ∗ Donko is a non-Nupe settlement, inhabited
by people of the Kamberi tribe. Names of Nupe sub-tribes thus GBEDEGI.

S.F.Nadel fecit 1939

THE KEDE: A RIVERAIN STATE IN NORTHERN NIGERIA

By S. F. NADEL

I. Introduction

THE Kyedye or Kede,[1] with whom this paper is concerned, are a section of the large Nupe tribe of Northern Nigeria, whose general culture and social organization I have described elsewhere.[2] The Kede have many cultural traits in common with their mother tribe; their kinship system is the same; they speak the dialect which is spoken to-day by the majority of the Nupe sub-tribes and has become the acknowledged language of the Emirate, Nupe 'proper'; they have also adopted the religion of Nupe kingdom, Islam. Yet combined with this cultural affinity we find certain marked divergencies. The Kede are a riverain group—the only purely riverain group among the various Nupe sub-tribes. Their economic pursuits and general social life centre round the river on which they live and from which they derive their livelihood. This means already that their social and cultural life must present certain features which are absent in Greater Nupe. Their political organization, moreover, contains certain distinctive and unusual traits—unusual even for Africa at large. It is for this unusual nature rather than for its relation to practical problems of African administration that I have chosen the political organization of this small Nigerian sub-tribe for the subject of this contribution.

II. Demography

The main body of the Kede lives to-day on the Rivers Niger and Kaduna between 8° 30′ and 9° 40′ North Latitude, inhabiting a narrow strip of land on both banks. The Kede share their territory with a number of other tribal sections of the Nupe, which lead a semi-riverain life, pursuing—unlike the Kede—agriculture

---

[1] The proper Nupe name is Kyedye. But the Hausa, Yoruba, and other neighbouring groups (as well as, to-day, Government officials) prefer the more easily pronounced Kede. We shall adopt, for the sake of simplicity, this latter name.

[2] See *Africa*, viii, 1935, and also my forthcoming book, *A Black Byzantium*.

beside fishing and canoeing. Their villages and hamlets are scattered between the Kede settlements all along the river banks.[1] The sharp division, cultural and tribal, between the Kede and the other semi-riverain groups is illustrated in the linguistic usage: for Kede the word *eyapaciʒi* (canoemen), is used almost synonymously, while the other groups are referred to, collectively, as *laticiʒi* (farmers). Tradition, too, has its contribution to make: it represents the Kede as alien immigrants who have come from outside into their present habitat and settled there among the 'aboriginal' population. This tradition (to which we shall return later) is again reflected in linguistic usage, the different semi-riverain groups which to-day are the neighbours of the Kede in the river valley being spoken of, collectively, as *kintsoʒi* (owners of the land—that is, original inhabitants).

We possess detailed population figures only for one part of Kede country, for what is to-day the Kede District of Bida Emirate. But we may take these figures as representative of the whole area inhabited by the Kede.[2] In a total population of 12,066, the Kede number 2,225, and the *kintsoʒi* (comprising various sub-tribes) 9,742, the small rest (99) being made up by non-Nupe strangers who live in Kede District. The Kede thus form a minority in their own country—the country which bears their name. But it rightly bears their name and rightly is called 'their' country, for the Kede minority represents the ruling group, and their chief the ruler of this whole territory and the different groups which inhabit it, Kede as well as non-Kede.

But Kede country is itself part of a larger political system, the Nupe Emirate. In pre-British times, the country of the Kede lay almost entirely on Nupe territory or, more correctly, on the territory ruled by the *Etsu* (king) of Nupe, under whom it enjoyed the status of a semi-autonomous, vassal State. Under British administration, Kede country, greatly affected by the re-alignment of the

[1] They comprise sections of the following Nupe sub-tribes: the Gbedegi on the upper stretch of the Niger; the Bataci, or Marsh Dwellers, on the lower reaches; a few groups of Beni near the confluence of Niger and Kaduna; the Kupa round Eggan in the south; Dibo or ʒitako near Katcha and Baro; and, finally, a group of Nupe from Gbara, the ancient capital of Nupe kingdom, on the Kaduna and on the Niger near Patigi.

[2] These figures are taken from an official, unpublished, provincial census, for the use of which I am greatly indebted to the Administration of Niger Province. While the figures are perhaps not correct in every detail, they are reliable enough for the purpose of this argument.

political boundaries, came to lie in three different provinces and six different (modern) Emirates or Divisions.[1] However, we shall see later that this distribution of a comparatively small group over so many political divisions is not due entirely to the re-alignment of political boundaries. It is also a result of movements of Kede groups in recent times, after the political boundaries had been fixed by the present Government.

By far the largest section of the Kede lives on the left bank of the Niger and Kaduna, in Bida Emirate. In this area the Kede have also maintained their political status of a separate political unit, with their own chief as the administrative head. In all other areas the Kede communities are absorbed politically in the districts on whose territory they lie, and live under the local, non-Kede chiefs and district heads.[2] The modern political situation has not, how-ever, obliterated the other features of their social life; the charac-teristics of their political organization, more specially, live on, though on a smaller scale, in the one area where it has been given official recognition. Although many of our political data will of necessity be derived from this one area, we may again take them to be representative of Kede country at large, and when speaking in the following of Kede, Kede culture and social system, we shall mean the group as a whole, disregarding the modern political subdivisions.

There exists, however, one subdivision of a different nature, deep-seated and of old standing, which we may not ignore. I have spoken so far simply of the Kede. But there exist in reality two Kede groups: the Kede *Tifin*, or upper-stream Kede, and the Kede *Tako*, or down-stream Kede, the boundary between the two groups lying roughly at Jebba Island (the two groups overlap for a short stretch north and south of Jebba).[3] Now, what I have said about the specific features of the Kede social and political system applies only to the down-stream group. The upper-stream Kede show none of the traits which give to the culture of the sister group

[1] The Kede on the right bank of the Niger belong now to Ilorin and Kabba Provinces, and to the Emirates, or political divisions, of Ilorin, Lafiagi, Patigi, and (in the south-west corner) Koton-Karifi. The Kede on the left bank of the Niger and on the River Kaduna belong to Niger Province (formerly Nupe Province) and to the Emirates of Bida, Agaie-Lapai, and Kontagora.

[2] In one place (Ogudu) a certain compromise has been effected, the head of the fairly numerous Kede community acting as a titled 'second-in-command' to the village chief.

[3] The upper-stream Kede are also called Kede *Gbede*, after the Nupe sub-tribe (Gbede or Gbedegi) with which they share their territory.

its distinctive character; nor do they share the position of political supremacy which the down-stream Kede have assumed. They are, culturally, a semi-riverain group, like all the other Nupe sections whose villages lie interspersed between Kede settlements, and politically, again like these sections, subjects of the (down-stream) Kede ruling group. Thus when we shall speak in the following of the Kede political organization, we shall refer to this latter group only. The upper-stream Kede will be classified under one heading with the other semi-riverain Nupe sections, as, indeed, in native eyes, they are closer to the *kintsozi* than to the 'alien' immigrant group on the lower river. But the comparison of the two Kede groups will become of special significance at a later stage of this analysis. This strikingly unequal development in what appear to be two sections of the same tribal group should help us to isolate the factors, social or otherwise, that have moulded the political structure which we are studying.

III. Economic System

A demographic and political constellation such as we have discovered in Kede country is clearly the result of considerable group movements, possibly covering a long period. To be fully understood, such situation demands, first of all, an analysis—historical analysis, if possible—of tribal settlement. Before discussing Kede settlement, however, it is necessary to give a short description of the economic situation in the country. For, as I propose to show, the nature of Kede economics has decisively influenced the planning of Kede settlement and, indirectly, the whole political development of the tribe.

We can be very short as regards the economic system of the semi-riverain groups. They are in the main farmers, who cultivate the fertile marshland areas in the river valley. They are, besides, fishermen on a small scale, fishing from their small dug-out canoes in the backwaters and creeks of Niger and Kaduna—never in the main river, where the Kede alone are entitled to fish.

The Kede, on the other hand, are fishermen and canoemen of renown. Their name is known all down the River Niger, in districts far outside Nupe country;[1] and in their own part of the

[1] Their familiarity with the river has led to a considerable number of Kede being employed as sailors, skippers, and pilots by the Royal Niger Company and the Nigerian Marine Department.

world they have almost monopolized river traffic.[1] Let me say a few words about the river trade which Kede canoes have carried for centuries up and down the River Niger: comparatively few of the trade goods are destined for inland trade; the majority come from and go to places outside Nupe country. The Kede ship south: gowns (of Hausa and Nupe make), horses from Hausa, potash from Lake Chad, Nupe-made mats and straw hats, fish and rice from the Niger; and north: kola nuts from the markets in Southern Nigeria, European salt, and palm oil.

In this river traffic the Kede canoeman assumes two different roles: he is either a contractor who hires his canoe and crew (consisting of himself and his family members) out to a trader for a specific journey or he is both trader and contractor in one, carrying his own goods on his own craft. A variety of the first kind of occupation is the extensive ferry service which the Kede have established in certain places; here the Kede canoemen carry people, goods, and animals across the river for a small payment.[2]

The work of the Kede canoemen, though lucrative and admitting of big profits, is strenuous, exacting, and not infrequently dangerous. They must be prepared to go on long expeditions, which still to-day may be expeditions into the unknown.[3] These river voyages mean long absence from home, often of many months, not only because of the distance of their destination, but also because of the many stops and long waits which they involve: thus the canoemen may have to wait in a certain place till the river becomes navigable again; or till they have filled their canoes with

[1] The division between fishermen and canoemen among the Kede is rarely rigid—members of a fisherman family may take to canoe-work or canoemen spend their leisure time fishing; we will ignore this division in the following and concern ourselves only with the canoemen, who are of most interest to us. Originally the Kede also used to build their own canoes. The deforestation of the river banks forced these craftsmen to move south, where to-day they form a small colony of Kede canoe-builders near Onitsha.

[2] The 'very lucrative' ferry service at certain riverports is mentioned in Laird and Oldfield, *Narrative of an Expedition into the Interior of Africa* (1837), ii, p. 316. The most important ferry service of this kind to-day is at Jebba Island, where the Kede compete with the railway bridge, offering a cheaper service to the people who want to save the bridge toll.

[3] The journey from Kede country to Onitsha and back—one of their regular tours—takes two to three months. In 1936 I saw ten Kede canoes being loaded in Jebba with petrol for the French Air Service in Fort Nyameh. The river journey up the Niger was new to the canoemen, and was expected to take three months.

G

trading goods, or till they have found another 'passenger' (in native phraseology) to engage them for a profitable return journey.

Here we grasp the significance of this productive system for the organization of settlement in Kede country. The long canoe expeditions necessitate fixed stopping and resting places, where the canoemen must be sure to find shelter and food and opportunity to refit their craft. The 'termini' of their river routes more specially will tend to become at least seasonal 'colonies' of Kede. The stopping and waiting places will naturally be chosen in accordance with commercial considerations. And, finally, there must be some system of political protection, which could ensure the safety (speaking of pre-British times) of these far-flung routes, the stopping places with their valuable stores, and the seasonal or permanent trading posts:[1] trading posts which, of necessity, tend to become political colonies—this gives us the formula of Kede settlement.

IV. Settlement

We are fortunate in possessing data which allow us to trace in detail the history of settlement and population movement in Kede country. Our data are derived only partly from oral tradition. The history of Kede settlement reaches into the well-documented era of Nigerian exploration and British occupation; its last phases are happening under our very eyes. In addition to these historical records, we possess evidence of a different kind, which, indirectly, contributes considerably to our understanding of population movement in Kede country: it lies, as we shall see, in the lay-out and organization of the present-day Kede settlements themselves.

According to Kede tradition, their tribal home was near the confluence of Niger and Kaduna, near Muregi, which, some time later, became their political capital. From there they are said to have extended their settlements, and rule at the same time, gradually over the river banks towards the north and the south

---

[1] A case in point is the uninhabited right bank of the Niger above Jebba, where constant raids by inland tribes (from Borgu) made settlement impossible. The left bank, on the other hand, could be adequately protected, and here the Kede established a settlement at Buka (it was later moved to Jebba). In the south, Kede canoes did not travel beyond Eggan in pre-British days. The river south of Eggan was the domain of the Kakanda, a warlike riverain tribe of non-Nupe stock, which refused Kede canoes admittance into their area. Trade goods for the south had to be trans-shipped at Eggan to Kakanda canoes.

till their villages covered the Niger Valley between Eggan and Jebba. At the time when the first European travellers appeared in Nupe country, we find the Kede already firmly entrenched in this part of the Niger Valley. Now, of the ten main villages of the Kede which exist to-day only one represents an independent, purely Kede settlement—the Kede capital, Muregi. It is a well-built village, with solid houses of sun-dried mud bricks, each compound walled in in Nupe fashion, with a big mosque and an imposing chief's house. It is, as I have said, a pure Kede town, a town inhabited entirely by the 'ruling race'—'*u de talakaʒi a*', say the Kede ('it contains no poor'—meaning persons belonging to the subject groups). All other Kede settlements, without exception, are built on or near the site of a village of 'original inhabitants'. In most cases the Kede settlement occupies the river bank itself, and the 'native' village the stretch of country immediately behind; in a few cases we find the Kede settlements on an island off the bank occupied by the 'native' village or on the opposite side of the river. The result is something like a twin-village, half 'native' and half Kede. The scene of Kede tradition, a tribal home and emigrant settlements, seems indeed visible in the present-day organization of Kede settlement, with its one all-Kede town and its many 'twin-villages' along the river valley.

The more recent history of Kede settlement remains true to this picture of a gradual territorial expansion. We know that towards the end of last century the Kede settled for the first time on the Kaduna River. Later, under the Royal Niger Company, the Kede were encouraged to extend their settlements still farther on Niger and Kaduna. It is easy to trace these new settlements, which were founded near the European trading posts and other places which had similarly gained commercial importance. Only some thirty years ago the Kede founded their latest 'colony'— on Jebba Island.

The villages differ greatly in appearance: some villages boast solidly built permanent houses, while others consist largely of more flimsy buildings, grass-walled huts, suggestive of temporary occupation rather than permanent settlements. The habitations of the Kede reflect the flexible, mobile nature of their system of settlement. The degree of permanence attempted in the buildings at the same time betrays the age of the settlement as well as its (past or present) importance as an economic or political centre. The Kede settlement at Raba is a typical instance of the more solidly built settlement. It was founded about 1840, when Raba was the capital of Nupe Emirate. The first settlers were five men with their families from Muregi, who belonged to one 'house'; to-day the Kede colony at Raba (which now also possesses a Niger Company storehouse) numbers seven 'houses'.

The Kede settlement at Katcha is an example of the other, poorly built, type, which gives the impression as if the settlers had not yet found time, or had not yet quite decided, to build themselves permanent quarters. The present Kede settlement dates back to 1905–10, at which time a group of Kede who had settled previously at Eggan, on the main river, abandoned this colony for Katcha, attracted by the opportunities of the place. Katcha, on a tributary of the Niger, owed its rise to importance to the introduction of steamer traffic on the Niger and the building of the first Nigerian railway from Baro, through Katcha, to Minna. Its five or six 'houses' of original Kede settlers have now increased to seventeen.

Our list of Kede settlements would not be complete without the mention of the purely temporary riverside camps, meant to last for one season or a few weeks only, which the Kede put up in the larger villages where they are wont to stop on their journeys up and down the river. During the main trading season, Jebba, Patigi, Wuya, or Katcha are crowded with these lightly built shelters, grass-huts, tent-like structures of grass-matting or —crudest of all—the wattle-and-matting awnings of the canoes simply pulled ashore. Kede settlement has not yet come to a standstill. Places which are gaining in importance still attract new groups of immigrants; and the seasonal shelters in a busy trading centre may at any time be turned into permanent quarters, as, indeed, it has happened repeatedly in the course of time.

Reviewing the history of Kede settlement, we find its dependence on economic factors fully confirmed. We may conceive of it as of a progressive realization of the dictates of the productive system of the country. The Kede, as we have seen, did not occupy new, uninhabited country, but settled in places where an existing population had already established a certain level of social and economic life. In the choice of places for settlement and in their subsequent development, the Kede were invariably guided by commercial considerations. They were, moreover, not satisfied with the position of immigrants who are dependent on the good-will of their hosts, but claimed with the territory in which to settle also the political rule over it. If they are thus not 'colonists' in the strict sense of the word, not caring for settlement in new, virgin country, they are 'colonizers' in a more special, political sense, being settlers, immigrants, and representatives of a ruling race in one.

Here a final point remains to be cleared up: the exact relation between the elastic territorial expansion of the tribe and the necessarily more inert and rigid expansion of political domination. From the history of modern Kede settlement we learn that there is a certain time lag between the first occupation of a new place by Kede immigrants (the nucleus stage of the seasonal camp) and its eventual rise to the status of a political outpost. The Kede, as a rule, attribute the founding of their various colonies to particular chiefs. The initiative taken by the Kede chief in the colonial enterprise refers both to the early growth and the final political incorporation of the new colony. He might himself send out settlers from Muregi to a new place which looked a likely centre for Kede activities (Raba is an instance of this), or he might direct settlers from other places to a promising new settlement (as was the case in Katcha). But not until a settlement was firmly established and numbered several families would he delegate an official representative of his to take charge of it, thus proclaiming the political incorporation of the new Kede dominion.

We learn, further, that Kede territorial expansion did not proceed step by step, in continuous stages, but rather in a series of leaps, which may leave gaps between outpost and outpost, or mother-country and new settlement. Thus there are 'uncolonized' spaces on the Kaduna River between Gbara and Wuya or Gbara and Muregi—that is, stretches of country with native villages which (unlike the interspersed *kintsozi* villages in the 'old' Kede country) have not been absorbed politically by the Kede. We may assume that the early growth of the Kede community followed the same line of development. If this was so, the compact political unit in the 'old' Kede country proves that political rule was later brought up to the new outpost, and the territorial gaps eventually absorbed in the extending political unit. To-day the firmly fixed boundaries of provinces and districts forbid, of course, a similar sequel to the founding of new settlements. The new economic development of the country, moreover, has attracted Kede emigration to places far outside the orbit of their political organization: thus at the busy trading-place on the confluence of Niger and Benue, Lokoja, a large and prosperous Kede colony has grown, which combines all the 'stages' of Kede settlement, permanent and semi-permanent houses in which Kede families have made their home as well as a large encampment on the river bank for the Kede canoemen from the north. But it seems that even in pre-British times the territorial expansion of the Kede had to leave certain 'gaps' in its network of settlements and political outposts. Thus the large Nupe town of Eggan on the right bank of the Niger, flanked to the north and south by (presumably old) Kede settlements, remained a powerful, independent political unit, placed directly under the King of Nupe. It is this characteristic scheme of Kede expansion which allows for territorial gaps and the founding of (at least temporarily) isolated outposts that justifies our speaking of Kede 'colonies' and 'colonization'.

V. Political Organization

The political system of the Kede corresponds in all important points to the concept of the State. On its small scale, it fulfils the essential conditions of State organization: its dominion is territorial and non-tribal (or inter-tribal); its administration is centralized; its machinery of government is monopolized by a special *ad hoc* appointed or selected body, which is separated from the rest of the population by certain social and economic privileges.[1] The first of these three features we have discussed already; as regards the second, we have learned that Muregi, the traditional home of the tribe, is at the same time the political centre of the country; and as regards the last point, we have seen that in a broad sense the Kede themselves represent, corporatively, the ruling group of the country. But among the Kede we find another, more precisely defined 'privileged group', in whose hands the government of the country is concentrated. This ruling group, in a narrow sense, consists of the Kede chief and his titled councillors and emissaries.

[1] With regard to this definition of the State, see *Africa*, vol. cit., and my forthcoming Nupe book. R. Lowie, *The Origin of the State* (1927) (chaps. iii and iv), recognizes territorial sovereignty and centralized authority as essential to the structure of the State; the factor of the special 'ruling group' has been elaborated by F. Oppenheimer, *The State* (1926).

The Position of the Chief. The Kede chief, or *Kuta*, resides in Muregi. In his hands used to lie the ultimate decision on all matters concerning country and tribe as a whole—above all, war and the founding of new colonies. The *Kuta* was also the judicial head of his country. The larger part of taxes, duties, and other revenues used to flow into his private treasury. He was (and still is), finally, the official representative of his country *vis-à-vis* the overlords of Kede, the Emirs of Nupe. Impressive paraphernalia and forms of ceremonial serve to display the exalted position of the Kede chief, the most imposing perhaps being the enormous State canoe, propelled by twelve paddlers (two to three is the normal crew of the Kede canoes), in which the *Kuta* travels. The authority of the Kede chief rests in the main on three facts: first, a moral sanction of Kede chieftainship lies in its hereditary nature and the fact of its being derived, in a straight line, from a mythical first *Kuta*, who had been invested with the rule over the Kede by Tsoede himself, the ancestor-king and culture-hero of the Nupe. (We shall hear more of him later.) Another support of Kede chieftainship, of more practical order, lies in the overwhelmingly strong economic position of the Kede chief. His resources allow him to acquire a large fleet of canoes—not only the chief means of livelihood, but also the mainstay of all military action in this riverain country[1]—and to attach to his household a host of followers and henchmen. The position of the Kede chief is made finally secure by the fact that the most important political offices in the Kede State are allotted to his blood relations.

The 'Offices of State'. Political offices among the Kede fall into two categories. One comprises a small group of rank-holders, *ticiʒi* ('titled ones'), who reside in the capital and represent the councillors of the Kede chief. A second category comprises titled official emissaries of the *Kuta*, *egbaʒi* ('delegates'), who are in charge of the various Kede settlements and colonies. To these two groups of 'real' office-holders we must add a third group of what the Nupe call 'private' or 'household' ranks, which the Kede chief bestows on faithful and able followers. The majority of them live with the *Kuta* in Muregi, acting as his messengers, councillors of a lesser order, and such like; a few are entrusted with emissary-ships.

[1] Laird and Oldfield (op. cit., ii, p. 279) mention that the Kede chief 'had twenty canoes of retinue'.

The councillors of the *Kuta* number five ranks, three of which correspond to more or less specialized offices: the administration of Muregi town, the guardianship of the sacred relics of Tsoede, and—in pre-British times—the leadership of military expeditions. In modern Kede, the District *Alkali*, the Mohammedan judge appointed by the Bida Native Administration for the District, is virtually a member of the chief's council in the same capacity of a 'departmental' official. With the exception of this last office, the ranks of the chief's councillors are hereditary and 'belong' to the various families which have held the ranks from times immemorial. The succession to a vacant office is not, however, automatic, but admits of a certain latitude, as for every vacancy there are bound to be several candidates of approximately equal seniority and equal claim. In the appointment of a new rank-holder by the chief and his councillors, due weight is given to the reputation of the candidate, his experience, intelligence, and economic success (as canoeman or river-trader). The position of a councillor appears to have carried no regular emoluments with it, except in the case of the official in charge of the town administration and thus the collection of taxes in Muregi. Occasional gifts from the chief and a share in the booty made on raids and warlike expeditions constituted their official income.

The rank list of the 'delegates' is both larger and more flexible than that of the councillors. It is frequently altered, increased, or decreased, according to the demands of administration. The members of this order of ranks are all recruited from the family of the *Kuta*. Their ranks are graded, and follow a strict system of precedence and promotion. Every promotion means a larger measure of power and influence, for it goes hand in hand with transfer to another, more important, and also more lucrative post. A new as yet untitled member of the chief's kin will as a rule be appointed to one of the lower ranks; the higher ranks and more responsible offices can only be reached by gradual promotion. Promotion and first appointment are, again, decided by the chief in consultation with the other tribal notables; here, however, the personal preferences of the electors count more than rigorous qualifications: in this system of ranks based on promotion, long experience is not regarded as a condition for a lower appointment, nor already achieved economic success for a rise in rank which carries with it increased economic benefits.

Succession to Chieftainship. Here we must turn back to the position of the Kede chief and the question of succession to Kede chieftainship. For the highest in the series of promotion which we have just been discussing, the ultimate promotion open to members of the chief's family, is promotion to chieftainship. The rank next to the chief's, *Egba* (here meaning 'deputy'), is in fact regarded as the rank of an 'heir apparent', and is as a rule held by the most senior among the titled relatives of the chief, his younger brother, or elder brother's son. Succession to chieftainship, more rigid than succession to the other political offices, thus allows the chief-to-be to consolidate his position in advance of his actual appointment. The tribal notables exercise a certain indirect influence: for in every one of the repeated routine decisions on the promotion of a 'delegate' they already decide to some degree his future chances as a candidate for chieftainship. But then, the ruling chief is himself one of the 'electors' and can easily turn the decision in favour of the candidate whom he supports.[1] Here becomes clear what I have said above about the kinship relation between the Kede chief and his 'delegates' tending to strengthen the position of the chief. The mere tie of kinship between them may conceivably prove a weak and unreliable support of his authority; but the fact that the delegates remain dependent on the favour of the chief for their promotion and political career in general turns it into a bulwark of chiefly power.

With 'councillors' and 'delegates' both dependent upon his goodwill, the Kede chief exercised an almost absolute authority—more absolute, I may add, than any other chief of Nupe. Repeated promotion and transfer, all decided in the capital, tied the delegates closely to Muregi and prevented them from making for themselves too independent a position in their temporary dominions. The 'absolute' power of the Kede chief thus appears as a necessary element in the control of this mobile political system which, with its scattered outposts and colonies, yet depended so much on smooth co-operation and concerted action. The weakness of the system lay in the fact that it allowed no legitimate check on the power of the chief. A more equitable balance of power could only be achieved by illegitimate means—that is, by feuds and

[1] It is significant, in this connexion, that the present *Kuta* introduced a new rank for his son when the list of traditional ranks was exhausted (see the chart of Kede ranks).

factional splits within the hereditary ruling class. The recent history of the Kede contains indeed evidence of such rivalry between the Kede chief and his officers of State, or between different claimants to Kede rulership, and the ensuing division of the country into rival factions.[1] Attachment to one of the rival factions is also the only means by which the subject classes, the commoners with no rank and office, could exercise an indirect influence upon the political management of their country.

Administration of the 'Colonies'. The following chart illustrates the different grades in the rank list of Kede delegates. The ranks are given in order of precedence, each rank together with the district to which its holder is posted. The last five ranks on the list do not belong to members of the chief's family, but to that group of 'household' ranks which are also occasionally vested with emissaryships.

Rank	Relation to Kuta	Posted to at present	Posted to formerly
Egba	Elder brother's son (classific.)	Gbara	Kpatagban (right bank)
Sonfara	Son	Lives in Muregi, no emissaryship	(A newly introduced rank)
Kofiē	Younger brother (classific.)	Raba	Raba
Ekpā	Younger brother (classific.)	Kpacefu	—
Tswadiya	Younger brother	Ketsogi	Ketsogi
Lefiti	Younger brother of *Egba*	Muregi, no emissaryship	Kpacefu
Liman Gyedwa	Distant relation	,,	Kpasha (right bank)
Tswadyagi	,,	,,	Kpasha

[1] Factional splits of this kind were occasionally utilized and fostered by outside Powers. Thus the Royal Niger Company supported an *Egba* in whom they found a valuable ally against the ruling *Kuta*, promising the former the chieftainship in return for the support of his faction. And once or twice the Emirs of Nupe backed the rival claimant of Kede chieftainship against the 'official' candidate.

Rank	Relation to Kuta	Posted to at present	Posted to formerly
Sodi	Younger brother	Katcha (unofficially)	Muregi, no emissaryship
Sheshi Kuta	Household-rank	Katcha	Eggan (right bank)
Tsowa Kuta	,,	Muregi, no emissaryship	Egbagi (right bank)
Capa Kuta	,,	,,	Wunangi
Mijindadi Kuta	,,	Jebba	Buka

The list shows that the assignment of posts to political ranks has undergone certain changes. They were due partly to the re-alignment of modern administrative divisions, which placed some of the former Kede areas outside of present-day Kede country (e.g. the Kede settlements on the right bank of the Niger). But partly also to changes in the economic and political importance of certain places and the corresponding change in their official 'appreciation'. Jebba and Katcha are illuminating examples. In Jebba we find a man of comparatively low rank in charge of the Kede community. He was posted there when Jebba was only just beginning to become the important place it is to-day. The *Mijindadi* is to-day a very old man, almost blind, and only nominally in charge of the 'colony'; he is generally expected to be succeeded by a high rank-holder whose rank would do justice to the importance of present-day Jebba. Katcha is, officially, in charge of the *Sheshi Kuta*, another 'household' rank; he is, however, unofficially assisted in his work by the *Sodi*, a relation of the *Kuta*, who also lives in Katcha and, in fact, only waits till this important Kede community will be handed to him as to the more suitable representative of the *Kuta*.

The dominion of the delegate varies in extent and composition. His district (especially if he resides in one of the twin-villages) may comprise both tribal groups, Kede and non-Kede; or the boundary of his dominion may be drawn round the Kede settlement, while the 'native' village (which would be some distance from the Kede settlement or on the bank if the latter is on an island) belongs to the country and political district inland. In either case, the dominion of the Kede delegate would stretch some way up and down the river, comprising hamlets and villages on (formerly) both banks. The 'native' villagers live under their own chief and elders, and are on the whole left to themselves, except for the political obligations towards the Kede rulers. In the carrying out of these obligations (to be examined presently), village chief and elders become mere subordinates of the Kede government. The Kede families, on the other hand, which live in the district of the delegate are his subjects in a different sense. They too have their obligations towards the government which he represents. But they share to some extent his privileged official position *vis-à-vis* the 'natives' of the country. The family heads of these Kede families assume certain titles in Nupe fashion, which are to mark them as 'elders' of their community. In this case, however, these are not the usual village ranks, nor are they *tici nya Kuta* ('ranks of the *Kuta*'), but are of the order of personal or 'household' ranks, which the Kede delegate may confer upon the family heads in 'his' town.

The official duties of the delegate relate to the three main concerns of Kede administration. He is charged with the collection of taxes on behalf of the Kede chief, the maintenance of law and order in the districts, and he finally acts as the agent of the chief in all matters requiring concerted action of the tribe as a whole. The first two duties have undergone but comparatively minor changes under modern administration. The last duty, the most important aspect of which used to be contribution to the fighting expeditions of the tribe, is reduced to-day to such relatively irrelevant activities as the arrangement of the periodical tours of inspection through Kede country of the Kede chief or the District Officer.

Taxation. The present system of taxation is based on an income tax on sliding scale, assessed among the Kede on the basis of the number of canoes owned. The tax is collected locally by the official Village Head, and is then transmitted by the District Head to the Native Administration Treasury in Bida. For Kede District read *delegate* for Village Head (a certain number of Kede 'delegates' having been made Village Heads under the Native Administration), and *Kuta* for District Head—in all other respects taxation among the Kede is the same as in the inland districts of the Emirate. This was not so in pre-British times. The *kintsoʒi* villages, like the other inland villages of Nupe, paid a certain annual money tax, assessed per village, which was collected by the *Kuta* and his delegates on behalf of the King of Nupe. The tax which the Kede themselves paid, on the other hand, was of two kinds: first, there was the tax proper, paid locally; at the village to which one belongs. It was an income tax in the modern sense, consisting in a percentage of the money income of every canoe-owner (i.e. profits from trade and transport). Second, there was the *albarka* (lit. 'blessing'), a tribute voluntary but in name, which canoe-owners were expected to pay to the delegates at whose place they were stopping and doing business. The tribute varied in amount: in Jebba it amounted to a 10 per cent., in Muregi to a 20 per cent. duty on all goods bought and sold. Failure to pay meant forfeiting the permission to call and trade in the district. The delegate returned to the *Kuta* half of his revenue from the tax proper, and one-fifth of the revenue from the *albarka*. The *Kuta*, in turn, handed about one-fifth of his total tax revenue (including tax on his private trade and canoe profits) to the *Etsu* in Bida.

Jurisdiction. The modern system provides for a professional Mohammedan judge (*Alkali*), who holds court in Muregi, and to whom all legal cases from the district have to be submitted. Native Administration police assist him on the executive side. The courts in the capital, Bida, are higher courts and courts of appeal for Kede as for all other districts of the Emirate. Under the new system, chief and delegate are allowed no judicial and only a limited executive authority.

In pre-British Nupe the maintenance of law and order devolved in different degree upon all existing political authorities, the local delegate, the Kede chief, and the Emir of Nupe, in accordance with the nature of the offence. The local delegate could only deal with very minor offences of the kind which involves no restitution and only domestic punishment, if any. All other aspects of public security were regarded as being of direct concern to the State—Kede or Nupe. Even the smallest theft came before the *Kuta* in Muregi; adultery, litigation about bride-price or inheritance similarly fell under his jurisdiction. Certain major crimes, on the other hand, were under the jurisdiction of the King of Nupe himself. The list of these 'crimes of the king' (as they are still called) comprises: highway robbery (including robbery on the river highways of the country), homicide, seduction, and the crime *lèse majesté* ('abuse of the king', in Nupe phraseology). In securing a criminal, the *Kuta's* own men would act as a police force; if the crime came under the heading of a 'king's crime' the same police force would take the prisoner to the capital, where judgement would then be passed upon him by the king and his councillors.

We can say that with the exception of offences against kinship rules (e.g. the incest taboo) and offences against religious rules— the various religious rules of the *kintsozi* which were of no concern to the Kede rulers—no serious breach of established rules of conduct was left to private settlement or to the informal sanctions of 'public opinion'. The comprehensiveness of the claims of the Kede State to enforce conduct within its boundaries must yet admit of one significant limitation: the Kede must surrender jurisdiction over certain major crimes committed in their territory to their overlords; they must, in other words, agree to a limitation of their autonomy in the interest of the Emirate at large. We shall presently encounter another aspect of the maintenance of 'law and order' in which the prerogative of the Kede chief must give way to that of the central government of the country, yet in which the relation between the two is, in the very nature of things, much less clearly defined: the territorial rights of the various subject groups which are united under Nupe rule.

Territorial Rights. The Kede, as the overlords of the *kintsozi*, guarantee to their own subject groups certain corporate territorial rights. The semi-riverain *kintsozi*, as we have seen, derive their livelihood to a large extent from fishing in the backwaters and creeks of the River Niger. The fishing rights of the different *kintsozi* villages were upheld by the Kede rulers and enforced if need arose by the full military power at their disposal. Nupe kingdom equally guaranteed corporate territorial rights to its various subject groups. The Kede, as one of these subject groups, enjoyed these territorial rights with respect to their undisturbed possession of the whole riverain area.

But the presence of a strong and expanding group like the Kede in the political framework of the Nupe State must invite conflicts over the territorial rights of other subject groups of Nupe which are neighbours of the Kede in the river area. As the more recent history of Nupe shows, conflicts of this kind have frequently arisen. Their occurrence or avoidance is clearly bound up with the interpretation put on Kede political autonomy—a point which we will discuss under a separate heading.

VI. The Claim to Autonomy

Let me say, first, that the administration of Kede country presents an exact analogy to the administration of Nupe kingdom. Emissaries from the capital, delegates recruited from the ruling house, are in charge of the administrative districts of the Emirate as they are of the district of Kede country. This analogy reflects the analogous political evolution in both countries: the rise to power of a small group over a large country with heterogeneous population. The only exception from this rule of administering the districts of the Emirate through royal delegates is Kede country itself, which remained under its own chief, who acted as the representative of the *Etsu* Nupe. Even for this exception there is a parallel to be found in Kede organization: the emissary system did not apply to the area of the upper-stream Kede. Their whole area was regarded as one sub-district of Kede country and was placed in charge, not of an emissary from Muregi, but of one of their own chiefs, the village chief of Bele, their southernmost settlement. The explanation for this privileged position of the two groups, the Kede *Tifin* under Kede and the Kede under Nupe, is most probably the same—namely, that their rulers would have found it difficult to control themselves effectively the territory of these subject communities: the Kede the country of the upper-stream group, which was not easy to reach with their big canoes (note that they made the chief in the place farthest down-stream the 'deputy' for the whole group), and the Nupe kings the whole river area.

To the down-stream Kede their autonomous position in Nupe Emirate is a sacred trust, dating back to their first chief who received, with the chieftainship of Kede, the 'Rule over the Water' from the mythical Tsoede. The Kede chiefs still style themselves *Etsu nya nuwã* ('King of the Water'), and, as their history shows, have always taken this title very literally. It meant to them more than merely the formal concession of assigning to a Kede chief duties normally discharged by a royal delegate, and they have in the past frequently attempted to acquire a larger measure of independence in taxation, jurisdiction, and political management in general.[1]

In this connexion, we must point out an important development in the history of Nupe kingdom, which in turn greatly affected Kede history. The royal dynasty of Nupe, which traced its origin back to the mythical Tsoede, was in power till the earlier half of last century, when Nupe kingdom, like most of the Native states in Northern Nigeria, fell under the rule of Emirs of Fulani stock who had conquered the country and deposed the indigenous kings. We have no data on the relation between Kede autonomy and the Nupe State under the old dynasty. But it is certain that under Fulani rule conflicts constantly arose, partly perhaps because the Kede (like many other Nupe sections) resented the alien rule, but to a large extent certainly because the Fulani kings, much more than the Nupe rulers before them, had to curb in their own interest the autonomous leanings of their Kede vassals. The Fulani, whose wars at that time were directed chiefly against tribes in the south, could not afford to let an all too independent section control the river—the southern boundary and at the same time the vital artery of trade and traffic of the country. Slave trade, the economic mainstay of the pre-British rulers of central Nigeria, traffic in arms and powder, and troop transports for their military expeditions, all had to cross the River Niger on Kede territory.[2] The Fulani overlords enforced their sovereignty in a number of wars and punitive expeditions, in the course of which (if the reports are true) hundreds were killed, thousands of Kede sold as slaves by the victorious Fulani, Kede notables executed in Bida, and whole districts of Kede country devastated. A typical instance is the Katcha War—the answer of the Fulani to the first attempt of

[1] There exists certain evidence to show that the Kede chiefs succeeded in enlarging their judicial power at the cost of their overlords and usurped a certain judicial machinery of the Nupe State which had evolved in the river area. To-day, at any rate, the Kede claim that this judicial machinery was under the authority of the *Kuta*, while other, non-Kede, informants state that it represented entirely a prerogative of the kings of Nupe. I am referring to the *Ledu* (lit. prison) villages on the banks of the Niger, which were so called because they served as prisons and places of execution for criminals convicted, by the king's court, of a 'crime of the king'. I have described this system and the attempts of the Kede to claim it as their own in *Man* (1935), 143.

[2] The importance, for example, of Raba as a river port for slave traffic to the south is pointed out by Lander (*Journal of an Expedition* (1832), ii, p. 298). Laird and Oldfield speak of 600 Kede canoes, 'all of which may be employed for Ful troops to cross the Niger on war expeditions' (op. cit., ii, p. 315).

the Kede to force the tributary of the Niger on which Katcha is situated and to occupy the town. The people of Katcha, under allegiance to Bida, claimed protection for their territorial rights from the central government. The Kede were routed by a Fulani army, and the political rights of the Katcha people restored.[1]

The feud between the Kede and the Emirs of Bida, and, above all, the strategic position in the defence of the kingdom which the river tribe occupied, was utilized in the Royal Niger Company campaign against Bida in 1897. With promises of political autonomy to the tribe and the chieftainship to the ambitious nephew of the ruling *Kuta*, Sir William Wallace, the commanding officer of the Niger Company troops, secured the support of the Kede. Their canoe fleet was placed under the command of a gunboat and massed on the river south of Bida; with their help, the relieving force of the Nupe, which at the time was engaged in a war in the south, was cut off and Bida captured. The Kede received the promised reward and were granted semi-autonomy, being made responsible directly to the British Administration instead of to their former overlords, the Emirs of Bida.

The political status of the Kede was later changed again. The *Kuta* lost a considerable portion of his territory when the new provinces and divisions were mapped out (1900–1905). At the same time, his autonomous position was curtailed, and Kede country placed again under Bida. A last element of autonomy is preserved in the regulation that the District Headship of Kede District should remain vested in the Kede chief.

The adoption of this curtailed autonomy for the purposes of modern government has not been an unqualified success. Administrative officers have had cause to complain of the declining authority of the Kede chief. The more evident supports of Kede chieftainship—the dynastic title, the privileged economic position of the chief (a comparatively high salary having taken the place of the former share in taxes and tributes), and his control over the officials of his State—have not been affected so fundamentally

[1] This first attempt was carried out in the early days of the Royal Niger Company. The second, successful, attempt of the Kede to gain a foothold in the Katcha River was carried out under an administration favourably disposed towards Kede expansion, and led to the peaceful occupation of the riverside at Katcha mentioned previously. This 'peaceful penetration', however, is hardly less resented by the Katcha people, who have lost through it their formerly undisturbed fishing grounds.

by the political changes as to account for the decline of chiefly authority. What has changed is rather the spiritual background, the conception, of Kede autonomous chieftainship. It has lost its place in the scheme of Kede political life, which is still growth and expansion. It has been shorn of the qualities of self-responsible and exclusive leadership, which, in this dynamic society, constituted the *raison d'être* of its once absolute power. What remains of the leadership vested in the Kede chief is a leadership moving in the narrow circle of modern administrative boundaries and under the patronage of another, higher, authority. It had to surrender its prerogative of guiding and protecting the movements of the group as they followed, farther and farther afield, the lead of the general economic and cultural development of the country.

This change in the whole political existence of the Kede is most conspicuous in the Kede groups which now lie outside Bida Emirate and the area ruled over by the *Kuta*. Here the liquidation of Kede autonomy could not have been effected without disturbing consequences had Kede chieftainship still held its old meaning. Sentimental bonds between the split-off groups and the mother-country are still conspicuous; but on the whole I have gained the impression that these groups do not (or no longer) seriously miss or resent the separation, or contemplate the possibility of some future reunion. The weakened appeal of political autonomy reflects the general development, political and cultural, that has overtaken the country and separated autonomy from its vital counterparts in social life: economic and cultural unity, and the solidarity of community life. To put it differently: cultural self-realization has become possible outside the narrow political boundaries. I shall have to return to this point; but let me mention here a certain proof of the statement just made—namely, the continued, and even increasing, emigration to those distant Kede settlements which could under no circumstances be anything else but 'minorities' under alien rule.

VII. Social Stratification

The division of political rights and duties in Kede country and, implied in it, the unequal economic advantage enjoyed by the different sections of the population constitute the basis of a rigid social stratification. Ethnic and cultural differences add their weight to it in that they coincide with, and are interpreted in the sense of, distinctions implying social gradation.

On the top of the social structure, we have the hereditary ruling class formed by the chief's family group, and below it the second stratum, which comprises the Kede of common status. Though the latter exercise no direct influence upon the policy of the State, they can yet in certain respects range themselves beside the ruling class: if the members of the ruling class decide the fate of the country and derive the main benefits from all political exploits, war or peaceful acquisition of territory—the Kede commoners take an active part in all activities on a tribal scale, even bearing the brunt in the most significant activity, colonization, and benefit to a considerable extent from the political successes of their rulers. Indirectly, by attaching themselves in subservient position to the households and factions of the ruling class, they attain a larger measure of political influence and certain economic advantages not warranted by their hereditary status. Moreover, their racial and cultural affinity with the class above, and the proportionate remoteness from the lowest class beneath, place the Kede commoners on one plane with the ruling group of the country. The lowest stratum comprises the 'original inhabitants', whom tradition paints as having been the subjects of the Kede from mythical times and having had no culture worth mentioning before the advent of the Kede. In fact, they are still, seen with Kede eyes, a 'primitive' and slightly contemptible group; they fail by the cultural standards which the Kede recognize, being pagans, inferior canoemen, and relatively poor. They were excluded from the tribal activities of the Kede and all benefits accruing from them; yet they suffered more than the other groups from the failures of their rulers' policy, unsuccessful wars or revolts, for their country might become the battle-field and their farms and villages be destroyed, while, unlike the ruling classes, they had no reward to expect in the event of success.

The question arises by what machinery the Kede maintained this rigid division into hereditary classes, kept intact the solidarity of their small minority, yet were able at the same time to integrate and bind to loyalty the heterogeneous sections of their State.[1] Our

---

[1] The strong bond of loyalty that existed between the Kede and their subject groups is illustrated in the historical fact that in the Katcha War certain *kintsoʒi* groups fought on the side of the Kede against the Emir of Bida.

examination of the political organization has revealed one such machinery: the machinery of coercion. We must ask now how far other, non-political, forms of integration lend their support, or possibly are made to lend it, to political unification. We can distinguish three types of such supporting integrative agencies: (1) integration through actual co-operation between the sections of the population; (2) integration in the spiritual sphere—in other words, through ideologies teaching or preaching unity; (3) integration based on both. Instances of the first type are economic co-operation and community life, of the second, tradition and mythology, and of the third, religious practice.

VIII. Integrative Mechanisms

Economic Co-operation and Community Life. The propinquity of the Kede and *kintsoʒi* settlements, combined with the difference in their productive system, invites a certain measure of co-operation in the economic field. The Kede buy farm-produce from their peasant neighbours, who, in turn, use to some extent Kede transport to dispose of their surplus on the large river markets. This co-operation is by no means exclusive and does not lead to complete dependence upon each other. The peasants also sell some of their farm-produce inland or take their fish directly, on their own canoes, to riverside markets; similarly the Kede buy a certain amount of their food on the various outside markets which they visit on their river voyages.

In their community life, the two groups hardly achieve a more intensive, or less casual, co-operation. The difference in occupation and in the main interests of their lives is not balanced by any other strong ties. The young folk of the Kede and *kintsoʒi* frequently join in each other's dances; here and there friendships are struck between individuals from the two groups. But apart from these contacts the two sections keep to themselves. The age-grade associations do not stretch across the tribal boundary and, above all, there is almost no inter-marriage: the *kintsoʒi* arrange their marriages with their tribal relations inland, and the Kede marry among themselves.[1] In these marriages between Kede villages distance plays no part, which is rather significant, for the (inland) Nupe generally dislike marriages between distant places.

---

[1] This is true of all the older Kede settlements; in the more recent settlements (e.g. Katcha) I found a few cases of inter-marriage with the *kintsoʒi*.

The various Kede groups are thus all related, not only, rather vaguely, by common descent, being all emigrants of common stock, but also very concretely, by repeated inter-marriage. Personal contact between fellow tribesmen, friends, and relations among the Kede, whatever the distance of their habitations, is maintained by occasional visits, and revived regularly every trading season, when the Kede canoes travel from place to place. Finally, the solidarity of the Kede community is strengthened periodically, when new groups of immigrants come out from 'home' to join fellow tribesmen who have emigrated earlier in their 'colony'.

Tradition and Mythology. The Kede share their traditions with their mother tribe, and, like the Nupe, trace their origin back to the mythical Tsoede or Edegi, of whom we have heard already (see p. 175). This Tsoede is said to have been a Nupe man who lived about 1400, and who was sent as slave to Idah, to which country Nupe was tributary at that time. He won the favour of the King of Idah, so much so that he evoked the jealousy of the sons of the king, and eventually had to flee the country. He set out in a bronze canoe, loaded with gifts from the king and manned by other Nupe slaves, to return to his country and to make himself king there, the rule of Nupe having been the King of Idah's parting gift to his favourite. On his flight to Nupe, Tsoede was helped by two men whom he met on the river—one sitting on a stone in midstream (*kuta*),[1] and one fishing with a fish trap (*ɛkpā*). When Tsoede established himself as King of Nupe he rewarded these two men by making them chief over the whole river and its tribes (*Kuta*), and a high rank-holder in the new river State (*Ekpā*), respectively.[2] These men were the ancestors of the present Kede, and the first to exercise the 'Rule over the Water', which has remained in the possession of the Kede since.

It clearly does not come within the compass of the present study to examine how far these legendary data might contain a kernel of historical truth. Their importance to us lies rather in the sociological significance of the 'truth' which they announce—that

[1] *Kuta*, stone, seems to be an old form of Nupe; it occurs in two obsolete Nupe dialects, and also in Gbari, a related language. The modern Nupe word for stone is *takū* (the syllables of *kuta* reversed).

[2] The Nupe are very fond of such puns. There exists another version of this legend which derives the title *Kuta* from the fact that the man on the stone was wearing two gowns 'on top of each other'—in Nupe, *ku ta doʒi*.

is, in the influence upon actual social life which the belief in this
'truth' entails. The Kede tradition of origin, as we have seen,
concerns itself above all with the beginnings of the political history
of the tribe. In the fashion of such myths of origin, it anchors
the existing system in a dim past, which, by its very remoteness
and its supernatural and sacred associations, endows the present
with an immensely convincing validity. The Kede tradition of
origin ranges its strongest spiritual support behind what we now
recognize to be the two fundamental features of their political
system: the fact that the extent of Kede rule is defined on the
basis of locality, and not tribe, and the fact that, within the larger
political unit of Nupe kingdom, the Kede claim a semi-autonomous
position. Let me emphasize that the knowledge of this tradition
is not limited to the Kede, but is common to all Nupe sections,
and among them the various *kintsoʒi* groups. The common
possession of the myth represents a spiritual link of utmost
importance: for with the myth the subjects of the Kede also
accept the system which it is meant to guarantee—the overlordship
of the Kede.

Religion. As I have mentioned, the Kede are to-day Mohammedans—very eager Mohammedans, in fact. In many settlements
you will find *mallams* teaching the Koran to boys and adults, often
pupils who are able to attend the classes only when their travels
happen to take them to this place and allow them a short sojourn.
The *kintsoʒi*, on the other hand, are still largely pagans. Moreover, against the solid religious unity of the Kede, the *kintsoʒi*
show a certain diversity of religious rites and beliefs, which reflects
the composite nature of this group.[1] However, there exist two
rituals, both essentially river rituals, which are common to all the
semi-riverain groups, and a third ritual, linked with the memory
of Tsoede, which exists in all the larger riverain (and partly also
inland) villages of Nupe. The first of these rituals is the *Ndáduma*
(the Nupe name for the River Niger), an annual sacrifice to the
spirits of the river, performed in all the different river villages

[1] We cannot say what the religious situation in the river valley has been in
the earlier periods of Nupe history. The probability is that the Kede, as most
Nupe sub-tribes, possessed certain special rites and beliefs, which were not
shared by the other tribal groups. The characteristic difference between Kede
and *kintsoʒi* to-day, between a solid religious unit on one side and a heterogeneous religious group on the other, would thus have been equally marked
in the pre-Islamic era.

and believed to procure, and at the same time to keep within limits, the annual flooding of the Niger. The second ritual is the *Ketsá*, a sacrifice to the spirit of the huge rock of the same name which rises abruptly from midstream near Jebba (known to Europeans as Juju-rock); this sacrifice is believed to cure illness and barrenness and to secure luck in fishing or trade. The third ritual is the sacrifice to the *Chain of Tsoede*, a sacred relic which secures fertility, prevents illness, and is also used as an instrument of ordeal.

Now, these three rituals also occur among the Kede; the first two have in fact been, as it were, usurped by them, and made to some extent their own concern. The Kede chief holds himself responsible for certain special, most conspicuous, performances of these river ceremonies. Once a year a special *Ndáduma* is performed in a place called Bazumagi, north of Jebba, the *Kuta* himself providing the sacrificial food, a white bull and honey. Unlike the local *Ndáduma* rituals, the *Ndáduma* of Bazumagi is enacted on behalf, not of a particular village, but of the whole population of the river valley. The chief's *Ndáduma* also shows another feature which is absent in the local rite: the priest climbs a rock in midstream and throws a stone towards the bank; the spot where the stone falls is believed to mark the line to which the river will rise that year. The *Ketsá* becomes a chief's ritual at the appointment of a new *Kuta*. About one month after his accession the new chief sends a bull (preferably white) to Jebba Island to be sacrificed there by the local priest, again on behalf of the whole riverain community, to inaugurate and secure a prosperous reign. A special *Chain of Tsoede* finally is kept in Muregi, in the house of one of the chief's councillors (see p. 176). He performs the annual sacrifice of beer and the blood of a sheep, beer and animal being again provided by the *Kuta* himself.

It is interesting to note that in none of these rituals may the *Kuta* or any member of his family be present. Thus the double nature of these rites, which, though stamped chief's rituals, are essentially rituals of the *kintsozi*, is conspicuously symbolized. The interests which they voice—the securing of safety and livelihood to the people on the river—are adopted and made their own by the Kede rulers. A single belief and a common cult comprise both rulers and ruled, notwithstanding the religious barriers which otherwise separate the two, and add to the political dependence of the *kintsozi* another, spiritual, dependence.

Conclusions. We may say then, in conclusion, that economic co-operation and community life only underline the political and tribal divisions which cut across Kede society. As integrative forces which could foster a solidarity pertaining to the political system at large, they fail. Only the ideological influences, myth and religion, succeed in this. They anchor the external political unit in more deeply rooted interests and sentiments. They add to political coercion the more subtle persuasion of supernatural arguments, of beliefs in the necessity and fore-ordination of the existing system.

I have been using the present tense with some liberty. It was applied correctly if we are thinking of the last ten or fifteen years, but inaccurately if we consider the immediate present and, above all, the future. The rite of the *Chain of Tsoede* is still performed annually, in completely Mohammedanized Muregi. The bull sacrifice at the *Ketsá* was performed when the present *Kuta* succeeded to the chieftainship; whether it will be repeated for his successor is open to doubt. The *Ndáduma*, at any rate, although still existing as a local rite, is no longer carried out by the Kede chief. We have spoken before of the decline of authority of the Kede chief. It may seem surprising that a chieftainship which had been forced to give up most of the qualities from which it formerly drew its strength should so easily discard these 'binding forces' of religion. The explanation lies, again, in the changed conception of Kede chieftainship. Kede rule has exchanged its dynamic and expanding nature for the secure, aquiescent authority under the Pax Britannica. It can dispense with the binding forces of religion, which used to uphold the autocratic rulership of a small minority; it can, above all, afford to discontinue a practice which, to the Mohammedan chiefs of Kede country, appears as a concession to their less enlightened subjects. Kede rule has thus paradoxically weakened itself in its new-found security. And in this the chiefs of Kede do not stand alone; this paradox is, I believe, a not uncommon feature of modern, static, Government-backed chieftainship in Africa.

The incipient dissolution of the 'binding force' of religion in the Kede State is only following in the wake of the general dissolution of the solidarity which it was meant to uphold. The economic development of the country led, as we have seen, to an extensive co-operation with outside groups and to the founding of colonies in areas to which political rule could never be expected to follow. Common interests and culture, community life, intermarriage stretch as far as these outposts. Moreover, cultural assimilation and intensified contact have removed some of the barriers which formerly separated the Kede from neighbouring groups. The facts of common culture, economic co-operation, and community life thus no longer converge to cement the solidarity of a ruling group, but merely outline the much vaguer unit of a scattered ethnic group which has abandoned all claims to political self-realization.

IX. The Evolution of the Kede State

Our examination of the Kede State and its history does neither support nor refute the theory of the origin of the State which, accepted to-day by many students of society, derives every State organization from an original invasion and eventual conquest of one ethnic group by another.[1] Our data have shown political domination of one ethnic group by another to be a factor of paramount importance; they also revealed the occurrence of clash and conquest—though not on the comprehensive scale implied in this theory of the State; but they do not prove an original group invasion, beyond that which we must relegate to the era of mythical and thus unverifiable events. Our data can, in fact, also be taken as evidence for an 'internal diversification'[2] and a gradual emergence to political supremacy of one out of a number of ethnic groups.

Our data relating to Kede expansion in recent times, on the other hand, tend to confirm another sociological theory which concerns itself with social origins—namely, the theory which holds that migration and colonization are never a result of over-population, but rather an expression of that 'spirit of hope' and 'enterprise' which is absent in countries with over-population.[3] Can we accept this description of the growing Kede society as a final statement? Is the emergence of a tribal section to a dominant political role fully explained by this reference to psychological characteristics?

Our analysis of Kede political organization has emphasized a somewhat different aspect; it outlined the political system in its

[1] See F. Oppenheimer, op. cit.
[2] R. Lowie, op. cit., p. 40.
[3] A. M. Carr-Saunders, *The Population Problem* (1922), pp. 299 n.

dependence on economic factors and, tied up with them, environmental conditions. The impetus to colonization and expansion, as we saw it, was already implied in the way in which the people gain their livelihood. We can render this argument even more conclusive; the cultural situation in the river valley itself offers us the comparative material from which to draw our deductions. We remember the upper-stream Kede, who, neighbours, fellow tribesmen and in many details of culture close relations of the down-stream Kede, yet do not share their political achievements—and also do not share their productive system and economic life in general. We can even go further and point to the environmental factors on which the economic system of the Kede in turn depends. The environment in which the upper-stream Kede live indeed forbids a development of river trade and traffic similar to that evolved by the sister group. The river in their area is narrow, barred in several places by rapids and rocky, frequently dangerous, passages, and generally impassable during half the year. On its banks there are few settlements, and the hinterland is thinly populated, inhabited largely by comparatively poor and backward groups. Hold against this the down-stream country: a broad river, navigable all the year round, the banks covered with numerous villages and the hinterland a rich, populous country with highly developed trades and crafts.

It will have been seen that I am speaking here of environment in a rather wide sense, including, beside the physical constellation of the country, also such factors as distribution of population and the existence of a certain type of civilization. Methodologically, these facts stand in the same category as physical environment proper. True, they are essentially historical facts, representing the results of various historical developments. These developments themselves, however, are beyond our line of vision; their results—the fact that the Kede area happens to lie in the centre of a rich and powerful kingdom—are to us 'unique events' in the phraseology of the historian, extraneous factors of chance, which, like environmental facts, we have to accept as ultimate data.

Let me admit that this causal chain, environmental conditions—economic enterprise—political system, is not fully conclusive. It is weakened by another aspect of our comparative evidence—namely, the fact that the *kintsoʒi*, who are also close neighbours and tribal relations of the down-stream Kede, and who share with them the same 'stimulating' environment, appear to have remained unresponsive to it. I have no explanation to give. Does this mean, then, that we have to fall back on the psychological interpretation of the kind quoted above?

But the environmental and economic 'determinism' which these conclusions have put forward was not meant to exclude completely the contribution of psychological factors—that is, the social motive power that may lie in the temperamental and general psychological dispositions typical of a group. Nor was it intended to minimize the decisive part that enterprising and far-seeing individuals must have played in the creation of the Kede State. The river colonization was undoubtedly the work of a people fully deserving the attributes 'adventurous', 'courageous', or 'possessed of a spirit of enterprise'; it must also have been closely bound up with the leadership of certain outstanding individuals: think of the man who was responsible for the Kede throwing in their lot with the British, or the Kede chiefs who so successfully utilized the encouragement of the Niger Company for the expansion of their country. But two facts must be borne in mind when defending this psychological and 'individualistic' theory of social origins. First, the psychological characteristics which might be made responsible for the achievements of the group are not *racially* determined (i.e. by heredity)—the dissimilar social system of the upper-stream Kede proves this to the full; they remain an expression of, and a perfect adjustment to, environmental conditions. And, second, these psychological characteristics do not reflect the effectiveness of some spontaneous, as it were, self-contained, psychological force, but are fostered and formed planfully by the existing social system and its cultural demands, to which the individuals, generation after generation, learn to adjust themselves. How much in the gradual social development of the Kede State was due to the selective effects of environment, and how much to the spontaneous actions of exceptionally gifted individuals who, at one point of Kede history, may have shown their people a new way of life, is one of these questions of social origins to which, again, we have no answer.

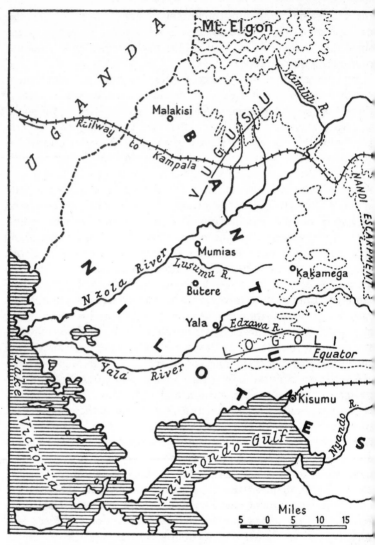

SKETCH MAP OF KAVIRONDO

THE POLITICAL ORGANIZATION OF THE BANTU OF KAVIRONDO

By Günter Wagner

I. Introductory

THIS essay proposes to deal with the political organization of two tribes living in the westernmost part of Kenya, the Logoli and Vugusu, which, together with a number of others, are usually referred to as the 'Bantu Kavirondo'. The tribes grouped under this name are politically quite independent, though culturally and linguistically closely related with one another. They do not call themselves by a common name. The name Kavirondo, although its origin and etymology are not entirely clear, was apparently given to them by Arab and Swahili traders.[1] It refers to the rolling, open plains that extend, broken by the Nyando Valley, from Mt. Elgon in the north to the Kenya-Tanganyika boundary in the south, as well as to the various Bantu and Nilotic tribes inhabiting these plains.

Migratory accounts and minor differences in language and custom make it possible to distinguish several larger divisions among the 'Bantu Kavirondo', each comprising a number of tribal groups.[2] Such a larger division has no common name either, but the tribal groups of which it is composed are conscious of their similarities and explain them either by a vague relationship in the distant past or by a long period of neighbourliness and intermarriage. Between tribes belonging to different divisions of this kind a more or less permanent state of warfare, broken by seasonal periods of truce, was the rule. There is no record, however, of combined warfare of one group of tribes against another. War

---

[1] cf. Johnston, Sir Harry, *The Uganda Protectorate* (London, 1902), vol. ii, p. 722 f.

[2] Two such larger groupings are (1) the Kitosh group, comprising the Vugusu of South Kitosh and Kimilili, the Tadjoni and some small groups of Nilo-Hamitic origin, such as the Ngoma (Ngomanek) and Lagu (El Bawgek), and (2) the Wanga group, comprising the Wanga proper, the Marama, and the Tsotso.

expeditions or raids were limited to the immediate neighbours, and tribes living more than twenty or thirty miles away were regarded as too remote to be either friends or foes.

The tribes immediately surrounding the 'Bantu Kavirondo', who are all of non-Bantu stock, lived in a constant state of war or tension with the Bantu. The Nilo-hamitic tribes to the east of Kavirondo,[1] who are predominantly pastoral, attacked the Kavirondo mainly for the purpose of raiding their cattle. The Teso and Luo in the west were bent on the conquest of territory and, as far as place-names and tribal traditions reveal, have gradually pushed the Bantu tribes eastwards. Their successive fronts of retreat run, generally speaking, parallel to the present Kenya-Uganda boundary. The pressure exercised by surrounding tribes upon the 'Bantu Kavirondo' does not, however, seem to have been excessive, for, in spite of their great similarity in language and culture, it did not weld them into a political and military unit. It may even be that their eastward retreat was at times and in some areas voluntary, as their present territory is at least as fertile and more healthy than the country from which they have moved.

In none of the approximately twenty tribal groups which make up the 300,000 Bantu of Kavirondo has political integration reached a very high degree, but it differs sufficiently in the various tribes to make generalizations from conditions in one area impossible. The following analysis, therefore, claims to apply to the two sub-tribes only of which a detailed study has been made, viz. the Logoli in the south and the Vugusu in the north. Both tribes have neighbours of non-Bantu stock along part of their boundary: the Logoli the Nilotic Jaluo and the Nyangori, a Nandi-speaking group, and the Vugusu the Teso, the El Kony, an offshoot of the Nandi living on the lower slopes of Mt. Elgon, and the Uasin-Gishu Masai, who frequently raided their country. In defence against these raids, the Vugusu lived in walled villages, the construction and maintenance of which demanded the co-operation of a large number of people, while the Logoli, like most of the other tribes, lived in isolated homesteads that were scattered over the whole countryside. The Logoli, who at present number approximately 45,000, inhabit an exceedingly fertile and well-watered stretch of country which permits of a very dense population. The Vugusu number about 40,000, but are dispersed over

[1] The Nandi, Uasin-Gishu Masai, and El Kony.

a less fertile, grassy plain, about seven times the size of the area occupied by the Logoli.[1] Like all Bantu Kavirondo, both tribes are mixed pastoral-agricultural. They practise hoe-culture to a fairly even extent, but while the Logoli own two or three head of cattle only per family, the average among the Vugusu is nine head per family, and individual herds of sixty to eighty head are not exceptional among them.

II. Definition of the Political Unit

The logical starting-point of any study of political organization is the demarcation of the political unit as the group and area of reference. In so far as the concept of the political unit involves the notions of power and authority, it would have to be defined as constituting that group of people which submits persistently and in an organized manner to leadership for the purpose of maintaining itself as a unit. It is thereby distinguished from other groups over which it exercises no authority and in contrast to which it recognizes and promotes its own unity. It may or may not maintain relationships with such other groups, and these relationships may either be friendly or hostile, depending upon the preponderence of common or mutual or of conflicting interests between them. The political structure of the unit thus defined would consist of the system of political institutions which maintain the unit as an entity, protecting it against disintegration from within as well as against dangers threatening from without.

A demarcation of the political unit and an analysis of political structure on the basis of this definition meets with some difficulty in the case of the Bantu of Kavirondo. In tribal societies in which political integration has reached the level where a central authority—a chief, a tribal council, &c.—is recognized, the tribal group is a clearly defined political unit: Externally, in that the central authority or government regulates all political relations with foreign groups, and internally, in that it forms the highest authority with regard to the inner maintenance of the group as a body politic. Even where this authority is delegated to smaller groups, the tribal society still constitutes the only political

---

[1] The respective density per square mile is 391 among the Logoli (of South Maragoli) and 73 among the Vugusu (of North Kitosh or Kimilili district). Census of 1932.

unit as long as these smaller groups are subordinated to it, i.e. derive their authority from the central government. In the case of the Kavirondo tribes, however, no such definition of the political unit on the basis of internal and external sovereignty can be given. As regards submission to political leadership, the largest groups, both among the Logoli and the Vugusu, are the exogamous, patrilineal clans[1] or clan groupings, consisting of one larger and several smaller clans, but not the whole tribal society. The tribal unit is marked by the belief in the common descent of all clans from one remote tribal ancestor, Murogoli and Muvugusu respectively, and by the occupation of a continuous stretch of territory. In addition, there are numerous institutionalized forms of co-operation and interdependencies between the different clans of the tribal group which distinguish inter-clan relations from inter-tribal relations, but there is no tribal authority which over-rules clan authority, either in its dealings with foreign tribes or in the management of its internal affairs. In terms of the definition given above, the clan would thus have to be regarded as the only political unit.

A number of considerations, however, make it seem more adequate to widen the definition of the political unit so that it comprises the tribal unit rather than the clan. In the first place, the fact that clans are exogamous and that marriage is regulated in such a way that all clans of the tribal group inter-marry, establishes a close connexion between the clans. The kinship bonds, maintained between every member of the clan and his maternal kin as well as his affinal relations, are so numerous and so strong that they establish bonds between the clans which, as we shall see, are in many ways as binding as if there were a central authority overruling that of the clans. Furthermore, the cult of a common tribal ancestor, to whom the Logoli sacrifice on a tribal scale at regular intervals, and the performance of the circumcision rites on a tribal scale create a feeling of unity which serves as a sanction for close co-operation in all matters affecting the tribal group.

The concept of 'political structure', likewise, requires a wider definition than is customary to become applicable to Kavirondo

---

[1] The clan (*oluhia, luyia*) is named after its real or supposed founder and its members tend to form a territorial unit. The various characteristics of the clan are discussed later on in this chapter in their respective contexts.

society. There is no political structure as distinct from the kinship and social structure; that is, there exists no system of institutions that serve explicitly and exclusively the purpose of maintaining the tribal unit as a whole. To enable one to understand the organization of the tribal unit, the emphasis must, therefore, be shifted from the concept of the political institution to that of the political function. The assumption that each function in a culture must have its corresponding institution—religious, economic, political, &c.—would cut short an understanding of the way in which cultures are integrated into a body politic, the institutions of which are not yet clearly differentiated according to different aspects, but which serve many functions at the same time. Even in advanced communities where institutions are highly differentiated, they present only a visible superstructure, while their bases, the forces that sustain them, extend throughout the whole structure of society.

The political unit must thus be defined in terms of a consciousness of unity and interdependence rather than in terms of submission to a central authority. The tribe, as a political unit, is a group of internally and externally 'sovereign' clans, which are conscious of having sprung originally from a common ancestor and which are interconnected by the bonds of intermarriage as well as by common practices and beliefs in such a way that they consider themselves a unit in contrast to surrounding groups with whom they do not maintain such bonds. This tribal political unit does not necessarily act as a body in all its foreign relations, but it is merely the largest unit of people which feels as a unit and which—on certain occasions—acts as one.

The term 'political' will, accordingly, be used with reference to any form of socially sanctioned behaviour which, directly or indirectly, strengthens the unity of the tribal group, whether that be its primary purpose or not. An institution thus has political significance if it fulfils a political function, regardless of what other functions it may perform besides. The political structure, in this sense, is the sum total of all forms of sanctioned behaviour which serve, directly or indirectly, intendedly or not, to integrate the political unit.

We shall examine now where in the cultural life of the 'Bantu Kavirondo' this political structure resides.

H

III. The Internal Political Structure

From the point of view of political integration a clear distinction between the external and internal aspects of the political structure is hardly admissible, as both aspects are closely interdependent. External pressure or other stimuli affecting the political unit from without form the strongest incentive for internal unity and, vice versa, the external action of the group depends very largely upon the nature and degree of its internal cohesion. For the purposes of an analysis of political functions, however, a distinction between the external and internal governmental functions of the tribal unit must be made, as both have different situations to meet. The internal maintenance of the tribal society involves three major political or governmental functions: (1) the enactment of laws, (2) the maintenance of law and custom, involving both their perpetuation in periods where they are inoperative and their transmission to succeeding generations; and (3) the restoration of breaches of the law.

(1) *Enactment of Laws.* The general body of tribal norms is, in native opinion, as old as the tribe itself. There exists no historical or legendary account of a law-giver. Law and custom are believed to have been handed down from unknown times from ancestor to ancestor, and it appears to be the cumulative weight of ancestral authority which serves as the most general sanction for the observance of traditional norms.[1] Normally, the suggestion of questioning the validity of tribal norms is rejected both by motives of fear and of suspicion. Fear is felt that deviation from established norms will evoke punishment by the ancestral spirits. Such punishment is not thought to be limited to the action of the immediate ancestors from whom one normally has to fear unfriendly acts, but to consist in a general, although vaguely defined, displeasure of the spirit-world which might have disastrous consequences of any kind. The suspicion of practising witchcraft is felt towards any person who deliberately and persistently defies established norms. If such a person cannot be brought back to reason by the

---

[1] Remarks such as: 'This is the rule since long ago which all our grandfathers followed', 'It has been ordered (*okulaga*) by our grandfathers (*avadada*)', or 'Our forefathers never did like that' are frequently made by the elders when discussing a case in the present-day tribal courts.

performance of sacrifices, he is socially ostracized and, in an extreme case, killed.[1]

There is, accordingly, no recognized authority which wields legislative powers; law is, in theory at least, unchangeable, and the degree to which an action, a claim, or an obligation are in line with the age-honoured tradition is the only criterion of their merits.

Nevertheless, there are a number of legendary traditions and even historical data which indicate that the system of laws and customs was not as rigidly closed against changes and innovations as one is at first led to believe. Apart from norms observed throughout the tribal group, there are numerous clan rules which differ from clan to clan, but which, within each clan, are made valid by the same type of sanctions as tribal law. Most important among such clan rules are certain food taboos or rules of avoidance concerning certain forms of behaviour. While in many cases the origin of these rules is unknown, in others the time is still remembered when the rule was not yet in force, and the account given for its origin often bears the stamp of a true historical tradition. Thus among the Vugusu a certain clan refrains from wearing finger-rings of coiled iron wire. In explanation of this rule, it is said that some generations ago a member of that clan suffered from a sore and swollen finger caused by his ring, which gradually became worse until he died without having been able to remove the ring from his finger. Before his death, he is supposed to have said that 'it was a bad thing for the people of his clan to wear iron finger-rings, and that all who would do so in future should die as he was now going to die'.

Numerous ceremonial rules, especially details of ritual in connexion with sacrifices, purification rites, &c., which are observed by some clans but not by others have probably been enacted in the same way. Although neighbouring clans are aware of the existence of such sacrificial rules, it would not ordinarily occur to them to copy them 'as they were not theirs'. If, however, an exceptional situation arose, e.g. the repeated and conspicuous failure of the traditional ritual procedure to achieve its desired ends, a man would either tentatively vary the procedure or copy a ritual detail from a neighbouring clan or tribe. More probably

[1] This attitude differs from that adopted towards a person who breaks a particular norm for obvious purposes; cf. J. H. Driberg, 'Primitive Law in Eastern Africa', *Africa*, vol. i (1928), p. 66.

he would go to a diviner (*omufumu*), who, after consultation of
his various oracles, might suggest an entirely unconventional
procedure which, if successful, would set a precedent and thus
be gradually adopted by the whole clan. The fact that some types
of sorcery which were formerly restricted to certain tribes are now
recognized and 'detected' by the diviners of other areas and
counteracted by new devices, shows that there are some loop-
holes in the generally rigid convention.

A wider power to enact laws and customs and to induce people
to take an unprecedented course of action seems to have been
wielded by the dream prophet and by certain clan elders who had
gained a reputation as warriors and successful arbiters in disputes
and thus stood out as leaders among their age-mates. As far as
I could discover, no dream prophet (*omung'oli*) of any importance
is living in Kavirondo at present, but stories are told of men
who for years ahead predicted the coming of droughts, disastrous
raids, epidemics, and even the advent of the white man and of
the railway and motor car. When one of their predictions came
true, they gained, of course, in prestige, and their advice to
engage in unusual or refrain from customary actions was followed
by the whole tribe. A former prophet among the Vugusu is said
to have persuaded the whole tribe to migrate from its former
home in the Bugishu country to its present domicile. The Nyole,
a tribe that lives next to the Logoli, refrained from circumcision
for a few generations, paying heed to a curse uttered by a man
called Masava. His prohibition was observed for six age-classes
until, in the year 1917, the old men of several clans decided to
call the circumcision operator again. They performed a ceremony
at Masava's grave, neutralizing the curse (*xukavusia eminwa*), and
at first circumcised a few people only to see if they died. They
survived and nowadays circumcision is again performed by the
majority of Nyole clans.

Thus although there is a strong resistance to breaking away
from traditional norms and although there is no governmental
organ which possesses recognized legislative authority, law
and custom are by no means entirely rigid. Changes were
brought about either by the initiative of a strong personality
whose word carried much influence, as he had gradually gained
confidence by the display of courage and wisdom, or by the
example set by any ordinary tribesman if particular circumstances

or successive events justified his action. It appears that diviners and dream prophets whose advice was supposed to be the outcome of supernatural inspiration had more influence over their tribesmen than ordinary people.

(2) *The Continuity of Law and Custom.* Law and custom which in their totality make up tribal culture are not merely an inventory of rules of conduct, but a coherent system of relationships between individuals and groups. These relationships do not merely entail the observance of certain actions and the avoidance of others, but ideologies and values, mental and emotional attitudes as well. Thus 'family law', in the fuller sense of the word, comprises the totality of relationships, as expressed in actions and attitudes, that knit the members of the family together into a social unit, while the formulated 'laws'—such as regulate paternal authority, the rights and duties of husband and wife, inheritance and succession, &c.—demarcate the main lines and limits only along and within which these relationships work. The maintenance of law and custom is thus equivalent to the maintenance of effective relationships.[1]

The continuity in time or perpetuation of these relationships tends to be disrupted by two factors inherent in the conditions of social life. One of these is that most relationships and the institutions of which they form part operate, not continuously, but at certain occasions only. Between these occasions there may be long intervals during which the relationship remains latent. This is the more so the wider the group between the members of which a particular relationship exists. Clan solidarity, for instance, comes into operation only when challenged by the murder of a clan member or some similar occasion, but the specific type of relationship between the members of the clan on which this solidarity is based has to be permanently maintained, so that the law of solidarity may come into action whenever the need for its realization arises.

The other potentially disruptive factor is the coming and going of the generations. Matrimony, parenthood, kindred, clanship, &c., are permanent relationship patterns or institutions, but they

[1] cf. B. Malinowski, Introduction to H. I. Hogbin's *Law and Order in Polynesia*, pp. xxx–xxxv. The theoretical approach in this present study of the political organization of the 'Bantu Kavirondo' has been greatly stimulated by this and other writings of Malinowski (e.g. *Crime and Custom in Savage Society*), even where this is not particularly acknowledged.

derive their reality only from the fact that they are actually lived by human beings. The fact that individuals grow old, die, and are replaced by others involves the need for the transmission of law and custom, for the constant re-knitting of institutionalized relationships in view of the changing personnel.

In advanced and especially in literate communities the continuity of law and custom in the face of these two disruptive factors is attained by a complex system of legal, scientific, and educational institutions. In a primitive and illiterate community there are no such distinct institutions. There is no codification of law and very little education in the sense of an organized imparting of knowledge and moral values. We have to examine, therefore, by what other means the need for a continuity of law and custom is satisfied and how these means are embodied in tribal life.

(a) *The Perpetuation of Relationships over Periods during which They are Inoperative.* An analysis of the various cultural institutions and the behaviour of the individuals who partake in them reveals a number of devices which serve to maintain the effectiveness of relationships, rights, and obligations over periods during which they do not come into play. These devices take, as we shall see, *mutatis mutandis*, the place of codification of the law in more differentiated cultures.

The most general way of keeping a relationship alive consists in the exchange of gifts and visits between the persons concerned and in the participation in common feasts by all persons who form a social group for some purpose or other. The same motives, it might be said, underlie hospitality and gift-making in any society. This is true, but the much greater formality and regularity of such observances in a society like that of Kavirondo than, e.g. in a modern European community, indicates that they serve this purpose of keeping relationships effective far more definitely and exclusively. Formal visits are clearly distinguished from mere sociability. The visitor announces his intended visit beforehand, and the host instructs his wife to prepare a proper meal while he himself looks for an appropriate gift which his visitor can take home. A person exchanges such formal visits at more or less regular intervals with members of his maternal kin (especially his maternal uncle), with his wife's brothers and sisters' husbands, and with those members of his paternal kin which belong to the same 'gate' or lineage. These are precisely those persons to whom he can turn for economic support, for help in a quarrel or dispute, for a share in garden land, or on whose goodwill he depends to conduct his marriage successfully. The frequency and formality of the visits are graded according to the type of the relationship and depend, to some extent, on the personal factor. But even now-adays, where new conditions have loosened traditional behaviour considerably, the formal exchange of visits is still observed with a regularity that allows only little room for personal likes and dislikes. The refraining from mutual visits, on the other hand, is equivalent to the absence of an effective social relationship. When the laws of exogamy were stated to me, the persons that may intermarry were frequently defined as 'the people who do not visit one another'. This absence or cessation of mutual visits is taken as a clear indica-tion of the absence of any social bond which might come into conflict with the establishment of the marriage bond. People who have had a serious quarrel break off their mutual relations by strictly avoiding common participation in a dance, meat-feast or beer-feast, even if they meet accidentally at a third man's place. If their quarrel has been settled, the relationship is resumed again by a ceremonial exchange of visits, accompanied by certain ritual observances. The same attitude prevails between a newly married man or woman and their respective parents-in-law. The initial avoidance between them is not personal, but extends to their respective houses. After the birth of the first or second child, they terminate the avoidance ceremonially by paying formal visits to each others' houses.

The exchange of gifts fulfils the same purpose and is usually linked with the exchange of visits, although it is here more diffi-cult to distinguish between the exchange of gifts as a means of maintaining a relationship and as the fulfilment of that relationship. Smaller gifts, such as accompany the ordinary exchange of visits, clearly belong into the first category. They are 'real' gifts in the sense that they are given voluntarily to a measure and that reci-procity is not strictly observed and checked up.

The larger gifts—of stock or grain—which are exchanged at definite occasions between definite categories of persons are rather mutual obligations than gifts, as they are not voluntary but strictly reciprocal. In case of refusal, the gift is either fetched by force or the relationship ceases to exist, as the reciprocal gift will, of course, be likewise refused. As, however, years may legitimately pass between gift and countergift, and as the occasions at which the gifts become due are usually such that the recipient can make good use of them, they are not merely means of strengthening a relationship, but they are also ends in themselves. The persons between whom such mutual gift obligations exist are primarily the closer relatives within the paternal kin-group, maternal uncle and nephew, wife's brother and sister's husband, and circumcision friends.

Common feasts, finally, serve to maintain the feeling of unity within the clan and age-group and the bonds that exist between two clans. The obligation to give such feasts rests primarily with the old men of the clan, who are expected to kill an ox for the benefit of their clansmen and for chosen representatives of other clans whenever they are in a position to do so. If they neglect this duty persistently, they lose standing among their clansmen and, in extreme cases, are publicly ridiculed by young men, who, on certain occasions, climb the roofs of the huts and shout remarks of abuse or who sing songs of mockery and derision at beer-feasts and dances which quickly spread through the country. The animal slaughtered for a common feast is known as the 'ox of splitting', and the purpose of the feast is explicitly stated to be a demonstration of the clan's strength and unity. The killing of the ox and the distribution of the meat do not take place at the homestead of the person who has supplied the animal, but on the public place, the *oluhia*. Each clansman may attend and, although strangers and especially children who happen to pass by are all given a share, the bulk of the meat is divided among the clansmen and those persons from other clans who have been told to come or to whom the meat is sent in recognition of previous hospitality enjoyed at their place. While the maternal kin and the in-law relations of the owner of the ox receive the largest share among the non-clansmen, it is significant that the distribution of meat is not restricted to relatives, but extended to the old and influential men of neighbouring clans. They represent their respective groups and in turn distribute the meat received among their own clansmen, who jealously watch that they receive their share in due course. On some occasions the animal slaughtered for a clan feast is not taken from the herd of an individual clansman, but from the spoils of war or from the compensation received by a group of clansmen on behalf of the whole clan for the death or injury of a clan member. In the case of the circumcision feast, the ox that is killed and distributed among all the initiates on the 'day of coming out of the hut of seclusion' is taken from an old man's herd, but it is secretly selected and then abducted by the initiates and thus becomes a 'public animal', over the distribution of which the former owner has no say.

Beer-feasts on a large scale, which, as a rule, take place separately from beef-feasts, likewise do not serve the purposes of individual aggrandizement and sociability alone, but of maintaining relationships between the clans and the sub-groups of each clan, and of promoting unity within these groups. After each harvesting season, the elders of one *oluhia* decide to hold a large beer-feast and choose from among them a man at whose place the beer will be brewed and drunk. All people of the neighbourhood contribute basketfuls of grain, each according to his means, till the necessary amount has been collected together. When the beer is ready for consumption, all who have contributed grain assemble at the chosen place to join in the common drink. The beer is shared with others who have not contributed any grain, but the different people who take part in the feast are kept in clearly distinct categories: The 'owners' occupy the favourite seats and get the best quality and the largest quantity of the beer brewed. The 'helpers', who have given no grain, but have lent a hand in the preparations, are assigned a place for themselves; the 'beggars', poor old men too weak to help, are also given their own place, and the 'servants' of the 'owners' may drink the remaining beer next day and sing songs of praise to their masters. Besides, each 'owner' may bring his friend or relative along with him; he will then in turn be invited to a similar beer-feast in his friend's *oluhia*.

The particular way in which a feast is organized serves as an incentive for the display of a social attitude and a co-operative spirit, as the individual members of the group participate in the feast exactly to the extent to which they have contributed their share of grain or labour. The feeling of unity in the group is thus strengthened, and at the same time a safeguard is provided against exploitation by parasitic elements.

The social groups which maintain and strengthen their unity by such common feasts are the sub-clans (*dzimbia*), the main clans, the age-grades and, in connexion with circumcision, also the tribal society. Whereas beer- and beef-feasts by the clan or sub-clan are given whenever an ox or sufficient grain are available, distributions of meat between the members of one age-class take place on the occasion of their sons' circumcision only. The beef is not eaten jointly, but the boy's father kills an ox or two and sends meat to all those of his age-mates (*vagogi*) whom he knows personally, while others may come or send their wives to ask for a share of meat on the strength of the fact that they were circumcised in the same year as he. As circumcision takes place every few years and as all the members of one age-class have to slaughter an animal after each son's circumcision, the occasion of stressing the age-grade relationship by the distribution of meat recurs frequently and for each age-class extends over a large number of years. Circumcision also provides the occasion for feasts on a tribal scale. Among the majority of the Bantu Kavirondo tribes, both the performance of the operation and the various feasts that terminate the convalescence and seclusion of the initiates are the occasion for the gathering of thousands of people comprising many different clans. Although the entire tribe does not actually assemble at one place, the various sub-groups celebrate the different phases of the feast on the same days and in the same manner.

Other feasts on a tribal or at least on an inter-clan scale were wrestling matches (now almost entirely replaced by football games) in which the best wrestlers of one clan fought against those of another, the procedure being hedged round with rules very much like those connected with European sporting events.

Religious observances that involve the assembly of people on a tribal scale I have been able to record from the Logoli only. In a cave on the slope of a wooded hill they perform a semi-annual sacrifice to an ancestral spirit (Mung'oma) and to an apparently vaguely conceived tribal deity (Asai). The purpose of the sacrifice is to evoke an ancestral and divine blessing for the quick ripening of the crops or, on other occasions, to pray for help when a calamity, such as a drought, an epidemic, or a series of ill-fated raids, endanger the whole tribal society. The ceremonial rules on these occasions, such as refraining from any kind of garden work, apply to all tribesmen, and members of all clans join in the common singing of ceremonial songs (*kukelemana*) at the bottom of the hill, while the sacrificers, together with their ritual assistants, perform the sacrificial ceremonies in the cave, to which only they have access.

Tributes to the rain-maker are rendered on a tribal scale by the Logoli, who do not have a rain-maker in their own tribe, but depend upon the goodwill of a powerful rain-maker living among a neighbouring and hostile people, the Nyole. The decision to collect offerings of grain and animals from the people is made by the elders of the different clans, who set a day (either in a general meeting or by communication through messengers), when a delegation of the principal clan elders will go on an expedition to the rain-maker to implore him to send rain and to negotiate the amount of the tribute which they will have to pay.

The exchange of visits and gifts and the participation in common feasts and ceremonial observances serve to maintain relationships and thus law and custom in a general way. But the absence of a codification of the law and especially of distinct legal authorities or bodies which could safeguard the validity of an agreement or claim, creates the necessity for some corresponding arrangements by which rules and agreements, concluded between particular groups or individuals, can be maintained valid. This need is met in a variety of ways. Whenever a dispute arises which is not settled between the immediate partners concerned, the case is discussed by the elders of the sub-clan at great length. Previous cases which have a bearing on the case under dispute are recalled and the settlement which was then reached is restated. It is significant that the restatement of previous cases is not limited to those which directly bear on the present one, but that it usually embraces a much wider range of cases. Each legal dispute—provided that it is complex enough to offer scope for a difference of opinions—thus furnishes an occasion for recalling the juridical traditions of the tribe. Thus what to the casual observer appears as a straying away from the point and an indulgence in telling 'irrelevant' stories, actually serves the very important purpose of keeping known the body of traditional law.

Similarly, agreements between particular individuals are kept valid by their public restatement on occasions where people are assembled who may later be called upon as witnesses. Every economic transaction, such as the sale of a cow or the division of a garden, to begin with, takes place in the presence of witnesses, who are invited to a beer-feast which marks the transaction. Later on, when the non-fulfilment of some other obligation is discussed before the elders or when property is re-distributed after somebody's death, various people make use of the occasion to restate their own claims, not because they want to realize them, but because they want to keep them generally known. The elders then nod in agreement and the validity of the claim is thereby publicly recognized. The surest way in which a liar is detected is by his inability to provide witnesses who can vouch for his claim.

(b) *The Transmission of Law and Custom to Succeeding Generations*. The second factor that disrupts the continuity of relationships —the coming and going of the generations—raises the problem of transmission of law and custom to succeeding generations. This problem has two aspects: It involves, on the one hand, the imparting of practical and theoretical knowledge, of ethical and moral standards of behaviour, and of general rules of etiquette which are common to the whole tribe or even to wider groups. On the other hand, it involves the initiation into the successive phases of life, i.e. the acceptance of the individual into different and ever-widening social groups or types of relationship, each of which is governed by its own set of customs, rules, and values.

The first aspect of the task of transmission, the imparting of general knowledge, values, and manners, chiefly takes the form of a general education through example and precept which is accomplished without organized effort by the up-bringing of the child in the family and its adjustment to its everyday surroundings. It does not concern us in this analysis of the political organization.

The second aspect, however, requires a closer examination as it demonstrates the process by which the individual gradually gains his place in the tribal structure. As every individual enters a new phase of life and thereby attains a new status, the rights and duties and the new types of relationships, implied in his new status, are marked by a ceremonial initiation. If we follow up the life-cycle of the individual among the Bantu Kavirondo, we can distinguish six major phases, the entrance into all of which is marked by a very similar ceremonial procedure: (a) Earliest infancy during which the child is not yet socially acclaimed. (b) Later infancy and early childhood, the entrance into which is marked by the 'feast of washing the child' and the name-giving ceremonies by which the child is acclaimed as a member of the individual family and the father's clan. (c) Boy- and girlhood, marked by the teeth-knocking rite and the child's formal acceptance into its maternal kin-group as well as its admission to the activities of boys and girls respectively. (*d*) Adolescence, marked by the circumcision rites, which raise the young men to the status of warriors and full membership of the tribal society by grouping them all together into an age-grade, which, cutting across the clans, comprises the young men of the whole tribe who have been circumcised in the same year. (*e*) Matrimony, marked by the wedding festivities which do not only establish a bond between husband and wife but between the kinsmen and clans of both and, finally, (*f*) parenthood, marked by the ceremonial setting up of an independent household and homestead and the acceptance of man and wife into full married status in the tribe which is indicated by the termination of avoidances with the actual and all classificatory parents-in-law. Old age, while not marked by a ceremonial initiation', implies a gradual elevation in status and influence, as the principle of seniority operates in all relationships.

These different *rites de passage* have a great similarity to one another. They all serve the same purpose, viz. to accept the individual into an existing group or relationship pattern and to bind him to the obligations and standards of behaviour which membership of the group or participation in the new relationship entail. The following features are found in all or nearly all of the rites that mark the entrance into the various phases of life: (*a*) A mutual ceremonial utterance of the term of address that signifies a particular relationship or membership of a group. The utterance of these terms is not incidental, nor is it a mere symbol, but it actually establishes the relationship, with all that it entails, just as its opposite, the avoidance of certain terms, severs a relationship or prevents it from being established. (*b*) The type of behaviour which characterizes the new status in the group or the nature of the relationship between certain categories of people is acted in a pantomimic performance. (*c*) Gifts are exchanged between the persons who enter a mutual relationship; when a person is initiated into membership of an existing group, a common feast and dance are held which at the same time strengthen the unity of the whole group. (*d*) Commandments are given to the initiate by a close paternal or maternal relative, in the course of which he is instructed in the standards of conduct which henceforth are expected from him. While these commandments are given, the initiate observes definite rules of ritual, and the person who speaks the commandments drives home each sentence by spitting beer on face and body of the initiate. In the case of infants and small children, e.g. at the naming ceremony, the place of the commandments is taken by the uttering of words of well-wishing over the child (*okugasidza*). (*e*) In connexion with the exchange of gifts or the common feast the goodwill of the ancestors is invoked by the offering of meat and blood to the spirits and the utterance of a prayer in which they are asked to come and partake of the food that has been offered to them.

We see from this survey of initiation rites that the task of transmitting tribal law and custom from generation to generation is not performed by distinct institutions, controlled by a central authority, but that the different social groups and relationship patterns continue themselves by handing down their own systems of values and standards of conduct through the formal initiation of new individuals into them. The different groups and relationships, however, do not exist side by side, detached from one another, but they overlap in various respects. In the first place, as they are based partly on kinship, partly on marriage, partly on age, and partly on common family status, every individual belongs to several groupings. A person is not only a member of his lineage and clan, but at the same time of his age-grade; he entertains well-defined relationships with his maternal kin as well as with his wife's kin and that of his brothers' wives and his sisters' husbands, and he shares the common status of a married man or a father with many other members of the tribe, irrespective of clan or marriage bonds. This overlapping of the different groups and relationships, as regards their personnel, clearly acts as a force that maintains and promotes the feeling of tribal unity and the homogeneity of law and custom and that counteracts the tendency towards rivalry and competition between clans.

In the second place, effective kinship bonds and membership of various groups increase in number and importance as the individual gets older. Each successive phase in life means, therefore, a rise in status, i.e. an increase in rights and privileges, but also, of course, in duties and obligations. This fact, along with the principle of seniority as observed in the family relationships with regard to the holding and transferring of property, likewise tends to integrate the relations between the groups, as it places the greatest authority into the hands of the old men who, by virtue of the wide net of kinship bonds and group affiliations in which

they are enmeshed, are best fitted to overcome group interests
and jealousies and thus to plead for the unity of the tribe.

(3) *The Restoration of Breaches of the Law.* Before discussing
the seat or seats of judicial authority in tribal life and the manner
in which it works, we have to examine the different types of
breaches or nonconformity that are distinguished and the nature
of the restoration that is aimed at. From the linguistic evidence, it
appears that offences are and were classed into four groups:
(1) *amagovi*, (2) *amagoso* (or *amahiolo*), (3) *amatava*, and (4) *emigilu*.
A person commits an *eligovi*[1] when he refuses to pay a debt or to
fulfil a customary obligation, such as may be demanded by the rules
of kinship or that may result from partnership in cattle or some
other possession. The term *eligoso* denotes a range of offences
that in Europe would be classed as both civil and criminal,
such as adultery (by or with a married woman), theft, assault,
arson, &c. The word *elihiolo* is often used with the same meaning,
but seems to imply that the offence is of a more serious nature,
such as rape, murder, or witchcraft. It nowadays has the connotation of a sinful and morally strongly condemnable act, but it is
uncertain to what extent this connotation is due to mission or
other recent influences. *Amatava* are offences against property
or life which have been committed accidentally or at least without
the full intention and responsibility of the offender, such as
physical injuries inflicted by carelessness in handling weapons,
or the accidental destruction of a neighbour's house by fire or of
his crops by cattle. *Emigilu*, finally, are violations of important
taboos or rules of ceremonial conduct, pre-eminently of such rules
as the prohibition of incest and the avoidance of one's mother-in-
law or the desecration of objects used in the ancestor cult.

The distinction between these different types of offences and
recognition of a particular form of conduct as constituting an
offence is common to the whole tribal society, with the exception
of a few rules that are observed by some clans but not by others.
The fact that the body of rules and customs that demand conformity is, generally speaking, valid in the whole tribe does not,
of course, entail the existence of a tribal judicial authority.

What does the distinction of these four types of 'breaches' of
the law mean from the point of view of the restoration of the
breach? In the case of *amagovi*, no actual wrong has been done

---

[1] The class-prefix *eli-* denotes the singular, *ama-* the plural.

which needs to be undone. The fact that a claim has become overdue does not involve the notion that the creditor is entitled to compensation for the delay suffered in materializing his claim. The dispute merely has to be decided in favour of one of the disputing parties. When *amagoso* or *amatava* have been committed, the offence has to be undone by inducing or forcing the accused person to compensate the damage he has caused to the accuser. If the offence was unintentional (*elitava*), he merely has to restore the damage or pay cattle equivalent in value, while in the case of an intentional offence (*eligoso*) the double amount has to be replaced or a fine in cattle is levied that is considered ample compensation. This double compensation was interpreted by my informants as aiming to restore the goodwill of the wronged person towards the offender and not as a fine in the sense of a penal sanction. This interpretation is corroborated by the fact that after the settlement of an *eligoso* or *elitava* the plaintiff, if he has won the case, is expected to make a counter-payment, or rather gift, to the defendant as a sign of his satisfaction and reconciliation with him. Breaches of taboo (*emigilu*), finally, are restored by performing the appropriate sacrifice or purification ceremony, after which social relations are resumed with the offender by his fellow beings, who have avoided him in the meantime. If the broken taboo involves another person—as in the case of a violation of the mother-in-law taboo—the purification rite is usually followed by the participation of both persons in a common meal.

It appears from this brief survey of the types of breaches recognized and the methods employed in dealing with them that the restoration of law and order aims at the settlement of claims and the reparation of damages rather than at the punishment of the offender. This fact has two important consequences. The one is that jurisdiction takes place only when solicited by the victim or victims of the offence, as all offences are conceived as being injurious to the interests of a particular person or group of persons, but not to the tribal society as a whole. It is a logical implication of this conception that, not only every material object, but also every human being has its 'owner' or 'owners'.[1] A typical

---

[1] The Logoli term *ovwene* refers both to 'ownership' of objects and of persons. It differs, of course, from our concept of ownership in several respects. Thus the *omwene* (owner) of a person is the one who has not only the foremost rights over him but also the foremost obligations towards him.

case which illustrates this principle is that of serious physical harm suffered by a small child owing to the negligence of its father or mother. If the injuries, e.g. burns, are attributed to the carelessness of the mother, the father of the child can claim damages from his wife's father or brothers (as those responsible for her conduct), if to the carelessness of the father, the child's mother's relatives can claim damages from the father of the child or his kinsmen. Compensation for damages is thus claimed by and received from persons who, according to European notions, are not at all or only very indirectly affected by the offence.

The second consequence which follows directly from the first is that there is no tribal judicial authority, but that justice is administered by and between those groups of persons who are affected by the offence in question. Since, as has been said, breaches of the law can be restored by the payment of material objects, it follows that compensation will be claimed—and given—by all persons who have a joint interest in the material well-being of the individual immediately affected by an offence. As property is held and inherited chiefly by virtue of membership of the patrilineal group, it is the group of paternal kinsmen and, by extension, the whole patrilineal clan which has such a joint interest in the well-being of all of its members. Within the clan, the size of the group which will take judicial action is determined in each particular case by the extent and nature of common interests which are affected by the dispute or damage done. It is not a definite type of offence, but the seriousness of the situation, the amount of social disruption that threatens from it, which determines the composition of the judicial body. The creation or maintenance of common or mutual interests within the clan is therefore of paramount importance to the individual immediately affected by a breach of the law, as he needs support from other persons if he is to realize his claims and reparations for damages. By sharing common interests—economic, social, ritual, &c.—the damage suffered by one member of the group (lineage, sub-clan, or clan) becomes a concern of all and, moreover, support of a member of the group in one case invites his reciprocal services in another. This identification of a given group within the clan with the rights and duties of each of its members is the second reason why it is impossible to make a distinction between civil and criminal law. Whether the initiative in taking judicial action comes from the wronged individual or from the clan or any of its sub-groups of which the individual is a member and the specific interests of which are affected, in both cases that group acts, in a sense, as the accuser and as the judicial authority at the same time.

A distinction, however, must be made between law administered within a given group and between different groups. When a legal dispute or an offence involves two clans, the clan of the wronged person tries to obtain justice by negotiation with the clan of the offender, which, in turn, stands behind the offender and either rejects the claim or assumes responsibility for his action. When, however, a breach of law occurs within a given group and the nature of the offence is such that it affects those interests which are specific to the group and not further divisible, a restoration of the breach by compensation is obviously impossible, as it would necessitate the splitting up of the group into two units, the one which gives and the other which receives the compensation, an action which would destroy the solidarity of the group. Thus, if a person commits adultery with one of his father's or brother's wives, the usual compensation of a heifer is not paid, as a father and his sons form a property-holding unit in which the payment of compensation by one member to another member would be pointless. If a person kills a member of his sub-clan, no compensation would be paid either (among the Vugusu), as they say that the loss of life affects the whole sub-clan and not merely the immediate kinsmen. The action taken in such and similar cases furnishes a clear criterion of the nature of the solidarity that prevails within the group in question. Where it is deemed that no legal action (i.e. the imposition of a compensation) can be taken owing to the indivisibility of the common interests of the group, merely a sacrifice is performed to propitiate the spirits and a purification ceremony which frees the offender from his ritual impurity and renders it safe for his relatives and neighbours to resume social relations with him.

In the case of repeated offences, the only possible procedure is to expel the offender from the group and to withdraw from him the right for protection by the clan as well as the clan's responsibility for his deeds. The attitude towards an habitual offender thus differs fundamentally from that towards an occasional offender. Whereas the latter—no matter how serious the offence committed by him—is considered to have acted within a set of particular conditions and circumstances and against the interests only of the people directly or indirectly affected by the offence, the habitual offender becomes a source of danger to everybody in the tribe. He is, therefore, placed outside legal protection of the clan and may be killed by anybody when he is caught in the act of committing his next offence. Thus persons who have come to be regarded as dangerous witches or incorrigible thieves are first driven away from their clan and then, at the next provocation, put to death by the method of lynching carried out by as large and mixed a group of persons as possible to avert the possibility of a blood feud from arising. Such group action in the face of threatening danger, taken spontaneously, i.e. without a hearing of the case and often on the spur of the moment, is clearly not the same as institutionalized jurisdiction by the tribal society through recognized judicial authorities. It is rather that in such cases the person of the accuser becomes multiplied and that the tribal group by being accuser and public opinion at the same time cuts short the usual judicial procedure. It will be seen, therefore, that the occurrence of indiscriminate group-action in the face of dangerous witchcraft and habitual crime does not invalidate the basic principle of jurisdiction, viz. that it comes into force only when solicited by the victim or victims of the offence and takes place only within and between those groups of persons whose common interests are affected by the offence.[1]

A brief discussion of judicial procedure will show how this principle of group solidarity along clan lines works in practice, comprising ever-widening groups as the significance of the offence widens. In the initial stages of each dispute over a material

---

[1] A similar view is taken by J. H. Driberg in his paper cited on p. 203 *supra*. Driberg, however, constructs a difference between two distinct categories of offences, those against individuals (or individuals representing a family, community, or association), and those directed against or affecting the whole 'body politic'. With the first category he classes such offences as homicide, theft, adultery, injuries, slander, &c., and with the second one— which he calls anti-social—witchcraft, incest, and sexual perversion. With reference to Kavirondo law this classification would not apply, as (1) from the point of view of their social repercussion, offences show a wide range of shades, affecting ever-widening groups as they increase in seriousness, and not the two distinct types which he labels 'anti-individual' and 'anti-social', and (2) the amount of social disruption caused by an offence does not depend on the kind of offence (whether murder or witchcraft), but upon the particular conditions under which it has been committed, one of them being the previous record of the offender, another one the motives underlying his action.

object or the non-fulfilment of an obligation an attempt is made to reach an agreement between the two immediate parties concerned. If a debt is not returned or the obligation not fulfilled, the claimant at first takes resort to self-help, fetching the object in question— usually an animal—by night, assisted perhaps by one or two brothers or friends. If a neighbour encroaches upon his garden, he goes there at night or while the neighbour is away and re- marks the boundary-line by digging new ditches or by pulling out his neighbour's seedlings wrongfully planted on his land. This form of self-help is still frequently resorted to, especially among the illiterate section of the community, and gives rise to much disciplinary action by the elders of the new tribal courts, who are anxious to settle every dispute in court for fear of losing their court dues. In other cases, where self-help of this nature is im- practicable or impossible, the aggrieved person takes recourse to the spelling of a curse or to engaging the services of a rain-maker to obtain justice. Curses are mainly employed by older people, as their efficacy is supposed to increase with the age of the person who utters them, or in cases where the offender is unknown or where the evidence against him is not conclusive. I have myself witnessed a few cases where stolen property was secretly returned within a few weeks after a curse had been uttered. Threats to engage the services of the rain-maker to divert the rain from the offender's garden or to devastate it by directing a hailstorm towards it are said among the Vugusu to have been the most common means of pressing the payment of a debt.

When disputes or quarrels could not be settled by self-help, the person who believed himself wronged appealed to the old men of his sub-clan, and the accused person, if he belonged to the same sub-clan, was called by them or he came on his own account to defend his case. The old men then listened to the case as pre- sented by the two disputants and any witness. The decision could be announced by any of the elders present as, with the facts ascer- tained, there was only one possible judgement which was common knowledge to all. Nor was there any organized judicial assembly. The elders of the sub-clan met every morning on a pasture, where, sitting round the fire (*oluhia*), they discussed the news and the gossip of the previous day. These informal gatherings provided the main occasion for dispensing justice within the sub-clan. If the evidence could not be established by hearing the two parties and the witnesses, an ordeal was administered in the presence of the elders of the *oluhia*. No further action was then required, as the ordeal was supposed to administer justice automatically.

An alternative to the appeal to the elders for arbitration was the continuation of mutual provocations between the disputing parties until a fight ensued. It was then the duty of the elders to intervene by separating the fighters and by persuading them to return to reason and settle their dispute peacefully. The ability of certain men in the sub-clan to carry through such intervention successfully was one of the main requirements for political leadership. 'The head of the clan [*omugasa*] is the man who talks gently and who can make the people listen to him when they quarrel or fight' is the usual definition given of a traditional 'chief'.

If the dispute or offence was of a more serious nature, if it involved serious injury or even the death of a person, the news of it would quickly spread to all clansmen, and the elders of the different sub-clans would rush to the scene of the offence and hold a meeting *ad hoc* (*ekiruazo*) to prevent fighting and discuss the situation and finally give judgement. In such assemblies of the clan council (i.e. of the elders of all sub-clans) there was again no hereditary or formally appointed 'chief judge' or leading sub-clan, but strong personalities who had gained prestige as warriors and givers of feasts were recognized as authorities whose opinion carried more weight than that of the ordinary elders.

The only sanction which supported the legal decisions given by the elders of the sub-clan or by the larger *ad hoc* assembly of all clan elders was the solidarity of the members of the respective groups in backing these decisions. Native statements assert that whenever the verdict was supported by all or the great majority of the clan elders, the defendant would not have tried to oppose. Were he to have done so without finding any support among a section of his clansmen, the verdict would have been enforced by the elders by appointing a number of men who would take the cattle, or whatever the compensation would be, by force. Besides, the fact that a person who evaded justice in his own clan could only with difficulty migrate and settle in another clan, because he would not have been hospitably received if the reason of his secession became known, would force him to submit to the decision of the elders.

A different situation arose when a dispute between two members of the same clan led to a dissension among the clan elders, each backed by a section of the clan, and neither section was willing to yield to the other. In such a case, the weaker section would secede from the clan land and join another clan or migrate elsewhere, and a new clan would thus come into being. The origin of many present clans is accounted for by such quarrels. The main clan and the section that has split off would at first avoid all social relations with one another and also continue to observe the rule of exogamy.[1] After a few generations, when the quarrel has been forgotten, a member of the seceded sub-clan would tentatively marry an *omwiwana* (a niece) of the main clan, i.e. a girl whose mother comes from that clan. If this marriage produces offspring and the children survive, the two clans begin to intermarry directly. Thus the independence of the seceded clan becomes fully established and the original clan name, which at first is maintained along with the name of the man under whose leadership the clan group seceded, is dropped.

But the judicial functions of the clan were not limited to the restoration of law and order within its own ranks. They also comprised the settling of disputes that arose between members of different clans. In such a case, the wronged person and his immediate kinsmen would go to the elders of the defendant's clan. If the case was serious enough to affect the common interests of the whole clan, the plaintiff was supported by all the elders of his clan and a number of warriors, who would accompany him in his search for legal satisfaction to demonstrate to the defendant and his clan that they backed his claim. This was deemed to be the case when the life of a clan-member had been taken or seriously threatened by assault or attempted sorcery, or when a quarrel over property had reached the point where peaceful negotiations between the immediate parties concerned had come to an impasse and the dispute threatened to lead or actually had led to fighting.

If no agreement could be reached between the two clans, which would happen when one side demanded exorbitant compensation or when the inter-clan relations had been strained by a series of

---

[1] In this case the observance of exogamy is based partly on the consciousness of still being related and partly on the existence of a feud between the two clans. Thus, close co-operation and its opposite, a state of hostility, both act as a bar to intermarriage.

previous disputes, the two dissentient clans would break off their relations with one another and enter into a state of vendetta. This continued until the warriors of the aggrieved clan had taken a life equivalent in status or until several lives had been taken on both sides and the equilibrium had thus been restored. It was then the task of the elders in each clan to work for reconciliation by lamenting the deplorable consequences of the feud and by appealing to the former neighbourliness and the common ancestry of the two hostile clans in their talks with the young men of the tribe. If both clans were willing to terminate the avoidance a feast of reconciliation was arranged (*okuhololizana*) which entailed a common meal and sacrifice, and the former relations between the two clans were resumed again.

Thus the restoration of law and order, when infringed by a member of another clan, was ultimately achieved by a showdown of force between the two clans concerned. To render this effective, the clan had to have a high degree of solidarity within and at the same time had to be of sufficiently large size. As, however, owing to the nature of the bonds that make up clan solidarity, an increase in the number of clansmen beyond a certain point renders the occasions for co-operation between them too rare and too vague, there must have been an optimum size for a clan. This was reached when a fair balance existed between its external power, as expressed in the number of warriors, and its internal strength, as expressed by the degree and frequency of co-operation between its members. The need for this balance explains why young clans which were still small in number sought affiliation with larger clans in the form of ceremonially confirmed clan friendships and alliances and why, on the other hand, large clans tended to split up into sub-clans which gradually become independent of one another.

As regards the restoration of breaches of the law the clans were thus sovereign groups, as there was no tribal judicial authority which could be appealed to in the case of inter-clan conflicts. The fact that numerous bonds of kinship and marriage existed between the members of all clans in the tribe and that strife between clans weakened tribal co-operation in warfare, served as an inducement for the elders of clans, not directly involved in a clan-feud, to intervene as arbiters, but there was no legally binding force behind such arbitration.

IV. External Political Structure

Before discussing warfare as the predominant type of political relation between the tribes, I shall briefly review other types of inter-tribal relations, as they lead up to the formulation of the problem of warfare as a political problem.

Trade relations between the tribes were only weakly developed, as natural resources were fairly evenly distributed over the whole of Kavirondo and technical skill and knowledge were of such similarity in all the Bantu tribes that there was no incentive for a regular and organized exchange of goods. The occasional bartering of crops for live stock and of the products of certain crafts (pottery, iron-work, and ornaments) was too erratic to lead to the establishment of permanent political relations between the tribes on economic grounds.

Individuals who had gained repute as rain-makers, circumcision operators, diviners, or herbalists were consulted by clients from neighbouring and even hostile tribes and also called to other tribes to perform their services. Thus the Logoli sent frequent expeditions to the Nyole rain-maker whose powers were acknowledged by half a dozen other tribes. Such relations, however, are said to have been maintained during periods of truce only and, besides, were of such a nature that it was in the interest of both tribes concerned not to interfere with them by committing hostile acts to individual visitors from neighbouring tribes. Specialists were called by members of a hostile tribe because their services were unobtainable within the tribe and they were therefore welcome visitors. Clients who went to consult experts in another tribe, likewise, were immune from attack, as they brought gifts to pay for the information that they received. I could obtain no records of any occasions at which such relations were abused, nor, however, is there any evidence to show that they ever led to a closer political alliance between the tribes concerned.

Intermarriage between generally hostile tribes was limited to the marriage of female war-captives, who were taken at an age of six to ten years and adopted into the family of the warrior who had captured them. When grown up, they were married off in the same way as physical daughters. Capture of adult women was, according to information given by the old men, not at all or only exceptionally practised, as they would have acted as spies or attempted to run back to their own people at the first opportunity for escape that offered itself. Regular intermarriage, based on a mutual agreement between the parties concerned, took place only between tribal groups who maintained friendly relations based upon a recognition of a remote relationship, such as existed between the Vugusu and Gishu, the Wanga and Marama, and the Tadjoni and Nyala (Kabras). A one-sided incentive for marrying women of a neighbouring tribe existed if it was poor in cattle—especially after an epidemic had ravaged—and therefore willing to marry off its 'daughters' for a low bride-wealth. However, as far as genealogical records show, intertribal marriages appear to have been exceptional between tribes that had marked differences in custom, as these caused difficulties in the marital relationship itself, as well as in the social relations between the husband's and the wife's group. Even nowadays intertribal marriages are disliked on these grounds, especially by the girl's kin and clan, and most of the cases noted down by me concern teachers, clerks, or others whose occupation takes them away from their own tribe. It seems, therefore, that intertribal marriages did not constitute a strong factor in establishing social relations between the tribes and in breaking down cultural differences between them.

The attitude towards any neighbouring tribe as a whole was chiefly characterized by a feeling of suspicion, to which was added either fear or contempt. Fear of other tribes is never openly admitted, either in personal talks, or in migratory accounts, or in texts on warfare. It is, however, implied in the absence of contempt and ridicule. The Uasin-Gishu Masai, who frequently raided the country of the Vugusu without ever being raided in return by them, are always spoken of in a solemn manner, and I could not discover that any terms or songs of derision were current with regard to them. On the contrary, many Masai terms relating to the conduct of warfare, as well as some of their weapons and the attire of their warriors, have been copied by the Vugusu. The Logoli refer to their chief enemies, the Nandi and Tiriki, as *avafumbwa* ('enemies who come by night'), a term which is obviously intended to convey a feeling of horror.

Contempt and derision are far more common attitudes towards other tribes and find expression in numerous sayings and proverbs. Within the group of Bantu tribes, expressions of contempt centre chiefly round minor differences in custom: Foods eaten or refused, peculiarities of dress or ornament, and mannerisms such as particular ways of walking or talking. To tribes of non-Bantu stock, despicable qualities and sinister intentions are usually attributed. To the Logoli, the term *avavo* refers to their westerly neighbours, the Luo, and has the connotation of something evil and inferior. The Luo are ridiculed for differences in their tribal customs. They are derided because they do not practise circumcision, and cowardly boys, in a circumcision song, are told to run off to the Luo country and marry there, as the Luo women are satisfied to marry uncircumcised men. Among the Vugusu, an analogous attitude towards their non-Bantu neighbours prevails. The El Kony are merely ridiculed for their weakness in warfare, while numerous derogatory comments are passed on the Teso who, next to the Masai, were the chief enemies of the Vugusu.

With such relations and attitudes prevailing between the different tribal groups, what were the motives for warfare? From accounts of war expeditions and an analysis of all the accompanying circumstances, it appears that the two immediate aims in attacking other tribal groups were to capture cattle and to inflict a loss of life upon the group attacked. While the first of these two motives is clearly economic and requires no further interpretation once the significance of cattle in the tribal economic organization is known. the second motive cannot be considered an end in itself, as it leads to the further question: 'Why do people want to inflict a loss of life upon a neighbouring tribal group?'

To a certain extent, the taking of life might be considered a necessary consequence of the raiding of cattle, as the owners will try to defend their cattle, so that violence naturally results. The conduct of warfare by the 'Bantu Kavirondo' shows, however, that open encounters with the enemy were not avoided whenever possible, but actively sought after. Apart from single-handed cattle-stealing, they employed very little cunning in their raids, but openly challenged the enemy once they had approached him.

In war and victory songs, the killing as such is praised as the main purpose and achievement in a fight, and undoubtedly the thrill or 'sport' which warfare furnishes and the fame and prestige which the display of courage and daring bestows upon a warrior was a powerful motive and perhaps the strongest immediate incentive

for waging war. But beyond this immediate motive the taking
of life served other purposes, which become apparent when the
whole organization of warfare and the groups that waged war with
one another are subjected to a closer analysis. Although between
most tribal groups in Kavirondo—especially those who lived in a
permanent state of hostilities—an uninhabited zone of a few miles'
width was maintained, the tribal territory did not remain static,
but either expanded or contracted as the result of extended periods
of warfare. Among the Logoli the conquest of new land for cultivation is expressly stated to have been one of the chief motives for
warfare. It does not, however, become apparent as an immediate
motive, as a war expedition was never terminated by the annexation of a given area by the victorious side and a readjustment of the
boundary line confirmed by the vanquished or any similar procedure. This would have required a much firmer military organization than existed and an organized protection of the borders, for
which the political structure of the tribal groups was much too
loose. The immediate result of a raid was rather to weaken and
intimidate the neighbouring tribe and to induce its members
gradually to retreat, so that the uninhabited zone would widen and
the grazing of stock and the cultivation of gardens could safely
be carried on in what was formerly no-man's-land. The territory
thus gained by a very gradual process came under the control of
the clan whose warriors had driven the enemy tribe into retreat
and was shared out among them.

Whether such a conquest of territory involved a real expansion
of the tribal area or whether the gaining of land on one side was
always accompanied by a loss on the other side is very difficult to
decide. As far as traditions go, it appears that changes in the
territory held by the various tribes were due partly to a general
tendency of an eastward migration caused by a pressure of the
Nilotic and Teso-speaking groups, the ultimate reason of which
would have to be traced back to the upper Nile Valley, and partly
to a real need for expansion. This need, again, arose from a variety
of causes. Of these the most important seem to have been (a) a
natural increase in population which, in view of the fecundity of
the Bantu people, must at times have been considerable even in
pre-European days; (b) an increase in the wealth of cattle, either
by natural increase or by conquest, requiring larger grazing areas;
and (c) the deterioration of the soil, owing to various forms of

erosion caused by shifting cultivation and excessive burning of bush for grazing purposes. Expansion, based on these causes, cannot, however, have been continuous. The first two of these causes were checked by epidemics and by adverse luck in war. The third was limited by the checks on the increase in population and live stock and also by the fact that, under traditional conditions at least, the deterioration of the soil was not permanent but temporary, so that periods of expansion were followed by periods of retreat to lands formerly cultivated. The system of land tenure indicates that neither the tribal group nor the clans attached value to the possession of land apart from those stretches actually used or reserved for cultivation and grazing.

The fact that the two ultimate motives in warfare were the raiding of cattle and the conquest of territory has a definite bearing upon the conduct of warfare, as it involves conflicting aims. While it lies in the interest of expansion to carry on aggression in a ruthless manner which drives the enemy away as far as possible, the aim of raiding cattle clearly requires the presence of enemy groups in the neighbourhood. Owing to the necessity of balancing these two aims, warfare tended to be conducted with certain restrictions, above all with provisions for terminating a period of hostilities and with generally observed rules regarding the treatment of slain warriors and of women and children. Such 'rules of warfare' were more pronounced in the conduct of hostilities between the various Bantu groups than between Bantu and non-Bantu. In the latter case, the mutual destruction of the hostile groups was the prominent aim, while in the encounters between groups of Bantu stock the hostile groups conceded their mutual rights of existence and maintained a type of relationship with one another in which warfare functioned chiefly as a regulating and balancing force, making for an approximately even distribution of power and wealth between the tribes

Secondary motives of warfare, the relative importance of which differed in the different areas, were the taking of captives and the raiding of crops. The first was limited mainly to the taking of small boys and girls between the ages of six and ten years, who were adopted and brought up in the family of the warrior who had captured them. As, under traditional conditions, children were of economic value to the family, the adoption of war captives meant a welcome addition to the family and the clan.

The raiding of crops was customary only in the densely populated areas and among predominantly agricultural tribes, such as the Logoli and Nyole, while the more pastoral Vugusu ridicule it as below the dignity of warriors.

It becomes apparent, therefore, that there was no need for a tribal military organization, but that each clan or a group of neighbouring clans would conduct their war expeditions, as well as their defence against attacks, on their own account. Actually, both for the Logoli and the Vugusu, there are no records of any 'wars' on a tribal scale, but only of fighting and raiding expeditions undertaken by the different clans. Since, of course, only the larger clans could venture to undertake raids and provoke an open fight, as only they possessed a sufficient number of warriors, the smaller clans either had to stay behind or to associate themselves permanently or temporarily with a larger clan for co-operation in raiding. Warriors of other small clans accompanied on their own initiative groups of warriors of larger clans, particularly those with whom they were related in the maternal line or by marriage or whose circumcision age-mates they were. Where hostile tribes lived on all sides of the tribal territory, as was the case both with the Logoli and the Vugusu, the clans living nearest those sections of the border which were most suitable for raids and attacks acquired leadership in warfare. Thus among the Logoli the clan of the Mavi which fought against their western neighbours, the Nyole and Luo, and the clans of the Yonga and Tembuli, which fought against the Nandi and Tiriki in the east, appear to have been the clans which were foremost in taking the initiative in fighting. Till to-day they boast of more famous warriors than the smaller clans.

Such leadership of certain clans in warfare did not, however, necessarily entail any political domination over the smaller clans. There was no 'calling up' of warriors, but participation in a raid was voluntary and the spoils of war were divided among all warriors according to the degree of their participation in the raid. The initiative to embark upon a raid came either from the young men or from the elders who, sitting on the *oluhia*, incited the young men to go out and capture cattle, 'as they had not seen meat for a long time'; or it arose from an incident, such as the murder of a tribesman by members of another tribe with whom peace had been concluded. If the raid was likely to prove difficult and to require a large number of warriors, messengers were sent round to the villages or homesteads of other clans to invite them to come to a given place where the further procedure was discussed and a leader (*omwemilili*) was chosen, whose duty it was to direct the movements of the warriors and to co-ordinate the action of the different sections. All raids were one-day affairs or, if the attack was undertaken at night, as in the case of the Vugusu raids upon the Teso, of a day and a night.

Apart from seasonal periods of truce, which, by tacit agreement between all parties concerned, were observed during the times of hoeing and clearing the fields, a more lasting peace was concluded by the performance of complex peace ceremonies. The main rite had the significance of an oath, and is supposed to cause death and other misfortune to the party which first breaks the peace. The conclusion of peace never involved 'peace terms' in the sense that one party would pledge to pay tribute or surrender cattle previously raided, or even territory. Peace agreements are said to have been made by the Logoli with the Nyole, Tiriki, and Luo, and by the Vugusu with the El Kony, Nyala (Kabras), and Kakalelwa, but never with their chief enemies, the Masai and Teso.

V. The Nature of Political Authority

Although, as has been stated at the beginning of this chapter, there were no individuals or bodies which wielded clearly defined political authority entailing explicit rights and duties, the preceding discussion of the various aspects of political organization has indicated a number of ways in which individuals could gain prominence over their tribesmen or clansmen and find recognition as leaders by certain groups within the tribal unit and with regard to certain activities. We shall now review these different ways of acquiring prominence and then try to define the nature of political leadership as it existed among the Logoli and Vugusu.

(*a*) *The Privileges of Primogeniture.* As primogeniture carries with it a number of privileges, there is a tendency in every family for the oldest son to be recognized as the person next in importance to the father. His authority is based on three factors mainly: the first is that he is in a privileged position to acquire wealth in cattle. Although ultimately all sons are entitled to an even share in the father's legacy, the oldest son has a preferential claim to make use of family property, a fact which gives him a much quicker

'start' in life than is offered to the other sons. He is the first to be
given cattle to marry and, if the father is poor in cattle, the second
son may have to wait for many years until the father's herd has been
replenished before he can take a wife. The oldest son also has the
first claim to the father's land, to the inheritance of his junior
wives, and to the management of the family cattle. The younger
sons have to wait till the cattle taken over by the oldest son have
increased sufficiently to permit of an equal division, and it is
usually only in long-drawn-out instalments that they can obtain
their share in the father's legacy. It will be seen that the privileged
economic position of the oldest son tends to have a cumulative
effect—up to a point—as one generation succeeds the other. As
a consequence of this tendency, the line of first-born sons often
becomes the wealthiest in the lineage.

The second factor is that, through his management of the
father's legacy in land and cattle, the oldest son exercises authority
over his younger brothers, who depend upon his friendship and
goodwill for the realization of their share in the father's property
that is ultimately due to them.

A third factor is that family tradition and the knowledge of law
and custom and, in particular, of outstanding claims to property
are always passed on from the father to the oldest son, so that
in the lineage group the senior line becomes the chief guardian
of tradition and its members the performers of rites and sacrifices
for the while lineage or even the sub-clan.

The stress on primogeniture, however, is not so marked that in
each clan there is necessarily one leading family, viz. the descendants in senior line of the founder of the clan, although such
families are found in a number of clans. In most clans there are
several elders who trace their descent in senior line back for eight
to ten generations, but they are not able to link up their genealogy
with the name of the founder of the clan. The privileges of primogeniture thus constitute one factor that makes for economic and
ritual differentiation within the clan and thus for leadership.

(b) *Wealth*. The wealthy person, whether he has accumulated
his possessions through inheritance or through personal effort, has
means of gaining prestige and influence both within and outside
his clan. In the first place, by his ability to offer everyday hospitality in the form of beer, his homestead becomes the gathering-
place of the elders of the neighbourhood. In addition, he gains a

more definite influence over particular individuals in his clan by lending them a goat or sheep for a sacrifice, a heifer for their marriage cattle, or basketfuls of grain if they run short of food. The person who often receives such support thereby assumes the obligation to praise his creditor, to oblige him by small services, or, if he cannot return the loan, to render more substantial help by herding his benefactor's cattle, clearing his gardens, and keeping his huts in repair. The traditional type of 'retainer' or servant who is found in some wealthy homesteads usually has come into that position as a war captive, as a widower without children, or as a debtor who could not return his debt.

Moreover, by giving feasts on a clan scale, especially by killing the 'ox of splitting', a wealthy person has a means of gaining popularity among all his clansmen. Through his right of directing the distribution of meat, he can favour those who respect and honour him and who, at the discussion of clan matters, submit to his views. Finally, as elders of other clans are invited to these feasts, the wealthy persons also become, in a sense, the representatives of their clan. When elders of other clans kill the 'ox of splitting' they are invited in turn, or gifts of meat or beer are sent to them, which they apportion to their own clansmen. They have thus an opportunity of gaining influence among their clansmen even when they are the recipients and not the givers of feasts.

(c) *The Quality of being an Omugasa.* Among the Vugusu, the leading elders of a clan are called *avagasa*, i.e. men who talk gently and wisely and who can make the people listen and return to reason when they want to quarrel or fight. The possession of these qualities is usually quoted as the most important condition of leadership. A son who as a herdboy begins to show reason and the capacity of making his age-mates follow him in the various activities in which herdboys indulge is pointed out by the elders as a future *omugasa*, and they welcome his presence when he sits near them and listens to their stories of long ago. When he has become an old man he acts as an *omuseni*, i.e. he is called to the people to speak to them and comfort them when they assemble after a funeral to distribute the property of the deceased, to decide who should inherit the widows and to settle outstanding claims and debts. The death of each clansman is a critical moment for the preservation of peace within and between the clans, as it invariably leads to accusations of witchcraft or sorcery as being the cause of the death that has occurred. It is then the duty of the *omuseni* to curtail all such accusations by pointing out that all people are born into this world to die and that people should not harbour grievances and accuse one another of sorcery, as such an attitude would merely increase the sorrow that had befallen them. The *omuseni* usually winds up his speech with a review of the great deeds of the clan and with exhortations to live up to that tradition and to forget petty quarrels for the sake of peace.

Similarly, the *omugasa* is expected to talk for unity when legal disputes are discussed before the elders of the *oluhia*. When homicide or murder has occurred and the kinsmen of both parties insult one another and show impatience to fight, he persuades them to give and accept compensation. The degree to which he succeeds in such efforts determines his recognition as a leader.

(*d*) *Reputation as a Warrior*. A further quality that in the past made for leadership was the reputation gained as a warrior. Success in warfare served as a means of gaining wealth, but it also brought prestige in itself. Both among the Vugusu and the Logoli the names of clan heads of the past that are remembered are associated with accounts of their deeds as warriors, their success being measured in terms of the number of enemies they have killed and the head of cattle raided by them or under their leadership. Whether the choice of a successful warrior as a leader in raiding expeditions was linked with a belief in his possession of superior magical powers is to-day difficult to determine; he is said by the old men to have been chosen for his courage and his ability of inducing the others to follow him in an attack. Since, as has been said above, war expeditions were frequently undertaken jointly by several clans, leadership in fighting, more than that acquired in other ways, tended to be recognized by several clans and thus to establish a superiority of one clan over others.

(*e*) *The Possession of Magico-Religious Virtues*. Although the persons most commonly called to offer private sacrifices to the ancestors are the members of the senior line of a lineage, this duty can also be performed by any classificatory father or elder brother, if his qualities of character are such that he is considered a suitable person. He must be known for his kindness and honesty; he must be past the age of sexual desire; and he must be some one 'who can feed the people'; in short he must be a person without *embala*, i.e. without any failures and blemishes in the record of

I

his past and present life, if his sacrifice is to be favourably accepted by the spirits. That elder in the clan who possesses these qualities to the highest degree is recognized as the *omusalisi munene* ('the great sacrificer') who is called to perform private sacrifices of great importance and, among the Logoli, also the *ovwali*, the public sacrifice to the tribal ancestor and deity. His office is not hereditary, but dependent upon personal qualities.

Among the various 'experts', the dream-prophet and the rain-maker appear to have wielded political power of a kind, as, through the practising of their arts, they could influence the activities, not only of single individuals, but of larger groups of people. The dream-prophet, as has been stated, was consulted on the probable outcome of war expeditions, on the advisability of migrations, the probability of epidemics, and on similar matters of wider concern, while the rain-maker, through his alleged ability of withholding rain and of directing the rainfall, not only in general, but in respect of particular gardens, had the power of an executive organ in the administration of justice. These two experts, however, form categories of their own. Their knowledge is by virtue of inherited secret medicines and spells, and they wield it independently of their clan—and, in the case of the rain-maker, even of their tribal affiliations. Their special knowledge, therefore, does not appear to have lent them authority beyond that implied in their specific practices.

(*f*) *Age*. Old age, finally, was the most general condition of political leadership and was socially marked through the institution of circumcision age-grades. The recognition of primogeniture for the regulation of inheritance and succession lends seniority a superior status in all kinship relations. Generally speaking, it is always the oldest member of a group of kinsmen whose opinion carries the greatest weight on matters concerning that group. Adult sons show more obedience and respect to their father's oldest brother than to the father himself, and after their father's death his authority is not immediately transmitted to the oldest son, but first to the next oldest brother who is still alive.

The authority implied in old age is further strengthened by notions connected with the ancestor cult. One of these is that old age is regarded as a necessary condition of performing sacrifices, as it requires a mind that is free from sexual desire and that possesses other qualities characteristic of old age, such as wisdom, gentleness, and freedom from greed and jealousy. The other notion is that spirits remember the treatment received while they were still living persons and that they spare or trouble their living relatives according to the treatment received. Old men, therefore, are more than others feared as potentially troublesome spirits, a fact which considerably adds to their authority. Their power of uttering a curse, and especially a dying curse, is an all-powerful sanction at their disposal.

This review of the different ways of gaining prominence in the clan and tribe shows them to be of such a nature that they are not mutually exclusive. The more qualities of leadership came together in one person, the higher was his authority and the wider the group that recognized it. While primarily based on the organization of the patrilineal kin-group, leadership could, as we have seen, extend to embrace the clan and even a number of clans through the channels of wealth, warfare, and sacrifice. If there were several people in the clan who possessed the different qualifications of leadership, it was divided between them, but such a division does not appear to have led to an institutionalized distinction between different types of leaders, such as war-leaders, judges, and priests. Provided that he possessed the other necessary qualities, the war-leader, as he became old, was recognized as an arbiter in legal disputes and called as a performer of sacrifices, as he had increased the power of the clan and pleased the ancestors. There was a division of authority only in the sense that the leadership of the old men in matters of jurisdiction and sacrifice was paralleled by the leadership of the active warriors in the conduct of fighting.

Political authority thus remained inarticulate. It was not linked up with clearly defined rights and privileges, such as are usually associated with institutionalized chieftainship. The leading elders of a clan or sub-clan were merely those persons whose opinion carried most weight when public matters were discussed on the *oluhia* and who were called to perform sacrifices. They had no rights that were inherent in their office, such as to collect tribute, to enact laws, to call up warriors for a raid, or to grant or refuse residence of strangers on clan lands. There is no generally accepted term for a clan or tribal head, but a leading elder is referred to by a variety of terms which can also be used with regard to any respected and honoured person. Finally, there was no formal appointment and installation of the head of a clan or sub-clan. Only when a leader in warfare was chosen, he is said, among the Logoli, to have been shaved and anointed with *ghee* in the presence of the elders of the clan and to have been presented by an old warrior with a head-dress of cowrie shells, a ribbon of colobus skin, and a cloak sewn up of pieces of the skin of various animals, a ceremony which, aside from lending distinction to the war-leader, had a magic significance. Finger-rings, rare feathers, wristlets, ivory armlets, and spears are similar 'insignia' of this kind which were ceremoniously given to a man recognized as a war-leader. They were kept by the person upon whom they had been bestowed, and when he had reached old age were passed on by him to his oldest son or to another worthy successor within the clan. Such insignia of leadership seem, however, rather to have been charms than proper regalia implying a clearly defined status, as they were not outwardly distinguished from similar ornaments worn by ordinary elders. They were neither limited in number nor clearly graded in importance.

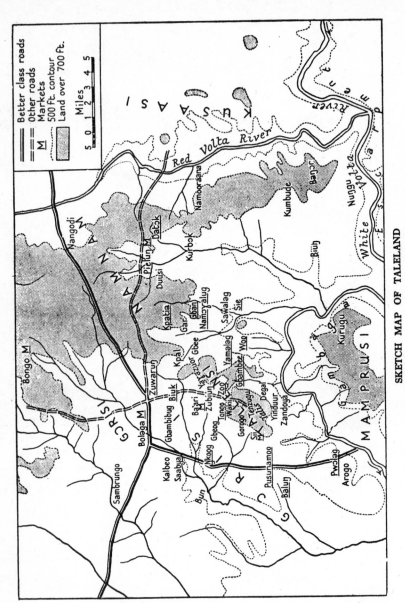

SKETCH MAP OF TALELAND

(Principal Namoo or part-Namoo settlements underlined thus : Tongo)

THE POLITICAL SYSTEM OF THE TALLENSI OF THE NORTHERN TERRITORIES OF THE GOLD COAST

By M. FORTES

I. The Country and the People

THE Northern Territories of the Gold Coast are inhabited by nearly three-quarters of a million people of negroid stock. They are part of a great congeries of peoples spreading far into French West Africa which speak related languages and share the same basic culture. To this congeries belong the Tallensi, who speak a dialect of Mole-Dagbane, a language prevailing in the eastern half, roughly, of the culture area under consideration. South of them, across the White Volta River, dwell the Mamprusi, speaking a dialect hardly distinguishable from theirs, but exhibiting a somewhat different variant of the culture. Economically and demographically, the Mamprusi show many contrasts to the Tallensi.[1] The other tribes adjacent to the Tallensi—the Gɔrisi (or Nankansi), Namnam, and Kusaasi, as they are commonly named—differ so little from them that they might all be regarded as subdivisions of a single cultural unit. Together they number some 170,000 people in British territory.

The Tallensi total about 35,000. To describe them as a tribe suggests a cohesive or at least well-defined political or cultural entity differentiated from like units. Actually, no 'tribe' of this region can be circumscribed by a precise boundary—territorial, linguistic, cultural or political. Each merges with its neighbours

---

[1] The Mamprusi have a population density of twenty-three to the square mile, whereas the administrative district which includes the Tallensi has a density of 171 to the square mile. The Mamprusi live in villages often widely scattered and varying in size from tiny hamlets to places with several thousand inhabitants. Their country, relatively low-lying by contrast with the high, well-drained plateau north of the White Volta, is reduced to swamp over considerable areas in the rainy season. Their economic system is much more complex than that of the Tallensi, and their religion has been influenced by Mohammedan communities settled in their midst. All population data are cited from the 1931 Census.

in all these respects. In the transition zones between two 'tribes' dwell communities equally linked by residential contiguity and by structural ties to both. Indeterminate frontiers roughly demarcate the Tallensi as an aggregate of communities speaking one dialect and having more cultural nuances in common and more social bonds with one another than any of them have with neighbouring 'tribes'.

Any inhabitant of Taleland calls himself Taləŋ by contrast with Mamprusi, Gɔrisi, &c. Among themselves, however, they distinguish the clans dwelling on and around the Tong Hills as the 'real Talis'.[1]

These and other Tale clans had to be subjugated by military operations which engendered a lasting respect for the power of the white man. Since then (c. 1911) a system of administration has been evolved under British control intended primarily to maintain peace and to provide the labour and materials necessary for opening up the country. Based in a rough and ready way on native institutions, it nevertheless endowed native functionaries with powers, backed by the sanction of force, both different and superior to any permitted them by custom.[2] Alongside of the system thus imposed by the Administration, though partially submerged by it, the native political institutions still flourish, however, because the ends they subserve vary considerably from those of the modern innovations. Apart from the Administration, no other contact agents are active within Taleland. The foundations of the native social system remain intact.[3]

II. Character of the Political System

Twenty-five years ago there was no one who had authority over all the Tallensi; no one who could exact tax, tribute or service from

---

[1] I use *Tallensi*, the form current in the dialect (Gɔrni) of the Gɔrisi for all the inhabitants of Taleland. In their own dialect (Talni), they speak of themselves as *Talis* (sing. *Taləŋ*), a form which, for the sake of clarity, I shall keep for the 'real Talis' only.

[2] In 1933 this system of administration began to be replaced by a new machinery of government based on the principles of Indirect Rule. This political experiment has already produced marked and valuable changes, but a consideration of them must be left for a later publication. I confine myself here to the period preceding 1934, the date of my first visit to the Tallensi.

[3] cf. my paper on 'Culture Contact as a Dynamic Process', *Africa*, ix, 1, 1936. Reprinted in *Methods of Study of Culture Contact in Africa, Mem. XV*, Int. Inst. of African Languages and Cultures.

all. They never united for war or self-protection against a common enemy. They had, in short, no 'tribal' government or 'tribal' citizenship, no centralized State exercising legislative, administrative, juridical and military functions in the interests of the whole society. Until British rule made them the subjects of a foreign State, obliged to render certain services and to obey certain laws and entitled in return to protection and freedom of movement, it was dangerous for anybody to travel outside his own community, except under the safe-conduct of kinsmen in other clans.

The indigenous political system of the Tallensi has a different character. It is based on a social structure which determines the status, rights and obligations of individuals and defines units —both territorial and associational—that transcend the domestic group and outlast changes in membership due to birth and death. A differentiated constitution provides for formal leadership and authority within each unit, and there are institutions binding them together in mutual dependence, compelling their co-operation for the common good and regulating their interrelationships, hostile or friendly. Finally, there are explicit sanctions maintaining the system.

III. Warfare

Formerly, war used to break out from time to time in Taleland. During the last three generations three large-scale wars occurred, involving almost all the Tale settlements, but, significantly, no neighbouring 'tribes'. Small fights were more frequent, both between Tale clans and between Tale and neighbouring non-Tale clans.

In general wars the alignment of forces always followed the major cleavage which runs through the whole society. The same communities always fought on the same side, assistance being rendered to one another on the grounds of clanship, local, community, or ideological ties. Armed conflict between units which supported one another in war sometimes occurred; but this was not regarded as war.

A general war consisted of a series of local skirmishes without organized methods of collective attack or defence or any military leadership, and lasted only two or three days. It ceased as abruptly as it usually began—as soon as the clans which initiated hostilities made peace.

Whatever the reason, it was a sin to instigate war. War occurred when members of one clan committed a grave injury (e.g. murder) against members of another from which theirs was divided by social barriers more powerful than any ties uniting them. It was not an instrument of policy, but an act of reprisal. Punishment, not conquest, was its purpose. Territorial annexation was incompatible with the social structure, nor could captives or booty be taken. It was a stern taboo to retain any of the food-stuffs or livestock pillaged in war. All had to be destroyed or immediately consumed. Yet war was clearly distinguished from armed self-help. To kill a man in war, though mystically dangerous, was not homicide, as it would have been if he were slain in a private quarrel.

War could occur only between contiguous communities or if the settlements intervening between the opponents were the attackers' allies. It implied the absence of clanship ties between the opponent clans, which could therefore intermarry. The highest frequency of marriage is with neighbouring communities; hence a man's kindred and affines would be amongst the enemy. Great vigilance was necessary, for it is both a sin and a serious breach of kinship ties to kill or injure such relatives. To take captives was impossible since they would generally be kinsfolk of the captor clan—people for whose welfare and on whose behalf elders of the captor clan must sacrifice to their ancestor spirits.

IV. The Network of Clanship and the Fundamental Cleavage of Tale Society

Tale warfare illustrates the basic principles of the native political organization. Any analysis of it must begin with a more precise definition of the units I have called clans. They vary significantly in their actual constitution, but the ground-plan of all is the same.

A settlement is referred to as a *tɛŋ*, a word which means primarily the Earth in its material aspect. It denotes also the Earth in its mystical aspect (see below, p. 254). *Ti tɛŋɔ* may mean the whole country of which Taleland forms a part, or Taleland only, or the settlement, according to the context of discussion. *Tɛŋ* in the secular sense is not a territorial concept, but indicates always a localized social unit, a community, or part of a community.

The skeleton of every residential aggregate is a clan, a part of a clan, or a group of clans. Such a local clan is conceived by the natives as an expanded agnatic lineage, all the members of which are 'kinsmen by consanguinity' (*dɔɣam*) to one another. Actually, the composite clan comprising two or more maximal lineages,[1] each occupying roughly its own section of the settlement, is the commonest type. Co-members of a maximal lineage are bound by the rule of exogamy. The correlative of this rule is the right of male members to inherit one another's widows, if kinship rules are not transgressed thereby.[2] These, the basic norms of clanship, are extended to other maximal lineages with which ties of clanship exist, whether of the same clan or not. The constituent maximal lineages of a composite clan, though relatively autonomous in relation to one another, are bound by clearly defined reciprocal duties and privileges, obligations and rights which emerge in ceremonial situations, economic and legal affairs and in the religious institutions.

A clan is referred to by outsiders as 'the people of such and such a place', e.g. *Tɔŋdɛm*. From the graves of their ancestors it can be inferred that the older settlements have been inhabited by the present local clans for at least three centuries. According to native theory, bonds of consanguinity, and therefore lineage membership, can never lapse. New maximal lineages cannot arise through fission of those in existence.

Like the constituent maximal lineages of a composite clan, though less so, the major segments of a maximal lineage are

---

[1] By a *maximal lineage*, I mean the most extensive group of individuals tracing agnatic descent from a single common ancestor. It comprises, therefore, all the agnatic descendants, male and female, of the remotest ancestor (eight to eleven generations back) known to members of the group. A maximal lineage has an hierarchical structure. It consists of two or more *major segments*, each a lineage of lesser span than the (inclusive) maximal lineage, whose members have a common ancestor one degree less remote than the founder of the maximal lineage. Each major segment comprises *lesser segments* constituted on the same principle; and so on down to the *minimal lineage* consisting of the children of one man. A composite clan therefore has no single common ancestor. The natives speak of a lineage as the 'house' (*yir*) or the 'children' *biis*) or the 'room' (*dug*) of So-and-So. There is no term for what I call a 'clan'. The lineage system operates completely independently of numbers. A maximal lineage of two members has the same status as one of 2,000 members in the same clan. I use *lineage* as the general term for a lineage of any order of segmentation and of any span.

[2] A father (son) may not marry the widow of a son (father). The classificatory extension of this rule differs slightly from one maximal lineage to another, according to its structure.

relatively autonomous genealogically, ritually and jurally, yet closely united by bonds of the same kind. The expansion of a maximal lineage through the course of generations, involving often territorial dispersion, enhances the centrifugal forces that promote the relative autonomy of its segments; but the centripetal forces of clanship, common religious cult, and often political interdependence continue to hold it together. In its temporal extension, every lineage represents a balance of these contrary forces. At a given time, it is a system of mutually balancing segments in which are vested the rights and duties through which the structural equilibrium is sustained. This tendency towards an equilibrium is characteristic of every phase of the social structure.

Descent being patrilineal and marriage patrilocal, the continuity of the lineage depends on its male members. Only they inherit property like land or cattle, succeed to office, and transmit the ritual and moral observances (totemic avoidances, &c.) distinctive of that unit.

Clanship has a further extension of political importance. Maximal lineages belonging to *different*, usually adjacent clans are asymmetrically linked by ties of clanship identical with those that unite constituent maximal lineages of the *same* clan, and cut across the latter ties.[1] Between such units, as within the clan, war was impossible.

This ramification of clanship ties corresponds closely to the local distribution of clans. Its greatest elaboration occurs among the 'real Talis'. Numbering about 10,000, they have some twenty-five territorially adjacent, composite clans interlinked by a network of clanship ties that embraces some clans of Goris as well. Thus

---

[1] Thus, for instance, three adjacent clans, A, B, and C, are interlinked as follows: A has three maximal lineages, A1, A2, A3; B has four, B1, B2, B3, B4; C has two, C1 and C2. Lineage A1 has ties of clanship with lineages B1 and C1, but *not* with the other B or C lineages, nor have B1 and C1 ties of clanship with A2 and A3. Members of A1, B1, and C1 may not intermarry; they may inherit one another's widows and have the reciprocal ceremonial obligations of clansmen. Members of A1 marry into the other B or C lineages, and B1 and C1 intermarry with A2 and A3. Similarly, A2 has ties of clanship with B4, but not with the other B or C lineages, and A3 has ties of clanship with B3. Maximal lineages linked in this way have the same relationship towards one another as the constituent units of a single clan, but the rights and duties pertaining to it are less rigorously effective than within the clan. Clan C has similar criss-crossing linkages with clan D, D with E, and so on.

every maximal lineage has its specific field of clanship, overlapping but not identical with that of any other maximal lineage of the same clan. It is both a constituent unit of a local clan and an intercalary unit linking that clan to another; and no clan is a closed unit. Thus any given sector of this network manifests an equilibrium of clanship and local ties balanced against genealogical and local cleavages. Loyalty to the local clan is balanced by the contrary loyalty to a component unit of a neighbouring clan. The resulting articulation of clan with clan gives the Talis a loose cohesion. They often speak of themselves as a unit differentiated from non-Talis by distinctive ritual and ceremonial observances. In fact, not all Talis have all these usages, and some non-Talis share them; characteristically, the Talis overlap with neighbouring aggregates of clans.

Interlocking with this nexus of clanship ties is an equally elaborate network of ties of ritual collaboration in the Great Festivals, the cult of the Earth and of the external *bɔɣar* (see below, p. 262). Ritual collaboration implies joint mystical benefits and responsibility and therefore amity and solidarity analogous to that of clansfolk. The two sets of ties, though not congruent, reinforce one another.

Fights between Talis clans were never, in consequence, regarded as war. Mediators linked to the combatants by ties of clanship, contiguity, or ritual collaboration immediately intervened. War to the Talis meant fighting their traditional enemies, the people of Tongo and their allies. Yet two Talis clans usually supported Tongo (see below, p. 257) and the Talis were and are bound to Tongo by stringent ritual ties, as will appear later.

By contrast with the Talis, their neighbours, the people of Tongo, are called Namoos. This nomenclature reflects the fundamental cleavage in Tale society. It is universally accepted that the founder of Tongo, Mosuor, was a fugitive from Mampurugu, where he had been forcibly ousted from the paramount chiefship. Mosuor found the primordial ancestors of four of the Talis clans occupying the country. Chief among them was the primordial Gbizug *tɛndaana*, who, the myth relates, terrified of the red turban, the flowing gown, the horses and the guns of Mosuor—these are the insignia of chiefs—fled to the Tong Hills. By a ruse, Mosuor caught him and declared that he had come to settle peaceably and to bring benefits to the community.

Therefore the *tɛndaana* allotted land to Mosuor and swore a covenant of eternal friendship with him and his descendants.

According to their lineal successors of to-day, the primordial *tɛndaanas* 'emerged from the Earth' or 'descended from Heaven'. Namoos scoff at these myths as physiologically absurd, but recognize that they express a claim to priority of occupation. The myth of Mosuor and the myth of the primordial *tɛndaanas* are complementary and are typical of the culture. Such myths conceptualize and postulate a beginning for the political and ceremonial relationships of chiefs and *tɛndaanas*, which they invest with the sanctity of unchallengeable antiquity.

Mosuor's agnatic progeny spread to Yamɔlɔg and Sie in Taleland and to Biuk on the frontier between the Tallensi and the Gɔrisi. Formally, the clan of *Mosuorbiis* (the children of Mosuor) constitutes a single maximal lineage distributed in these four territorially and politically independent units. The Tongo branch is senior to the others, as Mosuor's grave and the shrine (*bɔɣar*) dedicated to him remain in its custody. Each of these branches includes several accessory lineages united to it by some genealogical fiction and linked by ties of clanship with other clans. Tongo is linked thus to the Talis nexus, the other three branches to clans in the vicinity of each.

All those clans which claim descent from immigrant Mamprusi are designated Namoos. They have the same distinctive ritual observances. Living in close juxtaposition with the Talis are several other genealogically independent Namoo clans, each a local unit. Some fall within the political orbit of Tongo; others lie outside it. Around Yamɔlɔg and Sie dwell heterogeneous clusters of cians, Namoos and non-Namoos in close juxtaposition, some interlinked by clanship ties, others completely independent genealogically. Namoos and non-Namoos frequently form constituent lineages of the same clan, holding complementary ritual offices divided by the same structural cleavages as separate the Talis and the Tongo Namoos, but inseparably joined by equally strong structural ties and common interests. Most of these groups of non-Namoos claim affinity with the Talis as the autochthonous inhabitants of the country, though they are genealogically distinct from them, on the ground of similar ritual observances and prerogatives connected with the Earth cult. They have a role in the political system analogous to that of the Talis, but are distinguished from them by differences in the date and form of their respective Harvest Festivals.

The Talis and their congeners, claiming to be the autochthonous 'owners of the land', and the Namoos, presumed to be of varied immigrant origin, are territorially mingled, genealogically intertwined, and bound together by ineluctable ritual ties. But they are also separated by profound cleavages of equal import for their respective functions in the political system.

V. Limiting Factors: Kinship, Local Contiguity and the Economic System

Clanship, the most significant tie determining mutual assistance in war, did not operate automatically. Even segments of a single clan sometimes refused to help another segment if it was thought to have incurred just reprisals. Clanship also interposes genealogical barriers between units. For the individual, cognatic and affinal kinship ties breach the barriers. Great importance is attached to cognatic relationship, particularly to uterine (*soog*) kinship. But political relationships, like war, cut across these ties. Kinship, though it limits the insulation of lineage and clan and restricts the extent to which conflict can develop between such units, is marginal to the political system. This is obvious nowadays in the political intrigues which rend the country. Kinship ties between adherents of rival factions do not mitigate their political hostility. Conversely, however, the political rivalry of their clans does not deter individuals from the intercourse and reciprocities that kinship entails.[1]

Local contiguity also establishes ties and cleavages. The economic system, the lineage structure, and ritual ideology all put a premium on local cohesion as a factor of community solidarity. Where adjacent clans are genealogically distinct, they usually have ceremonial or community ties. The balance of ties and cleavages produces a state of tension liable to explode into conflict if one group infringes the rights of the other. Peace and non-provocation are stressed as the ideal relationships between neighbours. In this respect, contiguity imposes constraints similar to those of

---

[1] The web of kinship spreads so widely, both spatially and genealogically, that a native can travel as much as twenty miles, across 'tribal' frontiers, working his way from settlement to settlement through the hospitality and good offices of kinsfolk in each.

clanship,[1] but in consequence of the operation of different sanctions. The threat of war or, nowadays, of suspending friendly relationships is especially effective, since it endangers also community or ritual ties of fundamental import for the general good.

When ties of contiguity are added to those of clanship or of ritual interdependence, communities wider than the local clan emerge in certain situations. It is a matter of degree, of balance and contrast. The constituent units of such a community are more closely interconnected *inter se* than with other, similar units. Co-ordinated action for one end may be succeeded by independent, even conflicting action, following the lines of local and genealogical cleavage, for other ends.

Finally, the economic system is a limiting factor in the political organization. The Tallensi are peasants farming mainly cereal crops. The essential feature of their agriculture is fixed cultivation. They till the land surrounding their homesteads (*saman*) continuously, supplementing this with the less intensive cultivation of bush farms (*poog*) some distance from the settlement. The livestock they keep, though indispensable, is of subsidiary significance in their economy. Very few are wealthy enough to possess livestock equivalent in value to more than one or two head of cattle.

Peace and the introduction of British currency have brought about a tremendous expansion of local trade, but commerce is still mainly a casual occupation ancillary to agriculture. This is the case also with the few domestic crafts of the Tallensi. The only division of labour is that according to sex. Agriculture and animal husbandry are predominantly men's work; women attend to the domestic duties and engage considerably in petty trade.

Hunting and fishing, though pursued with zeal, contribute little to the subsistence level. The sylvan products of the untilled bush, however, supply commodities indispensable for their

---

[1] Thus it is an extremely heinous and therefore almost unknown offence to abduct a clansman's wife. It jeopardizes the very foundations of clanship as a factor both of political solidarity and of cult unity. The whole clan would be outraged and the elders would resort to the most drastic measures to set the matter right. The reaction is similar in the more frequent case of a man's abducting a woman married to a neighbouring clan; but this is due to fear of violent retaliation. In both instances, ritual reconciliation is necessary (cf. below, p. 270, where this is referred to again in another context).

domestic economy—firewood, shea (*Butyrospermum parkii*) fruit, &c. The products of the locust-bean tree (*Parkia filicoidea*) are exceptionally valuable, but not always freely obtainable (cf. below, pp. 258, 259).

The hazards of agriculture are enormous. The rainfall is precarious. An inopportune dry spell during the rainy season[1] may ruin the crops and create widespread privation. A generation ago, a prolonged drought spelt famine, when men in desperation seized their own or their neighbours' children to pawn or sell them into slavery among the Mamprusi for food. Nowadays such catastrophes can be averted by purchasing grain from more fortunate areas. Locusts are another unpredictable menace. Food is chronically insufficient; for even in an excellent season few people have the surplus to lay up supplies against a setback.

Fixed cultivation entails permanent and stable settlements and thus profoundly influences the political system. In the older settlements, the core of the society, an economically independent man farms land transmitted to him from his forebears, whose graves are beside his homestead. Security of tenure approximating to full proprietorial rights is the rule. In some settlements, farm-land (*kuo*)—i.e. the rights of tillage—can be alienated subject to the consent of potential heirs.[2] Elsewhere the sale of land is a sin against the Earth. In any case only extreme necessity will force a man to sell a farm. The home farms (*saman*) are a precious patrimony sanctified by the labour of former generations and held in trust for future generations. To sell this land is little short of sacrilege. To a lesser degree, this applies also to bush farms.

An essential element in the ecological adjustment of the natives has been a steady expansion into the uncultivated tracts bordering the older settlements. Pressure of population and low technical efficiency appear to have been the main causes of this process of

[1] In common with other parts of the Sudanese climatic zone, the Northern Territories of the Gold Coast experience two well-defined seasons, a rainy season yielding, in the region of Taleland, a mean annual rainfall of about 43 in., which lasts from April to mid-November, and an entirely rainless dry season lasting from mid-November to the end of March.

[2] Land is only alienated to clansfolk, kinsfolk, or co-members of the same local community, never to complete strangers. This is a consequence of the high degree of congruence between local grouping and genealogical grouping. Tale agricultural economy is more fully dealt with in M. and S. L. Fortes, 'Food in the Domestic Economy of the Tallensi', *Africa*, ix, 2, 1936.

local colonization, which has been greatly accelerated and amplified in range by the establishment of peace. It is a cycle in the history of a lineage. Young men shift to the periphery for a period; then, as the older members die, some return to take over the patrimony now left to them. The lineage system and the ancestor cult are the centripetal forces. The original home (*daboog*) of one's father is sacred; to abandon it is to incur the wrath of the ancestor spirits. New colonists, often younger members of the same lineage, replace those who return home. Gradually a permanent nucleus may be formed of descendants of men who did not return to their natal homes, and a new settlement arises. Such settlements are genealogically more heterogeneous than the older settlements. The dispersal of *Mosuorbiis* must have occurred in this way.

A maximal lineage, however widely it may be dispersed, never ceases to regard the original home (*daboog*) of its founding ancestor as its true home, very particularly associated with the spirits of its ancestors. Though dispersed, it remains anchored to a definite locality.

No one has an over-right to the farm-land a man holds by right of inheritance or purchase. No one can dispossess him of it, prevent him using it as and when he wills,[1] or resume any that he leaves untilled. Land can be borrowed; it cannot be rented. Chiefs and *tɛndaanas* (see below, p. 255) have no over-riding rights of ownership entitling them to rent, tax, or tribute for land. They have, indeed, no more land than they have acquired in the same way as any other elder.

Economically, therefore, the Tallensi are a homogeneous, sedentary, equalitarian peasantry. Every settlement has a few men of more than average wealth, due usually to the fact that they have many sons to farm for them. But no social privileges attach to wealth, though it is admired and envied. Wealth cannot be accumulated. It is partly utilized to add to the number of wives in the joint family, thus progressively increasing the drain on its resources, and is eventually distributed by inheritance. Thus it has only a temporary advantage. There are no economic classes cutting across and detracting from the solidarity of lineage, clan,

---

[1] This was remarkably demonstrated when the Tong Hills were re-settled in 1935–6. After twenty-five years, the people returned to take possession of their ancestral lands without a single boundary dispute or a single disagreement as to the ownership of plots.

and local community,[1] a fact of utmost importance for the political organization.

VI. *Authority and Responsibility in the Lineage System*

The principles of Tale social structure appear most conspicuously in large-scale activities like funeral ceremonies, the Great Festivals, hunting expeditions, &c. Rights and duties, privileges and obligations are vested in corporate units; and any authorized member can act on behalf of the unit. The principle of representation, rooted in the identification of lineage members with one another, is inherent in Tale social structure.

The range of participation determines what units emerge in a particular situation—the maximal lineages in clan activities, the constituent segments in lineage affairs, the clans in activies involving many communities. Concerted action is achieved by a balanced and symmetrical distribution of functions among the units involved. The solidarity of a unit varies accordingly. Segments bitterly opposed over divergent interests unite vigorously on matters of common interest. Co-members of any unit have a common interest in one another's welfare and in safeguarding one another's rights. Any of them will take reprisals for a wrong done against another.

The corporate identity and solidarity of the units thus delimited by agnatic descent and locality are functions of a differentiated constitution sustained by definite sanctions. Every lineage is subject to the authority of its senior male member (*kpeem*).[2] In a lineage of narrow span, i.e. with common ancestry placed four or less generations back, he is the most senior by generation; in lineages of wider span, age is the criterion, since generation seniority is no longer determinable. Throughout the social structure seniority confers authority.

The authority wielded by a lineage *kpeem* varies with its span. In the lineage round which a joint family is built up, the head

[1] Chiefs and headmen have become exceptionally wealthy through the exactions now within their power. They remain the individual beneficiaries of the new dispensation. No social cleavages based on differences of wealth have as yet grown out of this, though conflicts due to pecuniary competition are assuming a political complexion in some parts of the country.

[2] Wives are never assimilated into their husbands' lineages, though they gradually come to share the loyalties and interests of the latter. They are under the authority of their husbands, and *a fortiori* under that of any one exercising authority over their husbands.

has complete moral and ritual authority; he has the right to dispose of his dependants' labour, property, and persons; and he can use force or ritual measures to assert his authority. In a lineage of greater span, the head has only moral and ritual authority over his co-members other than his own dependants. The greater the lineage span, the older is the *kpeem*, the more prestige, respect, and honour attaches to his status, though it confers purely moral and ritual authority. Thus if the head of a major segment invites his co-members to hoe for him, it would be disrespectful but not a breach of sanctioned obligation to refuse, and they must be generously recompensed. The hierarchy culminates in the *kpeem* of the maximal lineage.

Every important transaction, secular or ceremonial, between constituted units brings into operation every grade of authority in the maximal lineage. The legal and economic rights of the family head cannot be exercised without the consent of the lineage heads senior to him. Each grade of lineage head has corresponding rights—e.g. in the gifts that legalize marriage. A specific right, though it is rigorously defined, is an element in the total configuration of rights.

Rights imply responsibilities. Every grade of right and authority is matched by an equivalent grade of responsibility. Those who can exact economic services from their dependants are economically and ritually responsible for their welfare and publicly liable for their actions. The head of a major segment has ritual and moral responsibilities towards and for the unit. He must provide the ceremonial contributions due from the segment on important public occasions, e.g. funeral ceremonies. He has no economic or jural liabilities for his co-members severally or jointly. The head of the maximal lineage has still more general moral and ritual responsibilities. This hierarchy of rights balanced against a hierarchy of obligations is the foundation of Tale jural relations.

The *kpeem* is the principal representative of the lineage, the focus of the forces maintaining its corporate unity and identity. All inter-lineage transactions are conducted formally through lineage heads; but whatever the issue, the whole unit must be consulted. Every member may express his opinion, greatest weight being attached to that of any one directly implicated, economically or jurally.

Ultimately, a *kpeem's* authority rests on a moral basis—the bonds of mutual dependence and common interest which unite co-members of a lineage, accepted as axiomatic in virtue of community of descent and most explicitly conceptualized in the ancestor cult. Every lineage, whatever its span, worships the shrine (*bɔɣar*)[1] of its ancestors separately. This is the primary index of its differentiation from other like units and the arch-symbol of its corporate identity and relative autonomy. To the hierarchy of segments constituting a maximal lineage corresponds a hierarchy of ancestor shrines. At sacrifices to a particular ancestor, every segment of the lineage sprung from him must be represented. Thus segments of a lineage sacrifice *separately* to their respective founding ancestors, *jointly* to their common lineage ancestor.

VII. *Tale Religion*

A man becomes head of his lineage by succeeding to the custody of the lineage ancestors' shrine (*bɔɣar*). He sacrifices to it on behalf of the lineage or any of its members and in his own name, especially at sowing, harvest and festival times. The Tallensi both fear and venerate their ancestors, seeking to placate and coerce them with sacrifices, so that health, fruitfulness, and prosperity may prevail.

This is native belief. Objectively, Tale religion is a potent instrument of social control. People who sacrifice together, whether as kinsfolk or through ties of ritual collaboration, must be at amity with one another, else they offend the ancestors. Because of this, death and the extinction of his issue is the mystical retribution falling on a man who murders a kinsman or clansman. For this reason, too, dissension amongst people thus united must eventually give place to reconciliation.

The custodian of any shrine must be treated with respect by those dependent on his priestly offices, else he may reject their sacrifices. This is the most effective sanction of a lineage head's moral authority. The ancestor cult, the supreme sanction of kinship ties, is a great stabilizing force counteracting the centrifugal tendencies inherent in the lineage system. However

---

[1] A *bɔɣar* is a particular catagory of *baɣar*. Any object or animal which has ritual significance may be called a *baɣar*. A *bɔɣar* is the *baɣar* which is the seat of all the ancestors of a lineage as far back as the one who founded it.

widely a lineage may be dispersed, its members can never escape the mystical jurisdiction of their founding ancestor. Cognatic descendants, too, fall under this jurisdiction as individuals.

The ideological framework of the lineage system is the ancestor cult; that of locality is the cult of the Earth (*tɛŋ*). It is not easy to formulate briefly the connotation of the word *tɛŋ*, in its mystical aspect. The natives distinguish between *kuo*, the arable surface, *tam*, the soil, and *tɛŋ*, the community, the locality, the land, or the Earth in its mystical aspect, according to context. Unlike ancestors, who differ from one genealogical group to another, and whose influence is confined to their own descendants, the Earth is single and universal; in theory, all peoples are subject to the mystical power of one and the same *tɛŋ*. Yet the Earth is manifold, too. Sacrifices must be offered to it at particular sacred spots (*tɔŋ-gban*), and the word *tɛŋ* (pl. *tɛs*) is applied to such places, meaning the sacred spot and its precincts. *Tɔŋgbana*, and hence *tɛs* in this restricted sense, have names and, like genealogical groups, differentiating taboos.

Between *tɛŋ* the universal and *tɛŋ* the particular sacred spot lies *tɛŋ* the locality embracing a number of sacred spots, but conceived as the widest precincts of one, the principal (*kpeem*) among them, and under the priestly jurisdiction of a single *tɛndaana*. This principal *tɔŋgban* is the ritual hub of the locality, the shrine of *tɛŋ*, the universal Earth, where important sacrifices are performed, especially at the times of the Great Festivals, and ritual atonement is made for sacrilege. As neighbouring *tɛndaanas* are usually connected by ties of clanship or of ritual collaboration, so neighbouring *tɔŋgbana* and *tɛs* are regarded in ritual and doctrine as 'kinsfolk' (*mabiis*). In conformity with the social structure, all the *tɛs* of Taleland and of some neighbouring non-Tale communities are regarded as 'kinsfolk', a metaphor which reconciles the diversity of sacred spots with the singleness and universality of the Earth.

The greatest sacrilege against the Earth is to shed human blood in strife. Atoning sacrifices must be made by both parties or they and their issue will perish. It is only less sacriligeous to keep anything found on the Earth (*tɛŋɔnpiima*), especially stray animals, objects of metal, or vagrant humans. Cloth may not be worn when sacrifice is offered to the Earth.

The Earth is impersonal, but 'alive' (*bonvor*)—that is, a controlling agency in the lives of men. Incalculable, like all mystical agencies, the source of prosperity, fertility, and health as well as of drastic retribution for sin or sacrilege, witting or unwitting, it is regarded with great awe. As lineage and locality are inextricably intertwined in the social structure, so *tɛŋ* and ancestors (*yaanam*) are indissolubly associated in Tale religion. The concepts mark two poles of the system, the ancestors being concerned primarily with the good of their descendants, the Earth with the general good. Every lineage worships its ancestors, but the priestly offices connected with the Earth are confined to particular maximal lineages.

VIII. Chiefship and Tɛndaanaship

The head of any lineage greater than the minimal is at the apex of a hierarchy of lesser heads. The head of a maximal lineage alone is not subordinate to one of higher degree nor balanced by the head of another segment of equal order. His status in the unit is unique, epitomizing its genealogical and corporate exclusiveness in comparison with all other similar units. He is the fulcrum of its relations with other units. Most heads of maximal lineages hold special offices sanctioned by the religious system and defined by myths of origin or descent. Through them a range of political relations transcending the limits of agnatic grouping is achieved.

In native thought, these offices comprise two major institutions: *na'am*, chiefship, and *tɛndaan*, the office of Custodian of the Earth. *Na'am* is the prerogative of one set of clans and lineages, predominantly the Namoos; *tɛndaan* that of the Talis and their congeners, in accordance with the major cleavage of the social structure. Actually, these two categories overlap. Several clans have both types of offices, held by different maximal lineages, and some offices (e.g. those held by the Hill Talis) have attributes of both. Homologous though they are in many respects, *na'am* and *tɛndaan* are polar functions indissolubly coupled together though opposed. This is the central factor in Tale political organization. The same configuration is found, with many local variations, throughout Taleland and the neighbouring areas. Its most precise elaboration occurs in the Tongo district. The Master of Tongo (*Tɔŋraana*) is the most eminent chief (*na'ab*) in Taleland. He claims nowadays to be the ruler of all the Tallensi; but this is a distortion in terms of the modern privileges of chiefship, of a status which is merely that of *primus inter pares* in the native system. His pre-eminence of rank is apparent from the deference shown to him by all other lineage heads in Taleland, as well as from the special taboos observed by him alone. Yet he has no administrative authority over any other community than Tongo, not even over the junior—but locally and politically autonomous—branches of *Mosuorbiis*. The Tongo *na'am* may be taken as a paradigm, for it differs from lesser chiefships only in degree.

'The chiefship belongs to all of us' ('*Na'am la a ti waabi bon*') is a maxim often cited. The office belongs to the maximal lineage, the clan, the community; a particular chief is only its temporary incumbent. This conception, expressing the identification of the whole group with the *na'am*, their loyalty to and pride in it, is the basis of a chief's moral and political authority. A chief cannot be deposed, nor will dissident segments secede, however objectionable a particular chief may be. They know that their turn to hold the chiefship will come round; for every member of the maximal lineage which has the prerogative of a particular chiefship is eligible for it. Rank is temporary in a given segment. Conversely, only agnatic descendants of the founder of a *na'am* may hold it, as only they can directly invoke the beneficence of the chiefly ancestor spirits.[1]

The Tallensi say that *na'am* is purchased (*da*). Theoretically, any eligible man, young or old, may compete for it. Actually men of junior status are considered to be unsuitable. Indeed, only elders commanding the services of many dependants could, formerly, raise the 'price'[2] enabling them to compete, partly from their own resources, but largely by borrowing from clansmen and kindred. Competition for a chiefship was a contest of segments, not of individuals. The higher a man's prestige and standing, the wider would be the span of the segment supporting him with loans and by their presence on the election day. The general level of economic equality made the purchase of *na'am* an indirect ballot.

[1] Thus theoretically every agnatic descendant of Mosuor is eligible for any of the chiefships held by *Mosourbiis*, and members of accessory lineages are ineligible. Actually, the political independence of each branch is asserted by the restriction of competition for its chiefship to its own members. Some minor chiefships may be held by members of two or more clans on the same principle.

[2] Minor chiefships 'cost' eight or nine cattle, important chiefships up to seventy head of cattle, as well as large sums of cowries—not to speak of the many presents that must be given to the elector's elders to obtain their good offices.

Na'am brings Taleland into the political orbit of the Mamprusi. The prototype and fountain-head of all *na'am* is the Chief of Mampurugu. To be valid, the mystical attributes which constitute its essence must be ritually vested in the holder by him or by someone endowed with *na'am* by him. *Na'am* is also an ancestral heritage and therefore most appropriately held by those who belong to the same stock as the Chief of Mampurugu, i.e. the Namoos. Accordingly, the elector of most Tale and many Gore chiefships is one of his sub-chiefs, the Kuna'aba. The *Tɔŋraana* alone among Tale chiefs elects subordinate chiefs, on the same princple. A hierarchy of chiefships results, all miniature replicas of the fountain-head *na'am* in structure and participating in its mystical virtue.

But the analogy of a feudal system[1] would be misleading. The chiefs appointed by a single elector—and by extension their clansmen—speak of themselves as 'kinsmen' (*mabiis*). In Taleland they assisted one another in war, sometimes to the detriment of ties of real clanship or of ritual collaboration.[2] They would also protect one another's clansmen from illegitimate molestation by their own people. Similarly, Tale chiefs refer to Kuna'aba as their 'father' (*ba*), implying that they owe him loyalty, respect, and ceremonial deference. They would not make war on his settlement nor he on any of theirs. They would try to protect clansmen of his travelling in Taleland from molestation, as he would their clansmen travelling in Mampurugu. But Kuna'aba has no economic, juridical, administrative, or military rights sanctioned by the native political system over any Tale chief. His ceremonial investiture by Kuna'aba is the crucial act conferring chiefship on a man (even if he is actually selected by an administrative officer). Nevertheless, Kuna'aba's modern judicial and administrative authority rests solely on the sanction of force represented by the Administration. It is significant that he was

[1] The Administration has always regarded Taleland as part of the 'Mamprusi State', under the ultimate rule of the Chief of Mampurugu, through his sub-chief and deputy, the Kuna'aba, who was considered to have full jurisdiction over 'Kurugu Division'. Kuna'aba and his councillors were created a Native Authority and Court in 1932 as the only official court in the Division vested with judicial and administrative authority. In the native political system, Kuna'aba's sphere of electoral authority does not correspond to a political or 'tribal' unit.

[2] e.g. the people of Sii, Talis by clanship ties and ritual observance but holding a chiefship from Kuna'aba, together with their clansmen the people of Yindu'uri, usually supported Tongo in war against their fellow Talis for this reason.

formerly treated with derision and his settlement often plundered by Tale clans which have no ties through chiefship with him.

An elector has, correlatively, no direct ritual, political, or military responsibilities for a clan whose chief he appoints. He is morally and ritually bound to select, in consultation with his elders, the best candidate for a chiefship, recking less of his pecuniary offer than of his reputation and pedigree. He must see that the office circulates, so that it is not monopolized by any one segment, thus stressing the common interest of the whole unit in the *na'am*.[1] An immoral choice would evoke the wrath of the ancestors. To this extent only has an elector a moral responsibility for the well-being of the community whose chief he appoints. He is the repository of *na'am*, so when a chief he appoints dies the insignia with which he was invested must be ceremonially restored to the elector pending the appointment of a successor. Thus the cycle is completed.

IX. *The Complementary Functions of Chiefs and Tɛndaanas*

Every Tale chief says, '*Man so ntɛŋ; ndame*' ('I own my land. I bought it'). In certain respects the rights and authority implied in this are precise. He owns the products of all locust-bean trees (*Parkia filicoidea*) growing within the precincts of his clan settlement, as well as certain stretches of river and of hunting bush, the exploitation of which is prohibited until they have been communally fished or hunted at the chief's instance. Big fish and special portions of any animal slain or found dead in his bush must be delivered to the chief. Stringent ritual sanctions uphold these rights. Vagrant humans (*da'abr*), stray dogs or cattle, and brass or copper ware found lying about must be delivered to a chief. These prerogatives have some, though limited economic value even to-day.[2]

---

[1] Owing to the advanced age at which chiefs were often appointed, the average duration of a chieftaincy was only about ten years. This conduced to a fairly rapid circulation of a chiefship amongst the segments of a clan.

[2] The right to vagrant humans has, of course, been abolished. Some minor privileges of chiefs corresponding to it in political significance have not been mentioned, as they are also falling into abeyance. In several cases, chiefship reduced entirely to these rights until the pacification of the country led to the establishment of permanent settlements on the fringes of what used to be merely hunting bush. Thus the chiefs of Biuŋ and Gbiog used to live amongst their clansfolk as members of communities dwelling within the zone of authority of other clan heads, though vested with rights over their respective tracts of river and bush, &c.

The products of locust-bean trees, river, and bush are luxuries not accessible to most commoners. Vagrant humans were sold; dogs and cattle sacrificed to ancestor spirits. The modern privileges of chiefship are sometimes described as substitutes for these traditional rights.

But to the natives their crucial significance lies in the correlative duties and responsibilities they involve. It was a grave moral responsibility, subject to mystical penalties, for any one but a chief to sell a wandering stranger into slavery. Fishing and hunting expeditions are dangerous. Only a chief can fire the bush. The fault for a serious accident falls on him. He must perform precautionary magic before an expedition, and offer placatory sacrifices to render river or bush safe again after an accident.[1]

These rights and responsibilities are indices of the complex configuration of rights and responsibilities through which chief-ship accomplishes what the natives regard as its supreme end—'to prosper the community' (*maal tɛŋ*). *Na'am* is a medium through which the mystical forces conceptualized in Tale religion are mobilized to ensure the welfare and fertility of humans, animals, and crops—the common good, in so far as it is determined by natural forces beyond pragmatic control. A chief's death brings famine upon the community. His blessing is as potent for good as his curse is dangerous. His office is sacred, imposing on him observances and taboos—very rigorous in the case of the *Tɔŋraana* —symbolizing his mystical powers and responsibilities. He is the guardian of the community, responsible for the organization of and major contributions towards sacrifices made by it to preserve the beneficence of the ancestors and for the conduct of the annual ceremonies of the Great Festivals. He is the custodian of the sacred objects that symbolize the continuity and perpetuity of the *na'am*. When a natural calamity threatens, the elders appeal to him for intercession with the ancestors. Most important is his power to regulate the rainfall.

These capacities, derived from the chiefly ancestors, are vested in a chief as the highest representative of his maximal lineage. He cannot exercise them arbitrarily, for his own ends, but only in conclave with representative elders of the clan or community for the

[1] Other aspects of communal fishing expeditions are discussed in my paper on 'Communal Fishing and Fishing Magic in the Northern Territories of the Gold Coast', *J.R.A.I.*, **67**, 1937.

common good. But he is also bound to exercise them; they are obligatory because, as trustee of the ancestors, he benefits by the rights of *na'am* bequeathed by them, which belong really to the maximal lineage. Hence a proportion of the economic goods he obtains through them must be distributed amongst the segment heads.

This configuration of rights, responsibilities and mystical powers binds a chief and his community in reciprocal dependence. Political boundaries are an innovation frequently causing acrimonious disputes between chiefs and headmen. A chief, in the native system, is the pivot of a community consisting of a series of zones of increasing amplitude and diminishing integration. At the centre is his own maximal lineage and clan. One or two contiguous clans may be closely associated with it, forming part of this central community in all but the genealogical sense. Its area of residence is approximately that within which the chief owns all the locust-bean trees. Beyond this stretches a zone of unrelated clans acknowledging the chief's mystical value for the common good and his correlative right to vagrant humans, but otherwise independent of, sometimes even hostile in war to, his clan. Divided by local, genealogical and ideological cleavages which may precipitate open conflict over divergent interests, such a cluster of clans emerges as a community in ritual collaboration for the common good, especially during the Great Festivals or if a natural calamity threatens. It represents a balance, usually, between Namoo and non-Namoo units, the pivot of which is the bond between chief and *tendaana*.

Without the blessing of the Earth, a chief's mystical powers are void. Thus the final phase of his investiture is his ceremonial reception by the *tendaanas* of the community in turn, who present him to their Earth shrines (*tɔŋgbana*) with pleas for blessings on his chieftaincy. Frequently thereafter he must send animals to them to be sacrificed to the Earth. He is powerless to ensure the welfare of the community without their ritual collaboration. He cannot hunt or fish his bush and river without a *tendaana's* blessing. Finally, on his death a chief is buried secretly by a *tendaana*. A community, whether it is a single clan or a group of clans, is politically defined by the complementary functions of chief and *tendaana*.

The relationship of chief and *tendaana* is one of polar opposition and mutual constraint limited by and maintaining their joint responsibility for the common good, validated by myths like that of Mosuor and symbolized in the taboos and prerogatives of each, those of tɛndaanas being mainly the exact contrary of chiefs'. As throughout Tale society, the structural relationships are conceptualized in and sanctioned by the ritual ideology.

A tɛndaana—Custodian of the Earth—is primarily a religious functionary. His office is homologous with chiefship, but oriented towards the Earth. He 'prospers the community' by ensuring the beneficence of the Earth for it. His ritual relationship with the Earth imposes certain taboos (e.g. he may never wear cloth, but only skins) on him and enables him to accept the responsibility of dealing directly with it. Hence all lost property not the prerogative of chiefs must be delivered to a tɛndaana. Lest the Earth be offended, a tɛndaana must pierce the soil for a new grave and turn the first sod for making a farm or building a homestead on virgin land. Portions of the animals sacrificed on such occasions belong to him. Tɛndaanas may not sell men; but if a chief sold a vagrant person he gave a cow to the tɛndaana of the area where the man was found as a piacular offering to the Earth. Because the Earth abhors bloodshed, tɛndaanas have ritual power to stop fighting and to mediate in disputes. They perform the sacrifices offered to the Earth to expiate murder. Their curse or blessing is more potent than a chief's, since the Earth is universal and can punish or bless a man anywhere.

Tɛndaanas, therefore, have great moral and ritual authority. But they cannot 'prosper the community' without the collaboration of chiefs for they have no mystical power over rain. Thus in the Tongo area, if flood or drought threatens, the representative tɛndaanas of the Talis call on the Tɔŋraana and exhort him to avert it. Though ancient animosities and structural cleavages divide their clans from his they are bound to collaborate ritually for the common good.

X. Tɛndaanas and the Wider Community

The office of tɛndaana is vested in a maximal lineage. Any male member of the lineage may at times deputize for the tɛndaana, and all its members must observe certain of his taboos. Tɛndaanas succeed by right of seniority or are chosen by divination from amongst the segment heads.[1] They are ritually installed by

---

[1] The Hill Talis have a variant procedure which is a compromise between this method of selection and the way chiefs are elected.

fellow *tɛndaanas* of lineages linked to theirs by ties of clanship or of ritual collaboration. This is one of many ritual ties that unite neighbouring *tɛndaanas*.

Composite clans have several *tɛndaanas*, one of whom is senior in status to the rest, but in ritual matters which concern the whole clan all participate, the key roles being distributed equally amongst them. *Tɛndaanas* of neighbouring clans, whether interlinked by clanship ties or not, usually have ritual ties, and any one of them can represent all in ritual relationships with a chief or another such group of clans. In the Great Festivals, the key functions are distributed amongst *tɛndaanas* representing such groups of clans and an equilibrium of mutual dependence is attained which is an extremely powerful sanction of solidarity, counteracting the conflicts due to divergent loyalties.

Every *tɛndaana* has his own *tɛŋ*, the area within which he sacrifices to the Earth shrines (*tɔŋgbana*) and exercises his other ritual prerogatives. He allots any unowned land in this area for farming or building, in return for gifts which have a ritual and not economic significance. People of other clans than his may dwell there, acknowledging his ritual rights, but not paying him rent or tribute.

A *tɛndaanas's tɛŋ* is roughly demarcated by certain natural landmarks, but it has no precise boundaries, since it is only a subdivision of the single, unitary Earth. Since neighbouring *tɛndaanas* usually have clanship or ritual ties, they regard their respective rights and responsibilities as specific devolutions of what are really common rights and responsibilities shared, in the last resort, by all *tɛndaanas*. Frequently neighbouring *tɛndaanas* have one or more Earth shrines in common.

The Earth cult, therefore, is at the same time a factor in the differentiation of structural units, accentuating their relative autonomy in relation to one another and their divergent interests, and a factor in the integration of the community. In the wider community, it balances chiefship; but in the narrower unit of a local clan or interconnected group of clans like the Talis, which has no chiefship, it is balanced by the cult of the 'external (*yɛŋha*) bɔγar'. Among the Hill Talis, this is an esoteric cult into which their youths are initiated, as well as a fertility cult which attracts pilgrims from places far beyond the borders of Taleland. Its devotees could visit these places safely, and this was a channel for both economic and cultural exchange. Such a bɔɣar is the core of the Harvest Festival of its congregation, which consists of a group of maximal lineages generally of different clans, each having the prerogative of one ritual office connected with the cult. This grouping cuts across the grouping in terms of ritual collaboration in the Earth cult. A bɔɣar is the seat of its congregation's ancestors, the opposite pole to the Earth in the religious scheme. Thus ritual sanctions and interlaced loyalties are counterbalanced to maintain the social equilibrium. Among the Hill Talis, the bɔɣar has the same mystical value and function as na'am in the wider community, and its principal officers are referred to as 'chiefs' among themselves, though they are tɛndaanas in relation to the Chief of Tongo.

The most conspicuous mechanism through which the ritual interdependence and joint responsibility for the common good of chiefs and tɛndaanas is maintained is the cycle of the Great Festivals.[1] Its centre is the Tongo area, but it embraces all the Tale settlements as well as several neighbouring non-Tale settlements each entering the cycle in its proper sequence. These festivals are periods of ritually sanctioned truce, when all conflicts and disputes must be abandoned for the sake of ceremonial co-operation. In each phase of a festival, every corporate unit involved has its specific ceremonial role, vested in its head and indispensable for the propitious outcome of the whole set of ceremonies; and in each the crucial act is the meeting of chief and tɛndaanas, or their deputies, jointly to perform ritual for the blessing of the community. The chief on whom the most important ceremonial duties devolve is the Tɔŋraana; but the rites and celebrations show that he represents all the chiefs whose common heritage is na'am derived from the Chief of Mampurugu and whose rights and responsibilities are interlinked through this fountain-head. Similarly, the principal tɛndaanas concerned represent all tɛndaanas.

In this festival cycle, therefore, the widest Tale community emerges; but it is so loosely articulated that for the members of any particular clan it forms merely a remote frame of social reference. It is not a fixed political entity but a functional synthesis. It brings out the common allegiance and ideological fraternity of all chiefs,

[1] See my paper on 'Ritual Festivals and Social Cohesion in the Hinterland of the Gold Coast', *Amer. Anthropologist*, **38**, 4, 1936.

the kinship of all *tendaanas* evinced in their common cult of the Earth, and the complementary functions of these offices. It means the dominance, for a period, of the forces of integration ever-present in the social structure—in kinship, clanship, neighbour-hood ties, chiefship and *tendaana*ship—but generally submerged by the sectional interests, springing from these same institutions, that divide Tale society into a multitude of independent corporate units. The festivals are annual events reputed to be of immemorial antiquity. This is proof of the relative stability of Tale society over a long period of time and of the well-adjusted balance maintained, in the long run, between the forces of integration and those of differentiation.

The mainspring of this synthesis is Tale ritual ideology. Principally, it is the notion of the common good as referring to human welfare and prosperity in their most vital and universal aspects, superseding all sectional interests rooted in the social structure. The mystical determinism postulated for it raises the common good above all mundane issues and subjects the obligation to collaborate for it to unchallengeable and eternal sanctions which it would be inconceivable to flout. It stands for the widest body of established custom, the 'rule of law' as the Tallensi understand it, which regulates their social life.

XI. The Secular Authority of Chiefs and Tendaanas

The secular powers and authority of chiefs and *tendaanas* have been radically altered by the advent of British administration. Chiefs are now the agents of the Administration, exercising judicial and executive authority in its name and with its backing. *Tendaanas* have no political status under this dispensation. Clans which have no chiefs are governed by headmen calling themselves 'chiefs' and exercising the modern powers of chiefs. They form part of the administrative machinery which has grown up to meet modern requirements—the provision of labour and materials for public works, such as roadmaking, formerly non-existent, and especially the maintenance of peace and the enforcement of law.

The significant characteristic of the new order lies in the Administration's monopoly of the sanction of overwhelming force. Chiefs and headmen nowadays exact taxes, tribute, and labour from their people which have made them fabulously wealthy compared with their predecessors. They stress jealously their territorial and political independence, instead of, as in the native system, the common basis of their rights and responsibilities. As agents of the Administration, they place their private interests first. To perform the duties and exact the rewards of their present administrative status, they rely on the assistance of their close agnates and of a new class of subordinate officers appointed by themselves; for the new sanctions deriving from the backing of Government could not operate through the hierarchy of lineage elders, who have no power to coerce fellow members.

The people accept the new powers and exactions of chiefs and headmen with a mixture of resentment and resignation. This does not affect their valuation of their traditional political institutions. For the new system and the native political organization are still largely discrete, though focussed partly in the same personages. The sanctions inherent in the native social structure are not effective in the framework of the new administrative organization. Chiefs and headmen are not restrained from what would be illicit extortions according to native values by the sanctions to which they submit unconditionally as members of the native social structure. Friction is inevitable when chiefs or headmen attempt to assert their administrative rights in situations defined according to the native political ideas by others; and factions coveting the wealth and power of office under the Administration are arising with claims to recognition based on their status in the native system.

At the same time, tendencies conducing to the fusion of the two systems are operating. Chiefs' and headmen's tribunals are especially important in this connexion. Though not recognized as part of the official judicial machinery,[1] they were encouraged by Administrative officers. They are rapidly becoming an integral part of the native political structure, though their authority is derived from the power of the Administration to enforce the peace

[1] The only officially recognized Native Tribunal in Taleland was, in 1934, that of the Chief of Kurugu (Kuna'aba). Its jurisdiction was limited to civil wrongs, with the exception of actions relating to land, inheritance, or damages or debts of over £5. Crimes fall under the jurisdiction of British courts, the District Commissioner sitting as magistrate. Actually, most cases dealt with by the Chief of Kurugu's court came on appeal from the unofficial chiefs' and headmen's tribunals, and appeal was allowed from this court to that of the Chief of Mamprusi, to which all land cases also went in the first instance.

they have been established to maintain. Their vigour is due to the abolition of traditional methods of obtaining redress for wrongs. Chiefs and headmen are the judicial officers, assisted sometimes informally and for reasons of etiquette and of ancient habit by a few elders. Their jurisdiction is confined to civil wrongs, and though they could until recently inflict fines in special cases, they lacked penal sanctions for the enforcement of their verdicts. The best of them tried, therefore, to arbitrate justly, so as to gain the acquiescence of both litigants. Generally a chief deals with cases in which members of his community are defendants. The hearing fees paid were a lucrative source of income until recently.

These judicial powers have enhanced enormously the prestige and authority of chiefs, especially within their own clans. Their judgements are influencing the development of Tale law and custom. Yet their administrative authority is still bounded by the cleavages of the native social structure. The *Tɔŋraana*, for instance, though recognized by the Administration as chief of the Talis, has no effective administrative control over them. The limit of his effective authority is the close-knit community consisting of his own clan and two adjacent clans, which have always been intimately united to Tongo by local, kin, and ritual ties.

In the native system, the secular authority of a chief or a *tɛndaana* is derived, on the one hand, from his ritual status, and on the other, from his supremacy in the hierarchy of lineage elders. Chiefs and *tɛndaanas*, especially those who are considered to be of senior rank, are always treated deferentially. Their ritual prestige and status in the lineage hierarchy has always enabled them to command individual or communal assistance from the whole clan in return for the customary recompense. They had no right to tax, tribute, or service. They were and are morally obliged to be hospitable and generous, especially to their clansfolk, but they have never had economic obligations towards them severally or collectively.

As head of the maximal lineage, a chief or *tɛndaana* must be informed of all important affairs that concern it. His assent is necessary in the conduct of many, especially if they involve relationships—jural, ceremonial, or economic, whether pacific or hostile—with other clans. A chief cannot, for example, allocate any land except his own to a new settler, but his consent and blessing are essential to permit the man to join the community and prosper.[1] If the common interests of the clan or of a close community like Tongo and its neighbours are infringed, e.g. if a member is murdered or a member's wife abducted, the action to be taken is decided and often carried out by a conclave of the elders presided over by the chief or *tεndaana*, or by a committee of all the *tεndaanas* and elders, in a composite unit. It was a grave sin for a chief or *tεndaana* to instigate war, but if an individual or a segment went to war, help would only be given by the rest of the clan if the chief or *tεndaana* consented, since his blessing and intercession with the ancestors and the Earth were indispensable for victory.

In these ways, chiefs and *tεndaanas* have always exercised considerable authority in the affairs of the clan; formerly, they had no judicial or administrative powers comparable to those of contemporary chiefs and headmen.

Associated with every chiefship—integrally part of it, according to native ideas—is a number of titled elders (*kpεm*) appointed by the chief in the same way as he is himself elected. Appointment to one of these titles is a signal distinction, though their value is mainly honorific. A conscientious chief distributes them fairly amongst all the segments of his clan, as well as amongst neighbouring clans closely bound to his. These elders never formed a regular council. In the affairs of the unit, the lineage elders played as great or greater part than they; but they, and through them their respective segments, have direct bonds of loyalty to the chief, independent of the lineage structure and counteracting the centrifugal forces of divergent segment loyalties. *Na'am* is thus, as it were, distributed amongst all the segments of the maximal lineage. In keeping with this, some of the titled elders have special duties and compensatory privileges connected with the chief's rights over locust-bean trees, bush, and river. The *Yidaana*, the most important titled elder, acted as the chief's deputy and spokesman in public matters. In the interval between the death of a chief and the appointment of his successor, when the *na'am* was carried on by his brothers and sons, a *Yidaana* could formerly exercise great influence on the conduct of affairs. These offices are not found in clans which have only *tεndaanas* and

---

[1] A *tεndaana* can allocate unowned land within the locality over which he has ritual jurisdiction as farming plots or house sites. The 'tenant', however, owes him only a ritual tithe in return, but no political allegiance.

analogous ritual lineage heads, who are more closely identified with the lineage structure than chiefs.

How, then, were the rights and interests of individuals or groups protected against injury thirty years ago? The general principles of what we should call legal procedure are the same now as they were then; for a case reaches a court only when other methods of effecting a settlement fail—when, formerly, the injured party would have resorted to armed self-help or drastic ritual sanctions.

The action taken to redress a wrong or assert a right depended on the structural relationship in which the parties stood to each other. The distribution of rights and responsibilities in accordance with the lineage structure makes every dispute an issue between groups—segments, lineages, clans, communities. Settlement by negotiation between the lineage heads, conducted through a privileged intermediary like a tɛndaana, or a kinsman of both units, or the head of a lineage connected with both, would be attempted, to begin with, and often succeeded. A dispute between clansmen creates intestine hostilities, disrupts co-operation, and undermines the clan's corporate unity. A misfortune attributed to the displeasure of the ancestors may intervene and compel a reconciliation to be effected. But if it is acute or involves two major segments, now as formerly it may be brought before the chief or tɛndaana, who with the elders threshes it out. Chiefs nowadays treat these like ordinary cases, but are swayed in their judgements as much by concern for the solidarity of the group as by considerations of strict justice. In any case, the weight of moral pressure brought to bear on the disputants is usually sufficient to settle the matter; but instances are known where clansmen fought one another as a result of a dispute.

Disputes between members of clans linked by ties of clanship, neighbourhood, or ritual collaboration were dealt with similarly. The injured group might force a rapid settlement by threatening to cut off reciprocal good relationships and to take to arms.

But if, owing to the distance between their settlements, the injured party could not make direct representations or threaten their opponents, recourse might be had to arbitration. Chiefs, assisted by their elders, were the usual arbitrators. The injured party would appeal to the head of their opponents' maximal lineage, who would send the disputants to a neighbouring chief in order to ensure an impartial hearing. This chief's recompense was a gift from the party for whom he found. He had no means of enforcing his verdict. The heads and lineage elders of the group adjudged wrong might attempt to do so in the interest of future good relationships. Sometimes, as still to-day, the issue would be left to mystical arbitrament. The disputants swear to the justice of their respective claims by the chief's skins or the Earth, and the prevaricator will, it is held, perish in due course. A chief could not impose fines even on members of his own clan or expel any one from the community. Like any head of a maximal lineage, he might, if he were gravely affronted, or if some one were a source of continual discord, curse the offender, who might migrate for fear of the ancestors' wrath. Public indignation might have the same effect; for such people endanger the community's welfare.

Compensation plays no part in Tale methods of adjusting wrongs. Homicide was and is regarded as equally a grave sin against the Earth and the ancestors, and an injury against the corporate unity of the victim's lineage and clan. If a man killed a clansman, whether accidentally or deliberately, the elders of the murderer's segment sent to beg the forgiveness of the chief or *tɛndaana* for this act which threatened to 'destroy the community' (*ŋma tɛŋ*). The chief or *tɛndaana* and the clan elders would then determine the number of cattle and sheep which must be offered by the culprit's family as expiatory sacrifices to the ancestor spirits and the Earth. The victim's family, too, must contribute animals to these sacrifices; for they serve not only to expiate the bloodshed, but to reconcile the two hostile segments. Vengeance is forbidden and, if necessary, forcible restraint or a ritual interdiction by the chief or *tɛndaana* would be used to quell hot tempers. The procedure was the same if the victim belonged to a different clan from the murderer. But if the two clans were traditional enemies in war, vengeance would be taken if opportunity offered by any clansman of the victim against any clansman of the culprit. Expiatory sacrifices would be made again, but no further reprisals ensue. Such murders, however, might formerly have led to war.

A thief caught *in flagrante* was severely beaten and publicly disgraced if he were a clansman of the sufferer. If not, his eyes were put out or he was otherwise mutilated. The disgrace was considered to be so great that no reprisals would be attempted.

Matrimonial rights are far more jealously guarded than property rights, for they are the concern of the whole clan, since all have leviritic rights to one another's widows and all children replenish the clan. This is a consequence of the elaborate differentiation of Tale society according to agnatic descent, and of the strength of exogamy as a factor of social cleavage. The abduction of wives—inconceivable, as we have seen, if ties of clanship exist between the abductor's group and the husband's—was and is regarded as a serious violation of a clan's rights. The injured clan would threaten to suspend ritual co-operation, or to retaliate in kind, or to go to war, and the lineage elders of the abductor's clan would immediately take steps to return the woman. This was indeed the most frequent cause of both small and large wars in the old days, as it is of much litigation to-day. Disputes over bride-price debts or over the possession of children form the largest proportion of cases brought to chiefs' courts. Formerly, they were a prolific source of armed conflicts and of cattle raids. Adultery provokes similar reactions, though it did not formerly precipitate war, since it does not usually break up marriage. If the adulterer belongs to the same clan as the wronged husband, a neighbouring clan, or one which has any ties with it, a ritual reconciliation is necessary. The lineage heads, sometimes with the aid of chief or tɛndaana, negotiate and arrange this. No compensation is exacted.

In all such cases, territorial remoteness from one another or wide social cleavages between the two groups concerned made it almost impossible to obtain redress for wrongs. The injured group had to await an opportunity to retaliate in kind.

In the background there lurked always the ultimate sanction—the right to resort to self-help, nominally permissible only if there were no ties between the two groups concerned, but sometimes employed even against clansmen. The commonest method was by raiding (ŋɔk), especially if claims to goods or livestock were at issue. The creditor, alone or aided by members of his lineage, would, at the risk of being shot, seize livestock belonging to any clansman of the debtor in payment of the debt. The latter would have to retrieve his loss from the actual debtor by putting pressure on him through their lineage elders, appealing if necessary to the chief or tɛndaana for support. He was entitled to receive only the number of livestock originally owed. Any loss in excess he might make good by a retaliatory raid; or he might appeal to the head of the creditor's maximal lineage, through an intermediary, to order the return of the excess livestock raided in the interest of peace between neighbours—an appeal as likely to fail as to succeed.

Tale jural notions and procedures are in conformity with the elaborately segmented character of the social structure. As there was formerly no completely dominant social unit or association, there could be no constituted legal machinery backed by irresistible force. Every region of Tale society, from the joint family to the whole vaguely delimited aggregate known as the Tallensi, exhibits a dynamic equilibrium—of like units balanced against one another, of counterpoised ties and cleavages, of complementary institutions and ideological notions. At every level of Tale social organization—kinship, clanship, economic relations, local relations, and the nexus of ritual interdependencies—the tendency towards an equilibrium is apparent. Overlapping and interlocking, these different orders of social relations reinforce one another. The principal mechanism by means of which this equilibrium is maintained is the balanced distribution of authority and prerogative, on the one hand, and of obligations and responsibilities—economic, jural, moral and ritual—on the other. Through this mechanism the component elements of any segment of the society control one another.

This does not mean that Tale society was ever stagnant. Tension is implicit in the equilibrium. It might explode violently when the specific interests of a unit were violated. But conflict could never develop to the point of bringing about complete disintegration. The homogeneity of Tale culture, the undifferentiated economic system, the territorial stability of the population, the network of kinship ties, the ramifications of clanship, and especially the mystical doctrines and ritual practices determining the native conception of the common good—all these are factors restricting conflict and promoting the restoration of equilibrium. War was the ultimate sanction against the violation or submergence of the specific rights of the corporate units constituting Tale social structure, and the ties of ritual collaboration the sanction preventing the complete disintegration of this structure into anarchically independent fractions. Social relationships in Taleland fluctuate between amity and discord, co-operation and conflict, for forces engendering both are always active; but in the long run an equilibrium is maintained. The political system of the Tallensi hinges on this principle.

THE NUER OF THE SOUTHERN SUDAN

By E. E. EVANS-PRITCHARD

I WRITE shortly of the Nuer because I have already recorded a considerable part of my observations on their political constitution and the whole is about to be published as a book.[1] They have, nevertheless, been included in this volume for the reasons that their constitution is representative of East Africa and that it provides us with an extreme political type.

I. Distribution

To discover the principles of their anarchic state we must first review briefly the oecology of the people: their means of livelihood, their distribution, and the relation of these to their surroundings. The Nuer practise cattle-husbandry and agriculture. They also fish, hunt, and collect wild fruits and roots. But, unlike the other sources of their food supply, cattle have more than nutritive interest, being indeed of greater value in their eyes than anything else. So, although they have a mixed economy, Nuer are predominantly pastoral in sentiment.

Nuerland is more suited for stock-breeding than for agriculture: it is flat, clayey, savannah country, parched and bare during the drought and flooded and covered with high grasses during the rains. Heavy rain falls and the rivers overflow their banks from June to December. There is little rain and the rivers are low from December to June. The year thus comprises two seasons of about equal duration. This seasonal dichotomy, combined with pastoral interests, profoundly affects political relations.

During the rains Nuer live in villages perched on the backs of knolls and ridges or dotted over stretches of slightly elevated ground, and engage in the cultivation of millet and maize. The country which intervenes between village and village, being more

---

[1] This record is printed in a series of papers in *Sudan Notes and Records* from 1933 to 1938. The research was done on four expeditions and was financed mainly by the Government of the Anglo-Egyptian Sudan and partly through a Leverhulme Fellowship. Rather than merely describe again what I have already described elsewhere, I have presented my material in a more abstract form than would be permissible were a descriptive account not accessible.

or less flooded for six months, is then unsuitable for habitation, agriculture, or grazing. Anything from five to twenty miles may separate neighbouring villages, while greater distances may divide sections of a tribe and tribe from tribe.

At the end of the rains, the people burn the grasses to provide new pasture and leave their villages to reside in small camps. When the drought becomes severe, the inmates of these intermediate camps concentrate on permanent water supplies. Although these moves are made primarily for the sake of the cattle, they also enable the Nuer to fish, which is generally impossible from village sites, and, to a lesser degree, to hunt and collect wild fruits and roots. When the rains set in again, they return to their villages, where the cattle have protection and the higher ground permits agriculture.

The distribution of the Nuer is determined by the physical conditions and mode of life we have outlined. During the rains, villages are separated, though by no means isolated, from their neighbours by flooded stretches of grassland, and local communities are therefore very distinct units. During the drought, people of different villages of the same district eventually concentrate on permanent water-supplies and share common camps. On the other hand, some families of a village may go to one camp and some to another, though the majority form a local community throughout the year.

Nuer seldom have a surplus of food and at the beginning of the rains it is often insufficient for their needs. Indeed, it may be said that they are generally on the verge of want and that every few years they face more or less severe famine. In these conditions, it is understandable that there is much sharing of food in the same village, especially among members of adjacent homesteads and hamlets. Though at any time some members may have more cattle and grain than others, and these are their private possessions, people eat in one another's homesteads at feasts and at daily meals, and food is in other ways shared, to such an extent that one may speak of a common stock. Food is most abundant from the end of September to the middle of December in a normal year, and it is during these months that most ceremonies, dances, &c., take place.

The Nuer have a very simple technology. Their country lacks iron and stone and the number and variety of trees are small, and they are generally unsuited for constructive purposes other than building. This paucity of raw materials, together with a meagre food supply, contracts social ties, drawing the people of village or camp closer, in a moral sense, for they are in consequence highly interdependent and their pastoral, hunting, fishing, and, to a lesser degree, their agricultural activities are of necessity joint undertakings. This is especially evident in the dry season, when the cattle of many families are tethered in a common kraal and driven as a single herd to the grazing grounds.

Thus, while in a narrow sense the economic unit is the household, the larger local communities are, directly or indirectly, co-operative groups combining to maintain existence, and corporations owning natural resources and sharing in their exploitation. In the smaller local groups the co-operative functions are more direct and evident than in the larger ones, but the collective function of obtaining for themselves the necessities of life from the same resources is in some degree common to all local communities from the household to the tribe.

These local communities are the monogamous family attached to a single hut, the household occupying a single homestead, the hamlet, the village, the camp, the district, tribal sections of varying size, the tribe, the people, and the international community the limits of which are a Nuer's social horizon. We regard the family, the household, and the hamlet as domestic, rather than political, groups, and do not discuss them further in detail.

The distribution of these local communities is very largely determined by physical conditions, especially by the presence of ground which remains above flood-level in the rains, and of permanent water which survives the drought. In any village, the size of population and the arrangement of homesteads is determined by the nature of the site. When perched on an isolated knoll, homesteads are crowded together; when strung out along a ridge, they are more widely separated; and when spread over a broad stretch of higher ground, several hundred yards may intervene between one hamlet and the next. In any large village, the homesteads are grouped in clusters, or hamlets, the inmates of which are generally close kinsmen and their spouses. It is not possible to give more than a rough indication of the size of a village population, but it may be said to vary from 50 to several hundred souls.

As explained, villages are separated by several miles of savannah.

An aggregate of villages lying within a radius which allows easy inter-communication we call a 'district'. This is not a political group, for it can only be defined in relation to each village, since the same villages may be included in more than one district; and we do not regard a local community as a political group unless the people who comprise it speak of themselves as a community by contrast with other communities of the same kind and are so regarded by outsiders. Nevertheless, a district tends to coincide with a tertiary tribal section and its network of social ties are what gives the section much of its cohesion. People of the same district often share common camps in the drought and they attend one another's weddings and other ceremonies. They intermarry and hence establish between themselves many affinal and cognatic relationships which, as will be seen later, crystallize round an agnatic nucleus.

Villages, the political units of Nuerland, are grouped into tribal sections. There are some very small tribes to the west of the Nile which comprise only a few adjacent villages. In the larger tribes to the west of the Nile and in all the tribes to the east of it, we find that the tribal area is divided into a number of territorial sections separated by stretches of unoccupied country, which intervene also between the nearest habitations of contiguous tribes.

As all Nuer leave their villages to camp near water, they have a second distribution in the dry season. When they camp along a river, these camps sometimes succeed one another every few miles, but when they camp around inland pools, twenty to thirty miles often separate one camp from the next. The territorial principle of Nuer political structure is deeply modified by seasonal migration. People who form separate village communities in the rains may unite in a common camp in the drought. Likewise, people of the same village may join different camps. Also, it is often necessary, in the larger tribes, for members of a village to traverse wide tracts of country, occupied by other village communities, to reach water, and their camp may lie close to yet other villages. To avoid the complete loss of their herds by rinderpest or some other misfortune, Nuer often distribute the beasts in several camps.

In western Nuerland, where the tribes are generally smaller than to the east of the Nile, there is usually plenty of water and pasturage, and it is possible, therefore, for village communities of the rains to maintain a relative isolation in the drought. But where, as in the Lou tribe, for example, scarcity of water and pasturage compels more extensive movement and greater concentration, people who are very widely distributed may have more social contact with one another than is the case in western Nuerland. The isolation and autonomy of local communities are broken up by economic necessity and the size of the political group is thereby enlarged. This fact has to be considered in relation to the further fact that to the east of the Nile wider stretches of elevated ground allow larger local concentrations in the rains than is usual to the west of that river. Moreover, seasonal concentration offers an explanation, though by no means a full one, of the location of tribal boundaries, since they are determined not only by the distribution of villages, but also by the direction in which the people turn in their move to dry season pastures. Thus the tribes of the Zeraf Valley fall back on the Zeraf River and therefore do not share camps with the Lou tribe, and that part of the Lou tribe which moves east and north-east make their camps on the Nyanding River and on the upper reaches of the Pibor and do not share their waters and pasture with the Jikany tribes, who move to the upper reaches of the Sobat and the lower reaches of the Pibor. Furthermore, that some of the larger Nuer tribes are able to preserve a degree of tribal unity without governmental organs may in part be attributed to seasonal migration, since, as explained above, the different local sections are forced by the severity of the latitude into mutual contact and develop some measure of forbearance and recognition of common interests.

Likewise, a tribal section is a distinct segment, not only because its villages occupy a well-demarcated portion of its territory, but also in that it has its unique dry-season pastures. The people of one section move off in one direction and the people from an adjoining section move off in a different direction. Dry-season concentrations are never tribal, but always sectional, and at no time and in no area is the population dense.

The total Nuer population is round about 300,000. I do not know the total square mileage of the country, but to the east of the Nile, where there are, on a rough estimate, some 180,000 Nuer, they are said to occupy 26,000 square miles, with the low density of about seven to the square mile. The density is probably no higher to the west of the Nile. Nowhere is there a high degree of local concentration.

Although dry-season movement produces more social inter-relations between members of different tribal sections than the rainy season distribution might lead us to expect, these contacts are mainly individual or, when they concern groups, only smaller

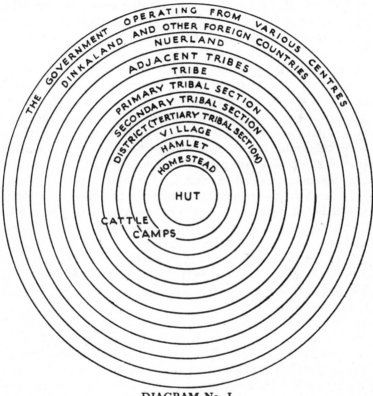

DIAGRAM No. I

local communities, and not the larger tribal sections, are brought into association. This is probably one of the reasons for the lack of structural complexity and of great variation of types of social relations among the Nuer. Outside small kinship groups and village and camp communities, there are no co-operative economic combinations and there are no organized ritual associations. Except for occasional military ventures, active corporate life is restricted to small tribal segments.

II. Tribal System

What is a Nuer tribe? The most obvious characteristic is its territorial unity and exclusiveness, and this was even more marked before European conquest than to-day. The population of a tribe varies from a few hundreds among some small tribes to the west of the Nile—if these are rightly regarded as tribes, for very little research was conducted in that area—to many thousands. Most tribes have a population of over 5,000 and the largest number between 30,000 and 45,000 souls. Each tribe is economically self-sufficient, having its own pastures, water-supplies, and fishing reservations, which its members alone have the right to exploit. It has a name which is the symbol of its distinction. The tribesmen have a sense of patriotism: they are proud to be members of their tribe and they consider it superior to other tribes. Each tribe has within it a dominant clan which furnishes a kinship framework on which the political aggregate is built up. Each also regulates independently its age-set organization.

None of the above-mentioned attributes clearly make a formal distinction between a tribe and its divisions. The simplest definition states that a tribe is the largest community which considers that disputes between its members should be settled by arbitration and that it ought to combine against other communities of the same kind and against foreigners. In these two respects there is no larger political group than the tribe and all smaller political groups are sections of it.

Within a tribe there is law: there is machinery for settling disputes and a moral obligation to conclude them sooner or later. If a man kills a fellow tribesman, it is possible to prevent, or curtail, a feud by payment of cattle. Between tribe and tribe there is no means of bringing together the parties to a dispute and compensation is neither offered nor demanded. Thus, if a man of one tribe kills a man of another tribe, retribution can only take the form of intertribal warfare. It must not be supposed that feuds within a tribe are easy to conclude. There is considerable control over retaliation within a village, but the larger the local community the more difficult settlement becomes. When two large divisions of a tribe are concerned in a feud, the chances of immediate arbitration and settlement are remote. The force of law varies with the distance in tribal structure that separates the persons concerned. Nevertheless, so long as a sense of community endures and the legal norm is formally acknowledged within a tribe, whatever may be the inconsistencies and contradictions that appear in the actual relations between tribesmen, they still consider themselves to be a united group. Then either the contradiction of feuds is felt and they are settled, the unity of the tribe being maintained thereby, or they remain so long unsettled that people give up all hope and intention of ever concluding them and finally cease to feel that they ought to be concluded, so that the tribe tends to split and two new tribes come into being.

Nor must it be supposed that the political limits of the tribe are the limits of social intercourse. People move freely all over Nuerland and are unmolested if they have not incurred blood-guilt. They marry and, to a small extent, trade across tribal boundaries, and pay visits to kinsmen living outside their own tribe. Many social relations, which are not specifically political, link members of different tribes. One has only to mention that the same clans are found in different tribes and that everywhere the age-sets are co-ordinated. Any Nuer may leave his tribe and settle in a new tribe, of which he thereby becomes a member. In time of peace, even Dinka foreigners may visit Nuerland unharmed. Moreover, we must recognize that the whole Nuer people form a single community, territorially unbroken, with common culture and feeling of exclusiveness. Their common language and values permit ready inter-communication. Indeed, we might speak of the Nuer as a nation, though only in a cultural sense, for there is no common political organization or central administration.

Besides being the largest group in which legal obligation is acknowledged, a tribe is also the largest group which habitually combines for offence and defence. The younger men of the tribe went, till recently, on joint raiding expeditions against the Dinka and waged war against other Nuer tribes. Raids on the Dinka were very frequent; war between tribes less so. In theory, if two sections of different tribes were engaged in hostilities, each could rely on the support of the other sections of the same tribe, but in practice they did not always join in. Contiguous tribes sometimes combined against foreigners, especially against the Dinka, though there was no moral obligation to do so, the alliance was of short duration, and the allies conducted their operations independently, even when in collaboration.

At the present time, Nuer are to the west and south bordered by
Dinka, who appear to have very much the same kind of political
system as their own, i.e. they comprise a congeries of tribes without centralized government. From the earliest times the Nuer
have been fighting the Dinka and have been generally on the

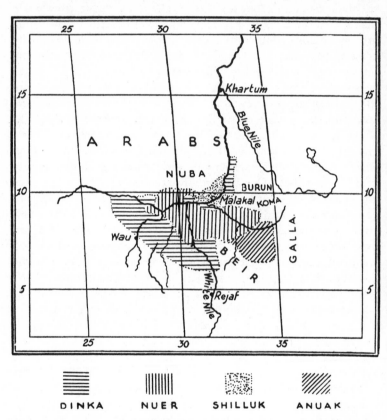

offensive. We know that during the first half of the last century
waves of Nuer broke from their homeland to the west of the Nile
on to the Dinka lands to the east of that river and that they conquered and absorbed the inhabitants in most of what is now eastern
Nuerland (the Nuer distinguish between *Nath cieng*, the 'homeland', or western Nuer, and *Nath doar*, the 'migrated', or eastern
Nuer). Fighting between the two peoples has continued till the
present time but there does not appear, if maps made by early

travellers are to be trusted, to have been much change of territory during the last fifty years. This eastwards migration is a fact that has to be taken into account, with those related earlier, if we wish to know why the eastern tribes are larger, territorially and numerically, than the western tribes, for it may be assumed that the struggle of conquest and settlement, and absorption of Dinka on an unprecedented scale, had some effect on the migrating hordes.

To the north, the Nuer are in varying degrees of contact with Arabs, the peoples of the Nuba Hills, the powerful Shilluk kingdom, and certain small communities in Darfung (Burun and Koma); while to the east and south-east they are bordered by the Galla of Ethiopia, the Anuak, and the Beir. Wherever the Nuer have direct relations with these peoples, they are hostile in character.

Arab slave-raiders from the Northern Sudan intruded here and there into the more accessible portions of Nuerland in the second half of the nineteenth century, but nowhere did they gain the upper hand or, indeed, make a marked impression on the Nuer, who opposed them as strongly as they resisted later the Egyptian Government, which undertook no serious operations against them. The Nuer likewise treated British rule with open disrespect till, as a result of lengthy military operations between 1928 and 1930, their opposition was broken and they were brought under effective administration. With the exception of this last episode in their history, the Nuer may be said to have reached in their foreign relations a state of equilibrium and of mutual hostility which was expressed from time to time in fighting.

A tribe is divided into territorial segments which regard themselves as separate communities. We refer to the divisions of a tribe as primary, secondary, and tertiary tribal sections. Primary sections are segments of a tribe, secondary sections are segments of a primary section, and tertiary sections are segments of a secondary section. A tertiary section is divided into villages and villages into domestic groups. A member of Z^2 tertiary division of tribe B sees himself as a member of Z^2 community in relation to Z^1, but he regards himself as a member of Y^2 and not of Z^2 in relation to Y^1. Likewise, he regards himself as a member of Y, and not of Y^2, in relation to X. He regards himself as a member of tribe B, and not of its primary section Y, in relation to tribe A. Thus, on a structural plane, there is always contradiction in the definition of a political group, for a man is a member of it in virtue of his non-membership of other groups of the same type which he stands outside of, and he is likewise not a member of the same community in virtue of his membership of a segment of it which stands in opposition to its other segments. ·Hence a man counts as a member of a political group in one situation and not as a member of it in a different situation, e.g. he is a member of a tribe in relation to other tribes and he is not a member of it in so far as his segment of the tribe is opposed to other segments. In studying the Nuer political constitution, it is therefore essential that we

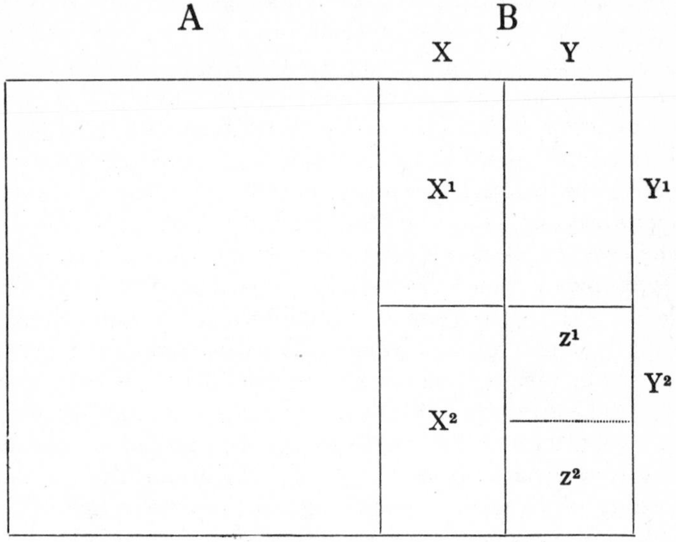

DIAGRAM No. II

view it together with those of their enemies as a single political system, for the outstanding structural characteristic of Nuer political groups is their relativity. A tribal segment is a political group in relation to other segments of the same kind, and they jointly form a tribe only in relation to other Nuer tribes and to adjacent foreign tribes which form part of their political system, and without these relations very little meaning can be attached to the concepts of 'tribe' and 'tribal segment'. That the distinction and individuality of a political group is in relation to groups of the same kind is a generalization that embraces all Nuer local communities, from the largest to the smallest.

The relation between tribes and between segments of a tribe

which gives them political unity and distinction is one of opposition. Between tribes, or federations of tribes, and foreign peoples this opposition is expressed, on the Nuer side at any rate, by contempt and persistent raiding, often carried out in a reckless and brutal manner. Between Nuer tribes, opposition is expressed by actual warfare or by acceptance that a dispute cannot, and ought not, to be settled in any other way. In intertribal warfare, however, women and children are neither speared nor enslaved. Between segments of the same tribe, opposition is expressed by the institution of the feud. A fight between persons of the same village or camp is as far as possible restricted to duelling with clubs. The hostility and mode of expression in these different relations varies in degree and in the form it takes.

Feuds frequently break out between sections of the same tribe and they are often of long duration. They are more difficult to settle the larger the sections involved. Within a village feuds are easily settled and within a tertiary tribal section they are concluded sooner or later, but when still larger groups are involved they may never be settled, especially if many persons on either side have been killed in a big fight.

A tribal section has most of the attributes of a tribe: name, sense of patriotism, a dominant lineage, territorial distinction, economic resources, and so forth. Each is a tribe in miniature, and they differ from tribes only in size, in degree of integration, and in that they unite for war and acknowledge a common principle of justice.

The strength of the sentiment associated with local groups is roughly relative to their size. Feeling of unity in a tribe is weaker than feeling of unity within its sections. The smaller the local group, the more the contacts its members have with one another and the more these contacts are co-operative and necessary for the maintenance of the life of the group. In a big group, like the tribe, contacts are infrequent, short, and of limited type. Also the smaller the group the closer and the more varied the relationships between its members, residential relations being only one strand in a network of agnatic, cognatic, and affinal relationships. Relationships by blood and marriage become fewer and more distant the wider the group.

It is evident that when we speak of a Nuer tribe we are using a relative term, for it is not always easy to say, on the criteria we have used, whether we are dealing with a tribe with two primary segments or with two tribes. The tribal system as defined by sociological analysis can, therefore, only be said to approximate to any simple diagrammatic presentation. A tribe is an exemplification of a segmentary tendency which is characteristic of the political structure as a whole. The reason why we speak of Nuer political groups, and of the tribe in particular, as relative groups and state that they are not easily described in terms of political morphology, is that political relations are dynamic. They are always changing in one direction or another. The most evident movement is towards fission. The tendency of tribes and tribal sections towards fission and internal opposition between their parts is balanced by a tendency in the direction of fusion, of the combination or amalgamation of groups. This tendency towards fusion is inherent in the segmentary character of Nuer political structure, for, although any group tends to split into opposed parts, these parts tend to fuse in relation to other groups. Hence fission and fusion are two aspects of the same segmentary principle and the Nuer tribe and its divisions are to be understood as a relation between these two contradictory, yet complementary, tendencies. Physical environment, way of livelihood, mode of distribution, poor communications, simple economy, &c., to some extent explain the incidence of political cleavage, but the tendency towards segmentation seems to be inherent in political structure itself.

III. Lineage System

Tribal unity cannot be accounted for by any of the facts we have so far mentioned, taken alone or in the aggregate, but only by reference to the lineage system. The Nuer clan is not an undifferentiated group of persons who recognize their common kinship, as are many African clans, but is highly segmented. The segments are genealogical structures, and we therefore refer to them as lineages and to the clan as an exogamous system of lineages which trace their descent to a common ancestor. The defining characteristic of a lineage is that the relationship of any member of it to other members can be exactly stated in genealogical terms. His relationship to members of other lineages of the same clan is, therefore, also known, since lineages are genealogically related. Thus, in the diagram below, A is a clan which is segmented into maximal lineages B and C and these again bifurcate

into major lineages D, E, F, and G. In the same manner, minor
lineages H, I, J, and K are segments of major lineages E and F;
and L, M, N, and O are minimal lineages which are segments of
minor lineages H and J. The whole clan is a genealogical structure,
i.e. the letters represent persons to whom the clan and its segments
trace their descent, and from whom they often take their names.
There must be at least twenty such clans in Nuerland, without
taking into account many small lineages of Dinka origin.

The Nuer lineage is a group of agnates, and comprises all living

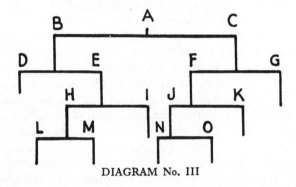

DIAGRAM No. III

persons descended, through males only, from the founder of that
particular line. Logically, it also includes dead persons descended
from the founder, but these dead persons are only significant in
that their genealogical position explains the relationship between
the living. The wider agnatic kinship is recognized the further
back descent has to be traced, so that the depth of a lineage is always
in proportion to its width.

The Nuer clan, being thus highly segmented, has many of the
characteristics which we have found in tribal structure. Its lineages
are distinct groups only in relation to each other. Thus, in the
diagram, M is a group only by opposition to L, H is a group only
by opposition to I, D is a group only by opposition to E, and so on.
There is always fusion of collateral lineages of the same branch in
relation to a collateral branch, e.g. in the diagram, L and M are no
longer separate minimal lineages, but are a single minor lineage,
H, in opposition to I, and D and E are no longer separate major
lineages, but are a single maximal lineage, B, in opposition to C.
Hence two lineages which are equal and opposite are composite in
relation to a third, so that a man is a member of a lineage in relation

to a certain group and not a member of it in relation to a different group. Lineages are thus essentially relative groups, like tribal sections, and, like them, also are dynamic groups. Therefore they can only be described satisfactorily in terms of values and situations.

Nuer lineages are not corporate localized communities though their members often have an association with a locality and speak of the locality as though it were an exclusive agnatic group. Every Nuer village is associated with a lineage, and though the members of it often comprise a small proportion of the community, it is identified with them in such a way that we may speak of it as an aggregate of persons clustered around an agnatic nucleus. The aggregate is linguistically identified with the nucleus by the designation of the village community by the name of the lineage. It is only in reference to rules of exogamy and certain ritual activities that one needs to regard lineages as completely autonomous groups. In social life generally, they function within local communities, of all sizes from the village to the tribe, and as part of them. We cannot here discuss the ways by which residential groups become a network of kinship ties—marriage, adoption, and various fictions— but the result tends to be that a local group is a cognatic cluster round an agnatic core, the rules of exogamy being the operating principle in this tendency.

Nuer clans are everywhere much dispersed, so that in any village or camp one finds representatives of diverse clans. Small lineages have moved freely over Nuerland and have settled here and there and have aggregated themselves to agnatically unrelated elements in local communities. Migration and the absorption of Dinka have been circumstances favouring the dispersal and mixture of clans. Being a conquering, pastoral people and not having an ancestral cult, the Nuer have never been bound to any particular spot by necessity or sentiment.

Nevertheless, there is a straight relation between political structure and the clan system, for a clan, or a maximal lineage, is associated with each tribe, in which it occupies a dominant position among other agnatic groups. Moreover, each of its segments tends to be associated with a segment of the tribe in such a way that there is a correspondence, and often a linguistic identification, between the parts of a clan and the parts of a tribe. Thus if we compare Diagrams II and III and suppose clan A to be the dominant clan in tribe B, then maximal lineages B and C correspond to primary sections X and Y; major lineages D and E correspond to secondary section X^1 and X^2; major lineages F and G correspond to secondary sections Y^1 and Y^2; and minor lineages J and K correspond to tertiary sections Z^1 and Z^2.

We speak of a clan which is dominant in a tribe as the aristocratic clan, although, except on the periphery of Nuer expansion eastwards, its predominance gives prestige rather than privilege. Its members are in a minority—often a very small minority—in the tribe. Not all members of the aristocratic clan live in the tribe where it is dominant, but many are also found in other tribes. Not all clans are associated with a tribe in this manner. A man is only an aristocrat in the one tribe in which his clan is dominant. If he lives in another tribe, he is not an aristocrat there.

There is consequently in every tribe some social differentiation. There are aristocrats, Nuer of other clans, and Dinka, but these strata are not classes and the second and third are properly to be regarded as categories rather than as groups. The Dinka who have been absorbed into Nuer society have been for the most part incorporated into their kinship system by adoption and marriage, and conquest has not led to the development of classes or castes. This is, perhaps, to be attributed, in part at any rate, to the fact that the Dinka, like the Nuer, are chiefly pastoralists and that in other respects their ways of life are very similar.

Without presenting all the evidence and without making every qualification, we attempt an explanation of why Nuer clans, especially the dominant clans, are segmented into lineages to a far greater degree than is usual among African peoples. In our view, they are segmented because the political structure to which they correspond is segmented in the way we have described. Social obligations among the Nuer are expressed chiefly in a kinship idiom and the interrelations of local communities within a tribe are defined in terms of agnatic relationship. Therefore, as the tribe segments the clan segments with it and the point of separation between the tribal sections becomes the point of divergence in the clan structure of the lineages associated with each section. For, as we have seen, clans and their lineages are not distinct corporate groups, but are embodied in local communities, through which they function structurally. Such being the case, it is not surprising that they take the form of the State which gives them corporate substance.

Those clans which are associated with tribes have generally greater lineage extension and depth than those which are not so associated, and the larger the tribe the more significance this association has for the Nuer. It is in the largest tribes, territorially and numerically, and those which have expanded most and assimilated most foreigners, like the Lou and Eastern Gaajak and Gaajok tribes, that we find the greatest attention paid to the distinct and dominant position of the aristocratic clans. Indeed, not only do political relations affect the clan structural form, splitting it into segments along the lines of political fission, but also the clan system may be said to have a corresponding action on the political structure. In a confusion of lineages of different clan origin and in an amorphous network of cognatic links, the political structure is given consistent form, in the language of kinship, by one clan—a single system of lineages—being made to correspond to the tribe and to its structure of opposed segments. Just as a man is a member of a tribal segment opposed to other segments of the same order and yet also a member of the tribe which embraces all these segments, so also he is a member of a lineage opposed to other lineages of the same order and yet also a member of the clan which embraces all these lineages, and there is a strict correspondence between these two sets of affiliations, since the lineage is embodied in the segment and the clan in the tribe. Moreover, the distance in clan structure between two lineages of a dominant clan tends to correspond to the distance in tribal structure between the two sections with which they are associated. Thus the system of lineages of the dominant clan enables the Nuer to think of their tribe in the highly consistent form of clan structure. In each segment the network of kinship ties are given unity and coherence by their common relationship to the lineage of the dominant clan that resides there, and as these separate lineages are composite in relation to other clans so the whole tribe is built around an exclusive agnatic framework. Though the sections may tend to draw apart and to split, a common agnatic value, shared by the dominant lineages contained in them, endures.

IV. Age-set System

Another tribal institution is the age-set system, which is socially more significant among the Nuer than among other Nilotic peoples of the Sudan. Nuer boys pass into the grade of manhood through a severe ordeal and a series of rites connected with it. These initiations take place whenever there are a sufficient number of boys of from about fourteen to sixteen years of age in a village or district. All the youths who have been initiated in a successive number of years belong to one age-set, and there is a four-year interval between the last batch of initiates of one set and the first batch of the next set, and during this interval no boys may be initiated. The initiation period is open for about six years, so that, with the four years of the closed period, there are about ten years between the commencement of any age-set and the commencement of the set that precedes or succeeds it. The age-sets are not organized in a cycle.

Nuer age-sets are a tribal institution in the sense that, in the larger tribes at any rate, all the sections of a tribe have the same open and closed periods and call the sets by the same names. They are also the most characteristic of all Nuer national institutions, for initiation scars are the sign of their communion and the badge of their supremacy. Moreover, though each big tribe has its own age-set organization, adjacent tribes co-ordinate their sets in periods and nomenclature, so that the Western Nuer, the Eastern Nuer, and the Central Nuer tend to fall into three divisions in this respect. But even when a man travels from one end of Nuerland to the other, he can always, and easily, perceive the set which is equivalent to his own in each area. The age-set system, therefore, like the clan system, whilst having a tribal connotation, is not bound by lines of political cleavage.

There is usually in each tribe a man whose privilege it is to open and close initiation periods and to give each set its name. This man belongs to one of those lineages which have a special ritual relationship to cattle and are known as 'Men of the Cattle'. He opens and closes initiation periods in his own district, and other districts of his tribe follow suit. Once a period has been opened, each village and district initiates its boys when it pleases. The age-sets have no corporate activities and cannot be said to have specific political functions. There are no grades of 'warriors' and 'elders' concerned with the administration of the country, and the sets are not regiments, for a man fights with the members of his local community, irrespective of age. In the rites of initiation there is no educative or moral training. There is no leadership in the sets.

There are probably never more than six sets in existence at any time, since six sets cover about seventy-five years. As each set dies its name is remembered only for a generation or two. Each set becomes more senior as the years go on, so that a man rises from a junior to a middle, and from a middle to a senior position in his community as a member of a group. The stratification of the age-set system is thus a further exemplification of the principle of segmentation which we have seen to be a characteristic of the political and kinship systems. There is further stratification within each set, but this is not of great importance, for the set sees itself, and is seen by others, as an undivided group in relation to other sets, and its divisions become merged as the set becomes more senior. A set once complete does not change its membership, but the sets are constantly changing their positions in relation to the whole system. There is also a certain relativity about these stratified sets similar to that we noted about tribal sections and clans, for, while they keep their distinction, there is often a situational fusion of two sets in relation to a third. This is especially apparent at feasts. Whether a set is regarded as junior or equal depends not only on its position in the age-set structure, but also on the status of a third set concerned in any situation, a tendency due to the connexion between age-sets and generations.

The most evident action of age-sets in determining behaviour is the way duties and privileges are effected by a transition from boyhood to manhood. Also, in virtue of the position of his set in the structure, every male Nuer is in a status of seniority, equality, or juniority towards every other Nuer man. Some men are his 'sons', some his 'brothers', and some his 'fathers'. Without entering here into further detail, we may say that the attitude of a man towards other men of his community is largely determined by their respective positions in the age-set system. Hence age relations, like kinship relations, are structural determinants of behaviour. The age-set system may, moreover, be regarded as a political institution, since it is, to a large extent, segmented tribally and since it divides a tribe—as far as its male members are concerned—into groups, based on age, which stand in a definite relation to each other. We do not consider, however, that it has any direct accord with the tribal structure, based on territorial segmentation, which we have recorded. The politico-territorial system and the age-set system are both consistent in themselves and to some extent overlap, but they are not interdependent.

V. Feuds and other Disputes

The political system operates largely, we think, through the institution of the feud which is regulated by a mechanism known as the 'leopard-skin chief', a title we retain, although the appellation of 'chief' is misleading. This person is one of those specialists who are concerned, in a ritual capacity, with various departments of Nuer social life and of nature. Leopard-skin chiefs belong to certain lineages only, though not all members of these lineages utilize their hereditary ritual powers. In most of Nuerland, the lineages are not branches of dominant clans.

When a man has killed another, he must at once go to a chief, who cuts his arm so that the blood may flow. Until this mark of Cain has been made, the slayer may neither eat nor drink. If he fears vengeance, as is normally the case, he remains at the chief's home, for it is sanctuary. Within the next few months the chief elicits from the slayer's kin that they are prepared to pay compensation to avoid a feud and he persuades the dead man's kin that they ought to accept compensation. During this period neither party may eat or drink from the same vessels as the other and they may not, therefore, eat in the home of the same third person. The chief then collects the cattle—till recently some forty to fifty beasts—and takes them to the dead man's home, where he performs various sacrifices of cleansing and atonement. Such is the procedure of settling a feud, and before the present administration it had often to be used, for the Nuer are a turbulent people who esteem courage the highest virtue and skill in fighting the most necessary accomplishment.

In so brief a description, one may give the impression that the chief judges the case and compels acceptance of his decision. Nothing could be further from the facts. The chief is not asked to deliver a judgement: it would not occur to Nuer that one was required. He appears to force the kin of the dead man to accept compensation by his insistence, even to the point of threatening to curse them, but it is an established convention that he shall do so, in order that the bereaved relatives may retain their prestige. What seems really to have counted were the acknowledgement of community ties between the parties concerned, and hence of the

moral obligation to settle the affair by the acceptance of a traditional payment, and the wish, on both sides, to avoid, for the
time being at any rate, further hostilities.

A feud directly affected only close agnatic kinsmen on both
sides. One did not avenge oneself on cognates or on distant
agnates. Nevertheless, we believe that the feud had a wider
social connotation and that therein lies its political significance.
We must first recognize that feuds are more easily settled the
smaller the group involved. When a man kills a near kinsman or a
close neighbour, the matter is quickly closed by compensation,
often on a reduced scale, being soon offered and accepted, for
when a homicide occurs within a village general opinion demands
an early settlement, since it is obvious to every one that were
vengeance allowed corporate life would be impossible. At the
other end of the scale, when a homicide occurs between primary
or secondary sections of a tribe, there is little chance of an early
settlement and, owing to distance, vengeance is not easily achieved,
so that unsettled feuds accumulate. Such homicides are generally
the result of intertribal fights in which several persons are killed.
This not only increases the difficulty of settlement, but continues
between the sections the mutual hostility that occasioned the fight,
for, not only the close agnatic kinsmen of the dead, but entire
local communities are involved. Feud, as a choice between direct
vengeance and acceptance of compensation, without the necessity
of immediate settlement, but requiring eventual conclusion, is
especially a condition that flourishes between villages of the same
district. The kinsmen of the dead man are near enough to strike
at the kinsmen of the slayer and far enough from them to permit
a temporary state of hostility between the local communities to
which the parties belong. For whole communities are of necessity
involved, though they are not subject to the rigid taboos that a
homicide imposes on close agnatic kinsmen of slayer and slain,
nor are they threatened with vengeance. Nevertheless, their members
are, as a rule, closely related by cognatic or affinal ties to the
principals and must assist them if there is an open fight. At the
same time, these communities have frequent social contacts, so
that eventually the mechanism of the leopard-skin chief has to be
employed to prevent their complete dislocation. The feud thus
takes on a political complexion and expresses the hostility between
political segments.

The balanced opposition of political segments is, we believe, largely maintained by the institution of the feud which permits a state of latent hostility between local communities, but allows also their fusion in a larger group. We say that the hostility is latent because even when a feud is being prosecuted there is no uninterrupted endeavour to exact vengeance, but the kinsmen of the dead may take any opportunity that presents itself to accomplish their purpose; and, also, because even when compensation has been accepted the sore rankles and the feud may, in spite of settlement, break out again, for Nuer recognize that in sentiment a feud goes on for ever. The leopard-skin chief does not rule and judge, but acts as mediator through whom communities desirous of ending open hostility can conclude an active state of feud. The feud, including the role played in it by the chief, is thus a mechanism by which the political structure maintains itself in the form known to us.

The leopard-skin chief may also act as mediator in disputes concerning ownership of cattle, and he and the elders on both sides may express their opinion on the merits of a case. But the chief does not summon the defendants, for he has neither court nor jurisdiction and, moreover, has no means of compelling compliance. All he can do is to go with the plaintiff and some elders of his community to the home of the defendant and to ask him and his kinsmen to discuss the matter. Only if both sides are willing to submit to arbitration can it be settled. Also, although the chief, after consultation with the elders, can give a verdict, this verdict is reached by general agreement and in a large measure, therefore, arises from an acknowledgement by the defendant's or plaintiff's party that the other party has justice on its side. It is, however, very seldom that a chief is asked to act as mediator, and there is no one else who has authority to intervene in disputes, which are settled by other than legal methods.

In the strict sense of the word, the Nuer have no law. There is no one with legislative or juridical functions. There are conventional payments considered due to a man who has suffered certain injuries—adultery with his wife, fornication with his daughter, theft, broken limbs, &c.—but these do not make a legal system, for there is no constituted and impartial authority who decides on the rights and wrongs of a dispute and there is no external power to enforce such a decision were it given. If a man has right on his side, and, in virtue of that, obtains the support of his kinsmen and they are prepared to use force, he has a good chance of obtaining what is due to him, if the parties live near to one another. The usual way of obtaining one's due is to go to the debtor's kraal and take his cattle. To resist is to run the risk of homicide and feud. It seems that whether, and how, a dispute is settled depends very largely on the relative positions of the persons concerned in the kinship and age-set systems and the distance between their communities in tribal structure. In theory, one can obtain redress from any member of one's tribe, but, in fact, there is little chance of doing so unless he is a member of one's local community and a kinsman. The force of 'law' varies with the position of the parties in political structure, and thus Nuer 'law' is essentially relative, like the structure itself.

During the year I spent with the Nuer, I never heard a case being conducted, either before an individual or before a council of elders, and I received the impression that it is very rare for a man to obtain redress except by force or threats of force. And if the Nuer has no law, likewise he lacks government. The leopard-skin chief is not a political authority and the 'Man of the Cattle' and other ritual agents (totemic specialists, rain-makers, fetich-owners, magicians, diviners, &c.) have no political status or functions, though they may become prominent and feared in their locality. The most influential men in a village are generally the heads of joint families, especially when they are rich in cattle, of strong character, and members of the aristocratic clan. But they have no clearly defined status or function. Every Nuer, the product of a hard and equalitarian upbringing, deeply democratic, and easily roused to violence, considers himself as good as his neighbour; and families and joint families, whilst co-ordinating their activities with those of their fellow villagers, regulate their affairs as they please. Even in raids, there is very little organization, and leadership is restricted to the sphere of fighting and is neither institutionalized nor permanent. It is politically significant only when raids are controlled and organized by prophets. No Nuer specialists can be said to be political agents and to represent, or symbolize, the unity and exclusiveness of local groups, and, apart from the prophets, none can be said to have more than local prominence. All leaders, in this vague sense of influential persons in a locality, are adults and, except for an occasional prophetess, all are men.

Owing to the fact that Nuer prophets had been the foci of opposition to the Government, they were in disgrace, and the more influential of them under restraint or in hiding, during my visit to Nuerland, so that I was not able to make detailed observations on their behaviour. Nuer are unanimous in stating that they did not arise much before the end of the last century and there is some evidence to suggest that their emergence was connected with the spread of Mahdism. However that may be, there can be no doubt that powerful prophets arose about the time of Arab intrusion into Nuerland and that at the time of British conquest they were more respected and had wider influence than any other persons. No extensive raids were undertaken without their sanction and often they led them, received part of the spoil, and to some extent supervised the division of the rest of it. Though there seems to be good evidence that the earlier prophets were no more than ritual agents, some of the later ones appear to have begun to settle disputes, at any rate in their own districts. However, their chief political importance rather lay elsewhere. For the first time a single person symbolized, even if in a mainly spiritual form, the unity of a tribe, for the prophets were essentially tribal figures, though—and this fact is also of great political significance—their influence often extended over tribal boundaries and brought about a larger degree of unity among adjacent tribes than there appears to have been hitherto. When we add that there was a tendency for the spirits which possessed prophets to pass, at their deaths, into their sons, we are justified in concluding that development was taking place towards a higher degree of federation between tribes and towards the emergence of political leadership, and in explaining these changes by reference to Arab and European intrusion. Opposition between Nuer and their neighbours had always been sectional. They were now confronted by a more formidable and a common enemy. When the Government overthrew the prophets, this development was checked.

VI. Summary

We have briefly described and analysed what we regard as Nuer political structure: the relations between territorial segments within a territorial system and the relations between that and other social systems within an entire social structure. We have examined intertribal relations. and the relations between tribal segments. It is these relations, together with the tribal and inter-tribal contacts with foreign peoples, that we define as the Nuer political system. In social life the political is combined with other systems, particularly the clan system and the age-set system, and we have considered what relation they bear to the political structure. We have also mentioned those ritual specialisms which have political significance. The political system has been related to environmental conditions and modes of livelihood.

The Nuer constitution is highly individualistic and libertarian. It is an acephalous state, lacking legislative, judicial, and executive organs. Nevertheless, it is far from chaotic. It has a persistent and coherent form which might be called 'ordered anarchy'. The absence of centralized government and of bureaucracy in the nation, in the tribe, and in tribal segments—for even in the village authority is not vested in any one—is less remarkable than the absence of any persons who represent the unity and exclusiveness of these groups.

It is not possible from a study of Nuer society alone, if it be possible at all, to explain the presence and absence of political institutions in terms of their functional relationship to other institutions. At best we can say that certain social characteristics seem to be consistent. Environmental conditions, mode of livelihood, territorial distribution, and form of political segmentation appear to be consistent. So do the presence of clans with genealogical structure and a developed age-set system seem to gc together with absence of political authority and of class-stratification. Comparative studies alone will show whether generalizations of such a kind are true and, moreover, whether they are useful. We cannot here discuss these questions and will only say, in conclusion, that the consistency we perceive in Nuer political structure is one of process rather than of morphology. The process consists of complementary tendencies towards fission and fusion which, operating alike in all political groups by a series of inclusions and exclusions that are controlled by the changing social situation, enable us to speak of a system and to say that this system is characteristically defined by the relativity and opposition of its segments.

SUPPLEMENTARY STUDIES BY CONTRIBUTORS
TO THIS BOOK

I. SCHAPERA: *Tribal Legislation Among the Tswana of the Bechuanaland Protectorate*. L.S.E. Monographs on Social Anthropology, No. 9, 1943.

Land Tenure in the Bechuanaland Protectorate, Lovedale Press, 1945.

The Tswana, International African Institute, 1953.

Handbook of Tswana Law and Custom, Oxford University Press, 2nd Ed., 1955.

S. F. NADEL: *A Black Byzantium*, Oxford University Press, 1942.

M. FORTES: *The Dynamics of Clanship Among the Tallensi*, Oxford University Press, 1945.

The Web of Kinship Among the Tallensi, Oxford University Press, 1949.

E. E. EVANS-PRITCHARD: *The Nuer*. Clarendon Press, 1941.

G. WAGNER: *The Bantu of North Kavirondo*, Volume I, 1949, Volume II, 1956, Oxford University Press.

INDEX

REPRINTED LITHOGRAPHICALLY
BY EBENEZER BAYLIS AND SON LTD
WORCESTER